The Rorschach Clinician

Scientific study of the Rorschach has barely begun but is now evidenced in studies which translate clinical theory intelligently into experimental designs and adopt proper methodology. A remarkable proportion of these attempts are successful in rejecting the null hypothesis, but failures of Rorschach hypotheses and low-level relations are frequent enough to demand revision of accepted interpretations.

—CRONBACH, 1956

The use of the test will be most fruitful if we understand fully the nature of the data we are studying in a Rorschach protocol. . . . This implies that we know what the processes are that lead to a response; which of these processes we single out and which we omit; what we emphasize and what we neglect when we assign a score to a response; and exactly what we do, what we assume and why we assume it, when we interpret a score or a psychogram, a response, a sequence of responses, or a total test protocol. We are far from knowing all this, and probably we shall never know it fully.

—SCHACHTEL, 1966

The Rorschach Clinician

A New Research Approach
and Its Application

CHARLES R. POTKAY, Ph.D.
Western Illinois University

Grune & Stratton
New York and London

To my wife, Catherine,
and our daughters, Sandra and Susan

Grune & Stratton, Inc.
757 Third Avenue
New York, New York 10017

Library of Congress Catalog Card Number: 76-133501

International Standard Book Number: 0-8089-0669-0

Printed in the United States of America (PC-B)

Contents

PART I   Sources of Rorschach Utility

v

PART II   Interpretations by Rorschach Clinicians

List of Tables

List of Figures

Foreword

by Frank J. Kobler

I have been teaching Rorschach's Test in my graduate courses in clinical psychology for almost 30 years, and have used it in consultation and private practice, and have conducted and supervised research on it for use in various journals and for doctoral dissertations. I have been reasonably well satisfied with the contribution that the Rorschach has made when confronted with a problem in personality assessment. Using the Rorschach has enabled me to learn more about a person, leading me to a better understanding of him, and permitting me to apply effective remedial procedures.

During the time I used the Rorschach there has been a considerable change in my method of use. This is the result of experience, the constant critical interaction with my graduate students and colleagues, and the continuing reflection on the overwhelming amount of published literature on the test. I saw from the beginning that there was little if any effective theory related to the test, which suited me well. I constructed my own dynamic explanation of each case, guided by all the information that could be obtained about the person and allowed the facts in each instance to determine that explanation. I felt that I was the "instrument" that was being used to understand and to help the person, and that the test played a subordinate and ancillary role in this process. There were many factors that led to my judgment, for example, of the intellectual level and effectiveness of a person, and the Rorschach was often one of these factors. As I acquired more experience in understanding and in making judgments about people, I was often incorrect, and a standardized instrument or test introduced a corrective that warranted my consideration.

In the beginning of my teaching and testing I was rigorous and precise in the use of this instrument, and I continue to be this way because experience and

---

Dr. Kobler is Professor of Psychology and Director of Clinical Training at Loyola University of Chicago.

research have taught that some instruments are better, faster, and more accurate than I am.

When I began using and teaching the Rorschach I depended almost exclusively on the quantitative and the sign approach. In some way it was comforting to add up a certain number of things, look for a relationship between them, combine a variety of factors in some appropriate way, and then draw a conclusion which could be written into an interpretation. There was something satisfying, definitive, even scientific about a certain number of M responses related to a certain number of W responses especially if one of the M responses appeared in an unusual or unique context. If, in addition, there was clearly discernible color shock on Card II there was little if any question about the results. Gradually the evidence accumulated both from the experience of others as reported in the literature and from one's own experience that this worked about as often as not. One of my students said you always had to fudge somewhat, either more or less, to make it come out. Perhaps this fudge factor in assessment has not been investigated sufficiently.

Certainly the Rorschach was not a psychometric instrument in the traditionally accepted meaning of the term. It failed to satisfy the usual criteria of a test on several counts and many people pointed this out in many places with clarity, conviction, and even a certain sense of elan. Others worked at great length and with some success to remedy this. Some of us were more successful than others. There are a number of good research studies on the Rorschach which, in my judgment, satisfy the criteria of science that are appropriate to the subject matter of clinical psychology. There could be more such studies and undoubtedly they will appear. Witness the present research by Charles Potkay.

Because I still use the Rorschach in teaching, in practice, and in research, I find that I use both the quantitative and the qualitative aspects of the test, with a greater emphasis on the latter. Over this period of time my use of the Rorschach has become like a sophisticated interview situation to which I bring to bear all that reading and experience have taught me. It begins, if there can be a beginning, when the subject or client is told that he is to take the inkblot or Rorschach Test. His reactions to me and to the situation, and mine to him take on an immediate interpretive significance. Hypotheses are formed almost instantly about the subject and about our relationship. I have not deviated from the traditional administration. There is a free association and an inquiry, and, in most instances, a testing of the limits. Scoring is accomplished immediately during the inquiry and may be done during the response proper and verified during the inquiry. The first response or the first few responses may tell much of the story. On the other hand the dynamics of the individual may be as opaque at the end of the test as they were at the beginning. Almost always, however, something of value appears during the testing. This can be a new idea or merely a confirmation of a hypothesis tentatively held. It is difficult to predict when the clues will appear. They may be in the use of the blot area, or in the manner in which the response is given, or in the ordinary or extraordinary content of the response, or in the card on which a significant action is depicted.

In using the Rorschach one knows quickly and with reasonable certainty how intelligent the person is. The amount and nature of his anxiety and how effectively he uses it or defends against it is also readily discernible. A picture of the defenses emerges rather definitively in many instances. The nature and the amount of hostility or depression, for example, is stimulated by the blots in a variety of situations. Quite frequently the subject's sexual conflicts and pre-occupations become evident. It is not too difficult to obtain some information on the level of emotional maturity and how effectively the subject relates to people or how comfortable he is with himself. Ascertaining a diagnosis from the Rorschach is a more difficult matter to decide, if indeed one wants this. The literature has indicated abundantly why this is so and the results contained herein confirm this conclusion. I have little hesitation, however, in concluding from this test whether or not a person's adjustment is substantially normal. With surprising frequency more specific diagnostic clues are available.

Dr. Potkay introduces a new and fruitful dimension into the research and the use of the Rorschach. He has selected three authentic Rorschach protocols (by Bell and Klopfer, by Beck, and by Bochner and Halpern) and submitted them to 36 highly competent and well known users of this test, asking them to reveal how they individually went about using this test. On one protocol he asked them to judge the intellectual level of the person, on the second protocol to gauge the level of anxiety, and on the third protocol he asked them to provide a diagnosis. He went about this in a very innovative manner. Every item of in-formation about the three protocols was placed on a small card and these cards were attached to a large folder. The data included the responses, all the scores used, the ratios, the background data on the subject, and other verbal com-munications. Each psychologist selected as many cards as he wished. He selected these cards in any order that he wanted to. As he selected each card he turned it over and saw the information that he requested. If the first piece of information he wanted was the number of M responses he selected this card and found what this information was. He continued this selection until he felt that he had the answer to the clinical question that was asked. Only those cards that he thought were necessary and sufficient to obtain the answer were to be drawn.

What a simple and ingenious device. With it one could see not only how much and what kind of information the clinician required, but also, and significantly, the order or process of his selection or his thinking. Now it could be determined what items of information were selected most frequently by the experts and which were more useful, i.e., selected earlier in the process. We have here *what* was used and *how* it was used. Through the use of this procedure we have the clinician entering critically into the research process, a condition little attended to in most Rorschach validity research.

With such a design certain potentially useful and essential hypotheses could be tested. One could discover if these expert clinicians functioned differently when the clinical question was different. They did. Again one could ask if the clinician's orientation was basically quantitative or qualitative did he then operate differently. He did. The expert clinician required the least information to answer the question about the intellectual level and he did it more accurately. The experts found that free association, background data, and numerical summaries and ratios were the most useful in the process of their thinking. On the other hand the experts as a group found that response scores, locations, content summary scores, and reaction times were of little value.

While each clinician used sources of test information in accordance with his interpretative approach, his approach was characteristically qualitative. The expert clinician in interpreting a Rorschach protocol works from the qualitative to the quantitative sources of information. The expert prefers to use the free association part of the Rorschach immediately. He likes to set up hypotheses which he checks out for support through the use of the quantitative indices. He is continually looking for confirmation of his hypotheses and makes anticipatory predictions with what he knows and suspects. Clinicians agree best on the information which was relatively useless. They also agree on being different or individualistic in how they proceed to their assigned task.

So here we have a research study being quite clear on utility. Although still somewhat short on validity, the study points the way to what is required to attain validity. It should come from using qualitative factors supported by quantitative factors. This leads me back to my own historical odyssey with the Rorschach. In this process I changed my emphasis on the quantitative to a new emphasis on the qualitative, and to the discovery that when I function qualitatively, and then use a quantitative support I can more generally say something useful and valid about the person. Results of the present study show that greater validity may be obtained by those experts who use this balanced approach to interpretation. To be qualitative alone, or to be quantitative alone in one's interpretative approach is more apt to prove fatal to accuracy. It is more useful and more valid to attend to a particular response in a particular card and not to a summary score. When I see a certain response I immediately begin to seek out other data in a variety of places to check a tentative hypothesis. And I am apt to do this differently and somewhat more idiosyncratically than my colleagues. Nevertheless we obtain much the same result. What Dr. Potkay shows is the essential unity of the clinician and his Rorschach. He finds that I am quite accurate in determining anxiety or intelligence, but not as accurate in making a diagnosis. But his conditions made it extremely difficult for the expert to be right on the diagnosis. Perhaps this can be changed in time as we learn more about the reliability and the validity of our diagnostic categories.

As a final note, it may interest the reader to see the names of the clinical psychologists who were kind enough to participate in the study.

Arnold Abrams, Charlotte H. Altman, Jack Arbit, Bernard M. Aronov, Edward J. Barnes, Robert P. Barrell, Samuel J. Benveniste, Frederick A. Braucher, Alvin G. Burstein, Alan S. DeWolfe, Frank Dinello, Bernard H. Gold, Morton Hammer, Shirley J. Heinze, William A. Hunt, Victor A. Jackson, Joseph C. Kaspar, Harold Klehr, Vita Krall, Ernest A. Kurtz, Charles E. Lane, Reid I. Martin, Robert L. McFarland, Marv L. Meyer, Gerald P. Motz, Ralph A. Nelson, Donald Paull, Melvin L. Perlman, M. Henry Pitts, Roderick W. Pugh, William G. Shipman, Paul R. Singer, Fred E. Spaner, LeRoy A. Wauck, George K. Yacorzynski, and Robert I. Yufit.

Acknowledgments

The present volume represents an expansion of doctoral research undertaken at Loyola University, Chicago, under the direction of Professor Frank J. Kobler. The teaching influence of Dr. Kobler, and of Dr. H. J. A. Rimoldi, provided the essential framework for the particular combination of Rorschach and problem-solving techniques employed in the study. Specific suggestions made by Roderick W. Pugh contributed meaningfully to the analysis and interpretation of the research data. Dr. Pugh and Dr. LeRoy A. Wauck were members of the dissertation committee.

The author wishes to give special thanks to Mrs. Catherine Potkay who aided in programming the data for computer analysis, with additional assistance coming from G. Neil Harper, Ph.D. and William B. Deeming of Skidmore, Owings and Merrill. Supportive commentary and suggestions were made by Bem P. Allen and Raymond N. Luebeck who reviewed the manuscript. Mrs. Mary Darby assisted in the preparation and typing of the entire manuscript, while Mr. Edward Streen and Mrs. Linda Cox helped with the proofreading. Jack S. Beacher, Herman I. Diesenhaus, Elizabeth Bankson Dorus, Herbert H. Krauss, and Dale G. Lenoue offered useful ideas regarding Rorschach scorings, procedure, and implementation during the time of the pilot study. Walter J. Flakus and John R. C. Morton of Western Illinois University were helpful in the final preparation of the text. Appreciation is extended to Mrs. Pam Landau of the editorial office at Grune & Stratton. Special thanks also are directed to John Bell, Bruno Klopfer, and Walter G. Klopfer for granting permission to reproduce selected excerpts from *The Case of Gregor* which appeared in the *Rorschach Research Exchange*.

Most of all, the author wishes to express his gratitude to the clinical psychologist participants who turned research possibility into research actuality. The influence of these individuals has been realized deeply both in relation to the specific Rorschach aspect of the research and to the incorporation of a collective impression of the professional clinician as willing, open, and competent.

February, 1971   CRP

Part I

Sources of
Rorschach Utility

Chapter 1

The Validity-Utility Discrepancy

Almost fifty years have passed since Hermann Rorschach first published his inkblot experiment. Today his technique is among the most used, and useful, of the projective instruments employed by clinical psychologists. Sundberg's (1961) survey of 185 clinical agencies and hospitals in the United States revealed Rorschach usage to be outstripping that of all other psychological tests. Surveys by Mills (1965) and by Crenshaw et al. (1968) showed the Rorschach to be leading all projective techniques in research use between the years 1947–1965. Jackson and Wohl's (1966) survey of 96 chairmen of selected psychology departments throughout the United States and Canada indicated that the Rorschach was the most emphasized clinical technique in the graduate curriculum, principally at the introductory level.

Rorschach's technique also has given rise to an estimated 3,000 publications. However, a critical number of the research studies have failed to demonstrate Rorschach validity by statistical means under conditions of controlled observation. Hunt (1950), writing in the first *Annual Review of Psychology*, judged traditional Rorschach technique to be inappropriate as a clinical method. Hertz (1942, 1952) has concluded critical reviews of Rorschach literature with statements that evidence of Rorschach validity at best has been uncoordinated, tentative, and suggestive only. Cronbach (1956) viewed the instrument as too imprecise and variant for use in clini-

3

cal decision making. Jensen (1958) stated outright that the Rorschach was worthless as a research instrument, having nothing to show for its applications in the personality field. Ainsworth (1954), in tones far gentler than those of most evaluators, cited the need for this "partly finished" instrument to be brought to a more finished state. Eysenck (1957) has compared the clinical accuracy of the Rorschach technique with the risky effectiveness of a diagnostically labeled die. A "charitable interpretation" of Rorschach evidence is that "it has not *yet* been shown to be of value *on its own*" (Horn, 1969, p. 654). Wrote Jackson and Wohl (1966),

> One becomes very curious as to what specific effects research has had. In spite of voluminous studies with negative findings and research reviews which are extremely critical (Buros, 1959, pp. 276–279), [psychology] instructors supported Rorschach practices in a manner expected of those who reject such research as inappropriate and irrelevant to Rorschach work (p. 132).

The discrepancy between clinical-academic utilization of the Rorschach and experimental failures to demonstrate Rorschach validity has been associated in recent years with a number of reconsiderations in psychologists' thinking about the blots. Alternative inkblot instruments have been developed (Holtzman, 1958; Levy, 1948; Harrower and Steiner, 1946; Zulliger-Behn, 1952), each accompanied by its own cache of research. Studies by Lazarus (1949) and Siipola (1950) have stimulated dramatic reconsiderations of the significance of color and color shock in Rorschach theory. Increasing attention has been given to stimulus qualities of the blots (Mitchell, 1952; George, 1955; Baughman, 1954, 1965).

The reconsiderations in Rorschach thinking referred to above may be illustrated by contrasting some traditional and current trends. Hermann Rorschach introduced his inkblots by stating that they lent themselves to interpretation as "accidental forms, that is, of nonspecific forms" (1942, trans., p. 51). Most workers today do not accept the idea of neutrality in relation to the blot stimuli. Individual blots are regarded as having distinct "card pull" (Ranzoni, Grant, and Ives, 1950; Klopfer et al., 1954), and specific areas of the blots are referred to as being symbolically meaningful (Brown, 1953a), or clinically predictive (Sapolsky, 1963).

> In scoring the answers given by the subjects, the content is considered last. It is more important to study the *function* of perception and apperception. The experiment depends primarily on the pattern (Rorschach, p. 19).

In contrast to this second statement in *Psychodiagnostics*, Zubin (1956) sought a shift in emphasis from the perceptual to the content aspects of the blots. Zubin's shift would eliminate the perceptual scorings on which Rorschach based his technique, and would lead to a conceptualization of the technique as a "systematic interview behind the veil of ink blots" (p. 189). Other contemporary workers have favored a content approach to Rorschach interpretation (Elizur, 1949; Wheeler, 1949; Lindner, 1950; Brown, 1953a).

Gordon (1959) wrote that Rorschach responses may be considered "samples of verbal behavior." The influence of some stimulus component, such as color, thus would hold less importance than the test subject's ability to verbalize the stimulus. No one-to-one correspondence would be assumed between actual and verbalized determinants. Consistent with the direction of Zubin's thinking, Rorschach responses would not be defined as directly perceptual. When a test subject spontaneously reports some instance of bizarre content, the principal meaning of this report for Gordon would be that of "poor social judgment," which always is of interest to Rorschach examiners.

Wagoner (1963) proposed a more radical formulation than that of Zubin and Gordon by suggesting that Rorschach response patterns are "really nothing but the number of times S has used nouns, verbs, and adjectives" (p. 419). A rejoinder to this proposed stress on the primary grammatical aspects of Rorschach responses was made by Arnold Binder (1964). Binder, admittedly biased in favor of the traditional perceptual framework, was able to offer his "personal feeling" that Wagoner's approach was misdirected.

Sarason (1954), in what Cronbach lauded as "the first major report on Rorschach which simultaneously adheres to the standards of scientific psychology and reflects faithfully the clinical use of the test" (1956, p. 183), described Rorschach test performance as purposeful problem solving. The latter description conveys strong emphasis on the cognitive aspect of personality functioning not originally conveyed by Rorschach himself.

Underlying the turnabouts in Rorschach thinking have been repeated failures of traditional frameworks to provide definitive evidence of validity. The Rorschach, however, survives. The Rorschach continues to find widespread application in clinical practice and in academic settings. The situation is similar to one discussed by Frank (1961) writing of the difficulties psychoanalysts have had in attempting to validate their slightly older theory and clinical procedures. Frank, noting the operation of a selection bias among psychoanalysts, was impressed by the observation that successful cases strengthen the underlying conceptual scheme while failures seem not to shake it. Nor do other of the projective instruments commonly employed in clinical settings stand in better stead (Murstein, 1963). In the case of the Rorschach, one may legitimately wonder whether the method has remained unshaken (Challman, 1951, p. 241).

The following commentary made by one prominent Rorschach expert of another may be considered representative of the existing state of Rorschach confusion.

> Except for the use of Rorschach's inkblot figures and some of his letter symbols, the technique has now so little in common with Rorschach's test, either in method or in some important basic presuppositions, that it represents a quite different approach. . . . It would go far in clearing up the present state of confusion if Klopfer and his associates ceased to identify their method by the term "Rorschach" (Beck, 1959, pp. 273–4).

The need for research which might clarify the validity-utility discrepancy characteristic of Rorschach history is clear.

Puzzlement over the major discrepancy between Rorschach utility and Rorschach validity served as the starting point of the research to be reported on in the present volume. The theoretical supposition was that before clinical Rorschach theory could be translated "more intelligently" into experimental design as adduced by Cronbach (1956), clinical implementation would first have to be examined more closely, particularly as this implementation came about through the activities of the professional clinician. *Clearer understanding of Rorschach utility must precede more meaningful evaluation of Rorschach validity.*

The idea of investigating the clinician as he implements the Rorschach in practice is not new. Armitage et al. (1955) cited the need for further explorations in the *utility* of the Rorschach. Chambers and Hamlin (1957) are among those whose research has been guided by the principle that "As the Rorschach is used in actual clinical practice, the clinician and the tool are an entity" (p. 105). Recent Rorschach studies have shown increased consideration for the significance of the concept "clinical use" in their designs. Hertz (1959), who has directed much of the blame for past Rorschach validation failures on clinicians, expressed similar recognition regarding the need for research on clinical utilization of the Rorschach.

> Indeed there is a need to do research on selection and training methods, on the clinician himself, and the clinical process . . . in the interpretation of a record, it is clear that Rorschach clinicians must exercise some self-discipline, standardize procedures to the extent to which they can be standardized, develop a consistent body of normative data, and train clinicians to handle the Rorschach as it should be handled (p. 47).

Ainsworth (1954) has stated that there is no sharp dividing line between validation research and the clinical use of the Rorschach technique. She views the two as going hand in hand. Her thesis that the Rorschach can be investigated most productively by classifying it less as a "test" of personality and more as a method of observation and appraisal reflects a lack of clear differentiation between the two outlooks. Her view is consistent with Zubin's (1956) conceptualization of the Rorschach as a veiled interview.

It would not appear to be coincidental that Beck, after having produced three instructional texts grounded in "sound, normative method" (1945, 1952, 1961), and after having conducted normative samplings of schizophrenic and normal populations, wrote in his 1960 text that his effort was "not to prove the test's validity but to demonstrate its working processes" (p. 8). While commenting upon the experimental nature of his Rorschach venture, he conditionally dismissed the dearth of validating data as an incidental shortcoming.

In sum, there are two general areas relevant to questions pertaining to Rorschach validity. Each area may be viewed as preceding actual validity study. Both areas have remained relatively unexplored in Rorschach research. The first area has to do with the *interpretative processes* of clinicians as the Rorschach is put to use. The second area concerns the nature of the interaction that occurs between *quantitative and qualitative* approaches to Rorschach interpretation. The present research was based on the belief that these two areas could be meaningfully combined into a single study. The study, while bearing a relation to the question of Rorschach validity, was concerned primarily with Rorschach utility. The study attempted to determine what information the clinician actually uses in his Rorschach interpretation and how he proceeds in his utilization of Rorschach information.

Identification of the *sources* of utility would relate to the question "What information do clinicians actually use in Rorschach interpretation?" Identification of the *processes* of utility would relate to the question "How or when do clinicians make use of information in Rorschach interpretation?"

Chapter 2

The Rorschach Clinician

Research interest in clinical judgment with the Rorschach has lagged behind traditional recognition of the instrument as "a highly complex multidimensional instrument which requires the full utilization of the skills of the clinician" (Hertz, 1959, p. 46). As phrased by Hertz, it is *the critical eye of the clinician* which leads to appropriate understanding of personality structure and the dynamics underlying behavior. Individuals show wide-ranging, unique, and often subtle levels of adaptive and defensive behavior. Appropriate clinical understanding of an individual thus must take into account a large number of internal and external variables, in combinations and in patterns, including perceptual capacity, intellectual functioning, anxiety experiences, interpersonal relationships, environmental influences, emotional stability, regularities in development, degree of integration, interplay of conscious and unconscious adaptation, and the direction and severity of any personality deviation that may be manifested.

Although many of the relationships between traditional Rorschach variables and personality functioning remain hypothetical, these assumed relationships are applied regularly in clinical interpretation. Contraindications in relation to routine application of Rorschach information have come from a number of sources. Rorschach workers readily acknowledge that test factors and configurations carry a variety of interpretative meanings, depending upon the context of the test data (Sargent, 1945) and the personality of the subject (Beck, 1935). Experimental investigators have also found rule-of-thumb Rorschach signs to be inadequate, including those related to normality (Brockway, Gleser, and Ulett, 1954). "Water" responses were found to be a specific indicator of alcoholism in Kentucky, but not in Massachusetts or Washington (Griffith, 1961).

Inkblot perceptions also may be affected by sex, age, race, intelligence, education, socioeconomic background, test situation, examiner characteristics, and other influences whose importance is only beginning to be evaluated systematically (Ames et al., 1952, 1954, 1959, and 1966; Williams and Nahinsky, 1968; Epstein, Lundborg and Kaplan, 1962; Schafer, 1954). The end result of this awesome Rorschach complexity has been to make the effectiveness of the Rorschach technique highly dependent upon the skills of its clinical users.

> The user of the method must rely upon a body of guesses as to the relationships involved—including those which have accumulated in the literature, plus his own experience with the test in particular, and knowledge of normal and abnormal personality in general (Schneider, 1950, p. 493).

Significantly, interest in clinical judgment appears to be on the increase in this country. Among the first to direct attention to the clinician, "psychology's forgotten instrument," was Henry Murray (1943). Recently active on problems related to validation of the clinician have been William Hunt and Ronald Walker (Hunt, 1946; Hunt, Schwartz, and Walker, 1965; Hunt and Walker, 1966; Hunt, Walker, and Jones, 1960; Walker and Hunt, 1965; Pribyl, Hunt, and Walker, 1968). Hunt's investigations have focused on clinical use of Wechsler's intelligence scales. Studies by Roy Hamlin of the clinician as judge have occurred within the Rorschach framework (Hamlin, 1954; Hamlin and Powers, 1958; Powers and Hamlin, 1955; Powers and Hamlin, 1957).

One study by Chambers and Hamlin (1957) bears on the importance of attending to both clinician and instrument in Rorschach investigations. Twenty psychologists were asked to identify Rorschachs according to clinical groups. Each psychologist received one record from each of five outpatient groups: involutional depression, anxiety neurosis, paranoid schizophrenia, brain damage from neurosyphilis, and adult mental deficiency. Under the relatively favorable forced-choice conditions employed, identifications were found to be accurate at a level better than chance. However, interjudge differences were large. Five judges contributed nearly 50 per cent of the correct identifications, while six judges contributed less than 10 per cent. Reasonable but not expansive claim for the Rorschach as a technique for identifying patient groups was considered justifiable by the authors, especially when the psychologists were classified into subgroups according to their success in making diagnostic judgments.

A number of relevant observations on Rorschach interpretation may be derived from Chambers and Hamlin's findings. First, highly successful use of "blind" Rorschach protocols was possible for some clinicians. Second, successful and unsuccessful judges differed in their approaches to Rorschach interpretation. Successful judges reached a higher level of abstraction from the raw data. They showed flexibility in shifting from one level of interpretation to another, suggesting greater capacity for adaptiveness and selectivity with regard to the data. Successful judges also adhered less to textbook statements and traditional "signs." They used fewer words to communicate their ideas. Third, significant differences could be noted in the level of difficulty associated with the diagnosis of various clinical groups. Mentally retarded adults were identified correctly in 90 per cent of the cases, while the remaining four groups were identified with only 50 per cent correctness. The highest single misinterpretation occurred between the organic and paranoid groups, organic patients being misjudged paranoid in 7 out of 20 instances.

Other variables influencing Rorschach interpretation have been cited. Hamlin (1954) reviewed ten studies dealing with the clinician as judge. He reported confirmation of his hypotheses that positive or negative outcomes in Rorschach research are related directly to (a) the complexity of the material being judged, and (b) the adequacy of experimental conditions in allowing the clinician to derive judgments from the material. In general, the more complex the material to be judged, the more negative the outcome.

> Increasing complexity beyond a certain point probably does not lead to meaningful global understanding, except under ideal conditions or in a clinical situation where data can be cross-checked, discarded as not pertinent, or synthesized in a manner that eventually results in a simplified picture derived from complexity (p. 235).

Cummings (1954) also reviewed the literature in the area of Rorschach judgment. He concluded that of the studies employing projective techniques, those most closely approximating the operation of the clinician-in-action often yielded positive outcomes, although not uniformly so. In conducting an investigation of his own, he limited the available data to single Rorschach card performances. His 8 judges showed moderate success in evaluating the adjustment of 50 white males. In comparing his basically positive results with negative results reported in similar studies (Grant, Ives, and Ranzoni, 1952; Newton, 1954), Cummings pointed out that the latter studies had utilized total Rorschach protocols as the judgment unit. Cummings concluded that his less complex, single-card units enhanced his judges' opportunities for intensive coverage of the data. His statements support those of Hamlin concerning the influence of *complexity of material* and *adequacy of experimental conditions* as variables in Rorschach research.

Powers and Hamlin (1957) limited the amount of data to be judged even further than did Cummings by presenting only Card I responses given by a 34-year-old male outpatient. Six clinicians were able to make "reasonably valid statements" from the limited data. The authors designated two levels of the judgment process, one descriptive and one speculative. In support of findings obtained by Symonds (1955), it was found that clinicians relied more on content factors than traditional determinant scores to back up their inferences. Determinant scores were called upon only secondarily. Powers and Hamlin further noted that success in Rorschach judgment was more characteristic of some areas of personality than of others, an observation which parallels that of Chambers and Hamlin (1957) with regard to differential difficulty in diagnosing various patient groups. Quoting from Powers and Hamlin,

> Agreement with the criterion measures was fairly good for the variables of intellectual level, intellectual efficiency, self concept and self attitudes, identification, and anxiety level; and agreement was least adequate for the variables of way in which subject relates to others and attitudes toward others, type of symptomatology, diagnostic category, and emotional control (p. 289).

Symonds' (1955) aim was to determine which aspects of Rorschach data expert clinicians would respond to in making "blind" judgments about a 27-year-old, female, high school teacher. Seven experienced judges were presented with a single Rorschach protocol. Large differences were observed in the fullness of the submitted reports and in the accuracy of the interpretations, with 65 per cent correctness overall. Accuracy of interpretation was checked against material revealed during individual therapy interviews. Only 44 per cent of the 200 interpretations were based on traditional Rorschach signs and determinants (accuracy = 60%), whereas 56 per cent were based on content (accuracy = 75%). The Rorschach judges again exhibited large individual variations in their patterns of determinant and content usage.

The finding that clinicians may rely more on content than on determinant scores as sources of information in Rorschach interpretation merits further comment. First, determinant and summary scores are derived from the response content appearing in a subject's "free associations" to the blots. Clinicians using these contents may make implicit determinant scorings which are not formally recorded, particularly in experimental studies. Clincians also may hold implicit expectations regarding the appearance of some determinant such as movement, shading, or popular percept on a Rorschach card, the absence of which would contribute meaningful information about an individual even though this information would not be scored formally.

Second, the critical cues in Rorschach interpretation may well have their origin in the free association responses. Included here would be the content of percepts, language idiosyncracies, and manner of associating (Turner, 1966). Lorenz (1959) viewed the formal pattern of language responses as an index of perceptual modes congenial to an individual, discerned through analysis of the classes of predicates the individual selects to represent his perceptions. Wagoner's (1963) proposal that Rorschach response patterns represent nothing more than number of times an individual has used nouns, verbs, and adjectives may be recalled in this context.

Turner (1966) found that predictions of personality adjustment based on free associations alone were as accurate as those based on entire Rorschach protocols. He expressed considerable doubt regarding the utility of certain traditional dimensions in Rorschach interpretation, even when professional experience was taken into account.

> Either all of the cues necessary to make judgments are available in the Free Association, or possibly the clinician is not taking advantage of any information which appears in the location chart, Inquiry, and Record Blank (p. 8).

Rodgers (1957) attempted to identify the sources of information entering into Rorschach interpretation. He had beginning graduate students prepare descriptive and self-concept Q-sorts from blind Rorschach evaluations of two nonpatient males. Although two months of course training were shown to have an influence on the students' interpretations, this influence was actually quite small, accounting for only 4 per cent of the total variance. The protocols themselves accounted for 20–23 per cent of the variance, while individual differences accounted for 15–19 per cent. The remaining 50–58 per cent was unaccounted for, and was considered to be error variance. Rodgers saw the latter as having "sobering import," but indicated that the error variance would be expected to be lowered markedly for experienced clinicians. Course instruction seemed neither to increase nor decrease stereotypy of interpretation.

Newton (1954) compared judgments of adjustment made by ten clinical psychologists with those made by psychiatrists. High reliability was obtained in all the judging tasks. The psychologist and psychiatrist groups were found to be nearly equal in their judgments of clinical case material (.94, .91). Reliability between the groups was lower (.86) but still significant, as was the psychologists' reliability when judging Rorschach protocols (.73). However, judgments stemming from Rorschach material were not found to correlate meaningfully with psychologists' judgments of case material (.09). Nor did the Rorschach judgments correlate significantly with diagnostic placements of the 50 subjects, 10 of whom were "socially adequate."

Corsini, Severson, Tunney, and Uehling (1955), related adequacy of clinical judgment to the length of time spent on the judging process. Three psychologists were asked to rank Rorschach records of 50 prisoners and 50 hired guards along a continuum of adjustment. One of the psychologists was requested to work rapidly and his "snap" judgments proved to be least adequate in comparison with the judgments of two other psychologists. The psychologist taking the longest amount of time showed the greatest accuracy, slightly higher than that obtained by a fourth psychologist who had administered the Rorschachs. All three judges performed better than an objective Rorschach checklist in separating the two groups.

The importance of length of time spent in Rorschach interpretation was mentioned in a study by Richards and Murray (1958). Three clinical psychologists, advanced graduate students, and nonpsychologists were asked to make global judgments of masculinity or femininity for 30 Rorschach protocols. Better than chance sortings were found for the trained psychologists, especially when "adequate time" was provided for making judgments. Wheeler's objective signs of homosexuality showed no relationship with measured femininity in males.

The amount of information required to arrive at a Rorschach diagnosis proved to be one of the most variable factors in Tabor's (1959) study of 30 clinicians. Variability seemed to be related more to the personal needs of the clinicians than to differences among the three diagnostic problems employed in the study. Individual clinicians were consistent in their information needs for the three problems.

Intelligence estimation represents an area of considerable interest in Rorschach research due to the greater consistency with which favorable outcomes have been obtained in comparison with the outcomes of diagnostic studies. Bialick and Hamlin (1954) found that four VA staff psychologists and trainees were able to make valid and reliable judgments of intelligence. Judgments were based on five Rorschach W responses, taken from each of 25 white, outpatient males. The authors chose intelligence as the judgment variable because they believed it to be the variable best known by the judges. Highest correlations were obtained by the experienced psychologists, .68 with Wechsler-Bellevue IQ's and .84 among themselves.

Complete Rorschach records, summary profiles alone, and lists of vocabulary words taken from Rorschach responses were incorporated in a study by Davis (1961). All three of his judges proved better than chance ($p<$ .01) in estimating the Stanford-Binet levels of intelligence of 70 white, young adult males. Judgments based on the vocabulary lists were slightly more successful than those coming from the total Rorschach records, supporting a parallel finding by Trier (1958). Clinical judgments made solely from the summary profiles were least effective.

As would be expected, not all of the research seeking to determine whether postulated relationships between Rorschach variables and IQ exist has been successful (Klopfer, Allen, and Etter, 1960; Pauker, 1963). "Usually, when low, significant correlations between Rorschach factors and IQ have been found, they have failed to hold up under cross-valida-tion" (Trier, 1958, p. 289). Illustrative of this type of failure was the study by Armitage, Greenberg, Pearl, Berger, and Daston (1955). These authors found 13 out of 19 Rorschach variables to correlate with Wechsler-Bellevue IQ's at the .01 level of significance ($N =$ 500 patients). However, when they applied their multiple regression equation based on the six highest contributing variables to 200 new patients, no better than chance accuracy in intelligence estimates resulted. The authors suggested that vocabulary and quality of perceptual organization may have provided cues to judges who were able to make fairly accurate estimates when given access to the protocols.

Trier (1958) employed advanced graduate students as judges, dividing them into three groups. Group I was given 16 Rorschach protocols, asked to list the seven "most sophisticated" words from each protocol, and then asked to make IQ estimates from these word lists. Each of the Group II judges, who did not have access to the protocols, was given one of the four sheets of word lists compiled by the Group I judges, along with information about how the lists had been derived. They were asked to make IQ esti-mates using only the word lists. Judges in Group III were given the proto-cols from which to make intellectual estimates. There were 16 protocols in all, four each from a diagnostically mixed group of patients falling within the following ranges of intelligence: 89 and below, 90–109, 110–119, and 120 and above. Estimates of IQ also were made from Thorndike-Lorge word frequency counts. A number of conclusions were drawn from the study. First, estimates of intelligence could be derived accurately from Rorschach vocabulary lists. Second, judgments based on total Rorschach protocols were no more accurate than those based solely on vocabulary, a finding which was not in agreement with Armitage et al., (1955). Third, estimates based on the Thorndike and Lorge word frequency counts resulted in accuracy roughly comparable to that achieved by the judges. Fourth, results for Group III were in agreement with those of Armitage et al. (1955), who reported a median correlation of .69 for estimates based on evaluations of total protocols.

Sommer (1958) studied the relationship between Rorschach M responses and intelligence. Test records of 77 male patients who had been given both the Rorschach and Wechsler-Bellevue were selected for analysis. The Wechsler-Bellevue scores were fitted into nine IQ categories, at 20-point intervals. The correlation between M and IQ was supported, even when Rorschach R and H variables were held constant. A further attempt was made to determine whether M responses given by subjects of varying verbal intelligence could be distinguished on other than quantitative bases. The M responses were ranked according to intellectual level by three groups of judges, including senior psychologists, interns, and secretaries. Similar to Armitage et al. (1955) and Trier (1958), Sommer noted the influence of such cues as grammar and vocabulary level in contributing to judges' estimates of intelligence. The interns and secretaries, for example, were able to rank qualitative differences in verbatim M responses at a level that exceeded chance expectancy. Unlike the other investigators, however, Sommer showed that when the verbatim cues were removed, only psychologists were able to make successful IQ estimates. In support of a traditional Rorschach assumption, he suggested that cues other than vocabulary and grammar are present in Rorschach M responses.

In sum, there appears to be a consistent line of evidence indicating that the critical influence in Rorschach interpretation may not be Rorschach's technique per se but the professional worker who puts the instrument to use, the Rorschach clinician. Results of Rorschach judgment studies have shown that clinicians interpreting similar Rorschach information vary not only in the accuracy of their outcomes but in their approaches to interpretation as well. The multidimensional nature of Rorschach information, along with the influences of interpretative context and the specific clinical problem being investigated, make it difficult for workers to formulate interpretative rules having constant applicability. As clinicians have been found to value Rorschach information differentially, and as the outcomes of Rorschach judgments have been shown to have a direct relationship with the complexity of the material being judged, *a priori* inclusion or omission of Rorschach data in a study may not encompass the informational needs of all clinicians participating in the study. Individual variations among clinicians have been found to be high, including the type of data used, the amount of data used, and the time taken to complete the interpretation process. Therefore, one of the most significant needs to be met in validation research would be that of incorporating the Rorschach clinician in an experimental setting which would permit him a representative yet flexible approach to interpretation, geared to his own experiences and needs. The contribution to Rorschach interpretation made by qualitative information in addition to the traditional quantitative scores and summaries also must not be overlooked. This especially would be true concerning the content of the test subject's free associations and language expression. As for the contributing influence of the Rorschach test itself, studies clearly have shown that information derived from Rorschach protocols can enhance the success of outcomes in judgment studies, although not necessarily when the approach incorporates too much information in an unselective fashion. Also, information derived from Rorschach protocols does not simply duplicate biographical and historical information, but frequently contributes to the modification of conclusions arrived at on the basis of case history material.

Chapter 3

Rorschach Interpretation:
Quantitative or Qualitative?

Approaches to Rorschach interpretation may be classified basically into two categories, the "sign" or quantitative approach and the "content" or qualitative approach. The quantitative determinant formulae and ratios of Klopfer are well known to Rorschach workers, as are Piotrowski's ten signs of organicity. The qualitative approach is represented in the writings of Schafer, Phillips and Smith, and Beck. Schafer's emphasis is on thematic analysis, while Beck stresses sequential analysis. The qualitative approach focuses on description and process, includes symbolic events, and attempts to answer the question "What's going on in the patient at this point?" (McCully, 1965). Although neither quantitative nor qualitative approaches remain exclusive in clinical practice, Beck (1942) has indicated that the criteria of the two are different and that validation is within two totally different spheres of reference. Armitage and Pearl (1957, p. 479) have written in a similar vein,

> Investigators report varying success in relating test characteristics to specific diagnostic categories. Some of these characteristics are the presence or absence of certain of the Rorschach determinants, their relative strength, patterns, ratios and their adherence to acceptable criteria. Other methods have relied more heavily upon the content of the record and its characteristics, while still others have employed both content and determinants in various combinations.

The Jackson and Wohl (1966) survey of Rorschach teaching in American universities indicated that half of the academic respondents relied on both psychogram and content data in making Rorschach interpretations. When considered separately, however, content data reportedly were given four times the emphasis given to psychogram data (38%:9%). The secondary emphasis reported for psychogram data was noteworthy because 70 per cent of the respondents wrote that they constructed formal psychograms as part of their typical Rorschach preparation.

The question of whether determinants or contents possess the greater importance in Rorschach interpretation is considered to be unanswerable by Shapiro (1959). Each dimension is required for optimal understanding of the other. Maximum accuracy in interpretation results from consideration of both dimensions. Shapiro does not suggest that determinant and content sources of information correspond in any fixed one-to-one relationship, nor that they should be given equal consideration *a priori*.

> My aim is not to convince you that you should rely just equally on content and on determinant interpretation in Rorschach work. It seems to me that perfectly legitimate differences of interest, natural inclination or background will tend to cause each one to give more weight to one side than to the other. Also, there is no doubt that there are differences in this respect among different Rorschach protocols; some, quite legitimately I think, seem to call for more emphasis on content interpretation. The aim here is, rather, to show that there is no reason intrinsic to the test to consider one aspect more important than the other, and, in addition, to show that each aspect can be properly understood only in the light of the other (p. 368).

A third source of information which has been gaining its due share of attention only within the recent decade is that of biographical data. Strauss (1968), for example, found that when anamnestic data on Rorschach subjects were made available to psychology trainees before testing, the trainees tended to favor this source of information in writing personality reports while ignoring test data and behavioral observations. Sherman (1952) and Bower, Testin, and Roberts (1960) reported that patient groups were differentiated more successfully when such background variables as age and education were introduced and combined with Rorschach data. The importance of age as a background variable was recognized, and controlled, by Chambers and Hamlin in their 1957 study. These authors withheld age information on patients whose protocols were being judged because they believed that such information would serve as a clue in the identification of diagnostic groups.

Few protocols describing the detailed working processes by which psychologists interpret Rorschach information have appeared in the journal literature (Hertz and Rubenstein, 1939), although they have appeared more frequently in Rorschach textbooks (Rorschach, 1942, trans.; Beck, 1945, 1952, 1960; Klopfer et al., 1954, 1956; Schafer, 1948, 1954). Published case illustrations have tended to highlight the interpreter's use of nondeterminant, qualitative variables in the interpretation process. The following textbook quotations are opening statements of interpretation taken from the first cases analyzed in each of the texts cited.

> The mood-chord which characterizes this record is announced in its first words, "a gloomy card" (Beck, 1952, p. 74).

> In the realistic case situations, it would be quite artificial, if not senseless, to interpret this record independently of the fact that it was produced by a five-year-old child. However, for the theoretical reasons discussed previously we will make such an attempt (Klopfer, 1956, p. 32).

> (a) As the opening response, this unusual image forcefully suggests emphasis on narcissistic-decorative values. (b) The orchid image also seems to include noteworthy passive-receptive connotations: to a woman an orchid is something she *gets* as a tribute to her attractiveness. (c) Note the utterly unreflective initial response to inquiry (Schafer, 1954, p. 198).

Hermann Rorschach, in an application published posthumously by his student Oberholzer, proves to be the interpreter of exception. Rorschach begins his analysis by noting that the variability of the case findings suggests no definite direction. He then takes the "generally safest" direction of focusing on the color responses which he states "have been found empirically to be representatives of the affectivity . . ." (1942, trans., p. 192).

Indeed, attempts to control and quantify some of the information utilized by Beck, Klopfer, and Schafer in the quotations cited would be problematical in experimental research. It is not surprising that research focus on such word variables as "gloomy" and "narcissistic-decorative values" has been avoided by past experimenters, or that the ambiguous influence of such background variables as age has received limited attention. The more conveniently quantifiable determinant variables and numerical formulae would be preferred data in Rorschach studies. Yet the question to be asked is whether quantitative data are in practice key sources of utility in Rorschach interpretation for experienced clinicians. Hamlin and Powers (1958) concluded that experienced clinicians drew upon "a wide variety of cues, many of which show little relation to traditional Rorschach scoring categories" (p. 242). The cues utilized were not found to be identical from case to case, or from one judge to another.

Levine (1959) sought to explain why investigators were unable to obtain positive findings when the Rorschach was used to make prognostic predictions of patient status following a period of hospitalization. He suggested that failures in this area may have resulted from an unselective empirical approach:

> It is possible that these unsuccessful investigators have been scoring the Rorschach for 'traditional' Rorschach categories while clinicians utilize different variables, perhaps without scoring them, in their day-to-day work (p. 439).

Hamlin and Powers (1958) recorded the running comments of experienced judges as they made diagnostic judgments between paired psychotic and nonpsychotic responses to single Rorschach cards. Included in the responses were inquiry information, time notations, and some minimal behavioral data. The judges were requested to write a brief report for each pair of responses. The report was to indicate the judges' reasoning as they proceeded in their analyses, the specific elements that influenced the development of their diagnostic choices, the final choices made, and the degree of confidence the judges had about each of their choices. Each of the three clinicians made 50 judgments, 25 independently and 25 in joint conference. Immediate feedback was provided concerning the correctness of each judgment as it was made. The results of one protocol analysis, termed "representative" by the authors, suggested that *expressive* response material was the variable chiefly drawn on by the psychologists to provide them with clinical cues. Little emphasis was given to "unconscious factors" or to classical structural indicators. The general interpretative procedure that emerged went as follows:

> In this example, the judge selects the non-psychotic tentatively, but correctly, on the basis of the first few words. This rapid, often correct, "hunch" was characteristic in the majority of the 100 choices. The judge then builds up several general inferences: (a) the non-psychotic is reacting to the examiner with affect, and with patterned defenses; and her expressions of uncertainty are related to this pattern; (b) the psychotic is uncertain of his perceptions; (c) the psychotic becomes "typically" both vague and concrete in groping for details to elaborate his responses; and (d) the psychotic cannot keep track of what he has communicated to the examiner (p. 242).

Artificial limitations present in Hamlin and Power's study need to be recognized before generalizations from their findings could be accepted. One limitation involved having the psychologists base their judgments on pairs of responses. In actual Rorschach practice, analysis is based on the total number of responses given by a subject, in the context of an entire record. The psychologists' observed reliance on "the first few words" thus could have been peculiarly enhanced by the experimental conditions. With little of the usual data available on which to base their judgments, educated "hunches" might have been practical necessities. A second limitation in the study centered around the psychologists' having received immediate feedback regarding the correctness of their judgments. External feedback of this type seldom is available to clinicians in professional settings. "Learning," reinforced by the additional feedback information, likely was influential in the making of judgments. A third point of interest had to do with the extent to which the representative judge in this study oriented her interpretative framework toward the Rorschach subject's interpersonal relationship with her. If in fact representative, the example suggests that *psychology's forgotten instrument* (Murray, 1943), the Rorschach clinician, has not been forgotten after all.

The question of which Rorschach data and cues clinicians may be utilizing in their interpretative analysis is a major one. Most validity studies done on the Rorschach have been based on the assumption that traditional variables are the ones being used most weightedly by Rorschach workers. However, it is not at all clear that successful Rorschach interpreters do utilize traditional variables in theoretically directed ways. Evidence to the contrary has been provided by Hamlin and Powers (1958), Levine (1959), and Armitage and Pearl (1957). Utilization of Rorschach data is a complex process and this process is not always a consistent one. When investigating clinical implementation of the Rorschach, therefore, it would seem to be essential "to ascertain those aspects of Rorschach utilization which contribute to [success] and to determine whether or not these aspects vary. . . ." (Armitage and Pearl, 1957, p. 479).

Armitage et al. (1955) attempted to identify Rorschach variables contributing to accurate estimations of Wechsler-Bellevue intelligence levels. Two approaches were employed, one an objective statistical procedure and the other subjective judgments by three VA staff psychologists, stemming from either psychograms or complete protocols. Predictions of intellectual level were least accurate when the method of analysis was strictly objective. "Unproductive" results were found when objective variables were used in combination (multiple regression equation) as well as when used singly. The authors concluded it doubtful whether any objective procedure could prove useful for individual prediction.

Greater accuracy of prediction resulted from the judgmental approach, which allowed for "the integrating factor of the clinician." Judgments based on psychogram data yielded less accuracy than those based on the entire protocols, but both forms of judgment were more accurate than the objective approach. Differences in accuracy occurred even though the same Rorschach information was used in both the objective and subjective approaches.

This suggests that the clinician makes use of these factors in a somewhat different way than can be accomplished through the objective analysis. It seems probable that he may be able to assign more subtle weightings to constellations of these factors than was possible in the objective aspect. Furthermore, the clinician probably capitalizes on inferences from such additional, subjective factors as (a) the use of specific content categories (e.g., science), (b) the kinds of blends utilized, and (c) the apparent presence of extreme anxiety (p. 327).

Although Armitage et al. termed their judges' estimates "fairly accurate" in most instances, the accuracy of judgments was insufficient for individual prediction. A similar outcome was observed for the objective procedure. Judgmental consistency among and between psychologists generally proved to be favorable. Differences among judges were greatest in relation to neurotic protocols. When asked to list the reasons and methods underlying their intelligence estimates, judges working from complete Rorschach protocols cited qualitative factors of vocabulary and perceptual organization as having aided them the most.

Inclusion by Armitage et al. of Rorschach protocols obtained only from persons suffering pathological symptoms would be expected to complicate accuracy in intelligence estimation. Judges first would have to evaluate emotional status and then relate this to intellectual potential and efficiency.

One of the limitations characterizing many studies which have attempted to use objective indices in making Rorschach predictions relates to the nonincorporation of some equivalent to human "past experience" which all Rorschach clinicians have available to them. Objective procedures might be more realistically applied were information regarding successful and unsuccessful applications to be provided in a sustaining way, perhaps in the context of some continuously updating computer program (Loehlin, 1968). Incorporation of such feedback in ways which would permit "reevaluation" of Rorschach information based on cumulative input also might be expected to improve the overall predictive accuracy of quantitative scores and summaries in Rorschach studies, especially in contrast with the relatively "static" approach used by Armitage et al. An updating feedback program would be analogous to "clinical experience" and could lend itself to objective Rorschach designs similar to the one mentioned earlier by Hamlin and Powers (1958). In the latter study, one-half of the judgments made by the Rorschach psychologists were accompanied by immediate information concerning the correctness of the judgments.

Caldwell et al. (1952) also found that judgments made from total Rorschach records tended to be more productive than those made from psychograms alone. Clinicians' ratings based on maximum information agreed more closely with psychiatric ratings than did those based solely on the scoring summaries. As the amount of Rorschach data available to clinicians was reduced, psychologist-psychiatrist discrepancy increased.

However, the discrepancy between psychologists and psychiatrists noted by Caldwell et al. was not serious. In addition, surprisingly little loss in Rorschach sensitivity occurred as the amount of Rorschach data was reduced. The authors had hypothesized that certain of the specific item contents would be vital for correct diagnostic interpretation. Three levels of data availability were defined. Level I included the subject's entire behavior: specific responses, scoring symbols, and test behavior. Level II included the response protocol only, as it would be given in "blind" Rorschach diagnosis. Level III included only the scoring summary, as it would appear in the psychogram. What surprised the authors was that the quantitative categories, by themselves, could be utilized meaningfully by the three relatively experienced psychologists. While individual Rorschach items did show differing degrees of influence in contributing to final ratings, sole reliance on the quantitative data appeared to sacrifice little information.

Findings from a 1957 study by Armitage and Pearl supported those of Caldwell et al. Armitage and Pearl used five VA staff psychologists with four to nine years diagnostic experience with the Rorschach. Each psychologist was asked to make 180 diagnostic judgments of patients distributed among four psychiatric classifications: neurosis, character disorder, and paranoid and unclassified schizophrenia. Sixty judgments occurred under each of three conditions—psychogram, protocol, and combined use of both. The number of judgments per day was limited to ten in order to relieve psychologist boredom and to minimize possible distribution biases. The psychologists were free to employ any method of judgment they desired and use any cues they could obtain from the material presented to them.

> No significant differences were found between judgments based on either
> *psychograms, protocols,* or *both.* Although missing the criteria of significance, some indications were present that the psychograms were somewhat better for the prediction of the neurosis and that the protocols permitted a somewhat more accurate judgment of paranoid schizophrenia (p. 482).

One conclusion that may be drawn from the above study is that some types of Rorschach data possess greater differentiating value than others in the evaluation of psychiatric groups. Although no significant differences were observed among judges in their use of a particular diagnosis, greater variability occurred with neurotic records compared with schizophrenic ones. A question also may be raised as to whether the variable of diagnostic category has been controlled realistically in past research studies on Rorschach judgment.

The hypothesis that formal Rorschach factors have greater value than content factors in differentiating schizophrenic from normal groups was tested by Sherman (1952). His hypothesis was supported only when the total number of Rorschach responses was low (R less than 19), and generally was less supported when level of education was controlled.

In a "sign" study of deviant quantitative and qualitative factors, Bradway and Heisler (1953) were unable to find any Rorschach item that had an exclusive relationship with a single diagnostic category. However, some statistical trends did appear. Among the 100 protocols, for example, no record with a total number of responses (R) greater than 40 or with greater than 7 popular (P) responses proved to be psychotic. A disproportionate number of records with R less than 8 were found among depressive persons. Frequent occurrences of "eyes" and self-reference responses were slightly above expectancy for patients diagnosed as paranoid. These trends are consistent with standard interpretations of single Rorschach scores, although other trends reported by Bradway and Heisler contradict traditional lines of interpretation. The authors cautioned that no Rorschach variable should be considered pathognomic in itself and emphasized the need for integrated, holistic evaluation of Rorschach data.

Sherman's hypothesis was not supported by Bower, Testin, and Roberts (1960) who investigated the capacity of three types of quantified Rorschach scales to differentiate groups of hospital patients. The scales were derived from content, thought processes, or determinants, and were considered to be sensitive to different levels of ego functioning. The scales were applied to 30 cases each of obsessive-compulsives, personality trait disturbances, psychotic depressives, and catatonic and paranoid schizophrenics. Content scales appeared to differentiate the schizophrenic groups more successfully than determinant scales, but they did not differentiate the depressives. The determinant equation differentiated nonschizophrenic groups, selecting out depressives, but tended to misclassify schizophrenic groups. The thought process scale contributed to diagnosis in a general way but lost power when broken down into subscales. When relevant background variables such as age and education were introduced and combined with the Rorschach data, agreement between Bower, Testin, and Roberts' discriminant function with original diagnosis was elevated from 56 per cent to 76 per cent.

In Rorschach analysis, content interpretation frequently occurs at a symbolic level. A given response content may convey a variety of meanings, depending upon the context in which it appears and the clinician making the interpretation (Phillips and Smith, 1953). Much of the interpretative foundation used in deciphering the meaning of Rorschach responses has been provided by personality theories, particularly those of psychoanalytic orientation, by past experience, and by specific case illustrations. Halpern (1953), for example, viewed the response "rock" as symbolizing "security." Explained Rychlak (1959, p. 456),

> What the clinician must mean in this suggestion is that a meaning is conveyed by the construct Rock. He—the clinician—has learned to identify this less frequent association which people have between feelings of security (object) and rocks (sign).

Rychlak wanted to determine the extent to which content interpretations could be generalized without losing their validity. He adapted a method employed by Osgood (1952) to assess whether or not subjects would agree in their choices of clinical meanings often assigned to contents. If Rorschach constructs really signified the meanings often ascribed to them, the various experimental groups would be expected to show consistencies in their selection of forced associations to the constructs.

Twelve familiar Rorschach contents were investigated by Rychlak: Boots, Smoke, Bear, Mask, Fur, Fire, Clouds, Rocks, Hair, Bat, Island, and Mountain. Subjects were asked to assign a positive or negative valence to each of the constructs listed. They also were asked to assign one of six arbitrary meanings to each of the constructs: Ambition, Love, Security, Depression, Fear, and Anger. Included among the 160 experimental subjects were introductory psychology students, extension students, and state hospital mental patients. Distribution of males and females was nearly equal.

Allowing for expected differences between psychologists and unsophisticated subjects, the major prediction in Rychlak's study was verified. Consistencies in forced associations were reflected by the groups, cutting across sex and mental health lines, and many of the clinical interpretations were found to hold. Among the more typical findings were that (a) "Security" was associated to "Rocks" by both normals (62%) and patients (63%); (b) a positive valence to "Fur" was more likely to be assigned by women (94%) than men (80%); and (c) male patients chose "Security" and "Love" more frequently in assigning meanings than did normal males, who selected "Ambition" more frequently ($p < .01$). Little reversal was noted in the valence assigned to any of the constructs.

The semantic differential was employed by Goldfried (1963) in order to determine the connotative meaning of some Rorschach animal symbols among college students. Forty male and 40 female undergraduates rated

10 animal symbols on each of 12 bipolar adjective scales. Results failed to confirm the generality of symbolic meanings with "universal" consistency. Some of the interpretations presented in the Phillips and Smith (1953) text were confirmed: Alligator as active and destructive, Butterfly as passive-feminine. Most of the interpretations, however, were either only partially confirmed (Spider as wicked, but not feminine) or not confirmed at all (Ape not as a threatening, destructive figure).

A different approach to validating clinical hypotheses concerning the meaning of Rorschach responses and test behavior was taken by Halpern (1957). He converted his own interpretative reactions to his subjects' percepts into questions which he then posed directly to the subjects. What he was seeking was "a simple, face-value attempt at checking what the psychologist feels his S is communicating" (p. 16). The questions represented a variety of experiential levels, including personal history, feelings, fantasies, impulses, and behavior. Two types of "impressive evidence" were claimed by Halpern in favor of his idea that questions asked by the examiner reached a deep, meaningful level for patients. The first type of evidence was the appearance of metaphors similar to a subject's original percept, while the second had to do with the enthusiastic reactions of the subjects in response to being asked the questions.

Halpern's procedure may be seen as heavily laden with subjectivity and directive leading. The procedure may be more representative of interview processes than of traditional Rorschach technique. On the other hand, there is reminiscent similarity between his approach and Allport's (1955) belief that one too frequently overlooked method for gaining understanding of an individual is to allow that individual opportunities to tell about himself. "We are still in the dark concerning the nexus of John's life. A large share of our [clinical] trouble lies in the fact that the elements we employ in our analyses are not true parts of the original whole" (p. 21). Halpern did ask his subjects about particular aspects of their experience, as he and they perceived them. His striving was toward a more realistic representation between an individual's Rorschach performance and the individual's characteristic feelings and ways of coping with and expressing his feelings.

Schafer (1954) distinguished between static conceptions of content interpretation and the more dynamic form of thematic content analysis whose origins stemmed from psychoanalytic theory. While foreseeably running the risk of "wild psychoanalysis," thematic analysis was seen as a requirement in Rorschach interpretation because it integrated the interplay that occurs among inkblot, perceptual style, and personal imagery. Risks of naive psychoanalysis could be offset partially by standardization of context in Rorschach interpretation and by avoidance of one-to-one interpretations between individual responses and pathognomic categories.

The influence of a static yet traditional content approach to Rorschach interpretation proved to be disruptive to the general findings in a dissertation study by Tabor (1959). Tabor obtained process analyses of 30 Ph.D. clinicians as they interpreted three Rorschach protocols. The content approach was implemented only by a single clinician and was such an unusual departure that it lowered the clinician's subgroup agreement in comparison with other subgroups analyzed in the research. Elimination of the performance of the one clinician who "proceeded largely on the basis of content analysis" raised the level of comparability of his subgroup quite markedly.

The latter observations would not conflict with Schafer's ideas concerning the meaningfulness of content analysis from a thematic frame of reference. The content information available to Tabor's clinicians was limited mainly to the major content categories, typically in quantitative form, and did not lend themselves to thematic treatment. Schafer's approach relies on specific response contents which are evaluated in sequence and then related to card context, including analysis of pre- and post-responses.

In sum, it would appear that the relative influences of quantitative and qualitative sources of informaton in Rorschach interpretation have not been established. The demand cited by Cronbach (1956) for revision of accepted interpretations of Rorschach hypotheses may be in order. Some favorable support for the separate use of the two approaches has been provided experientially and experimentally, especially when information has been evaluated and put to use by experienced Rorschach judges. However, there has been no "universal" application reported for any one type of Rorschach information—no single pathognomic or classificatory indicator, quantitative or qualitative—and holistic applications incorporating both approaches have proven to be most successful. Personal historical data recently has entered into the Rorschach picture more explicitly as an integral aspect of interpretation, necessitated by actuarial considerations and varying norms related to sex, age, socioeconomic status, and so on. Although both sources of information typically have been made available to Rorschach interpreters in most practical settings and in some research situations, it has not been uncommon for observers to note a differential weighting of one informational source over the other. The task of determining the specific nature of such a weighting, including the interaction between quantitative and qualitative sources, to date has been an impossible one. Separation of the two forms of Rorschach data encourages an approach to interpretation which is unrepresentative of actual Rorschach practice, while inclusion of both data forms results in contamination. Among the influences found to be associated with differential use of quantitative and qualitative information have been the theoretical orientation of the clinician; the clinician's training, Rorschach experience, and personal preferences; existing theoretical guidelines, tested or assumed; the researcher's methodological considerations; and, the type of clinical problem at hand. One underlying theme has been that qualitative sources of Rorschach information—the expressive cues, vocabulary, perceptual organization, and situational interaction between subject and examiner— too regularly have been overlooked as a key source of information, especially in experimental investigations of Rorschach validity. Currently in question is the function of "traditional" objective scoring information, along with "traditional" assumptions as to how such quantitative data is put to use. Reliance on a strictly objective Rorschach approach to interpretation frequently has resulted in outcomes which have been disappointing. Such a reliance also has dispensed with *the integrating factor of the Rorschach clinician* which likely represents the single most critical factor in the interpretation process. It is the Rorschach clinician who is able to decipher, weight, hold to or deviate from "traditional" applications, and who senses and takes into account such unpredictables as the subject-examiner interaction and the particular uniqueness of a test subject's Rorschach record.

Chapter 4

The Applicability of
Rimoldi's Technique

In an unpublished doctoral dissertation, Tabor (1959) analyzed the interpretation processes of 30 clinical psychologists who were asked to determine the diagnoses of psychiatric patients through "blind" Rorschach evaluation. Tabor's study implemented a problem-solving technique developed by Rimoldi (1955), who originally employed it to investigate the processes by which physicians diagnosed medical problems (1956, 1958).

The major feature of the Rimoldi technique rests in the step-by-step procedural recording it permits as isolated increments of information are selected, gathered together, and synthesized by a clinical worker. Data related to a specific clinical problem are written on separate information cards, one unit of data per card (questions). The worker is requested to solve predetermined problems by deriving his information from the data cards available, one question at a time, in a manner which then is left to the worker to decide upon for himself. The sequence of card selections (questions asked) is called a "tactic." Instructions emphasize that the worker select only information cards deemed "necessary and sufficient" in order to maximize the more systematic features of his approach and to minimize inclusion of relatively irrelevant data. The technique allows the experimenter to control (a) the problem to be solved, (b) the type of information made available, and (c) the amount of information given in a card unit question.

The Rimoldi technique has been used in a variety of contexts. Haley (1963) used it to assess the effects of training on medical diagnostic skills. Rimoldi and Devane (1961) assessed the influence of training on cognitive problem solving. The technique has been used to study thinking processes through different ages (Rimoldi et al., 1962), mathematical abilities (Reidel, 1963), and changes in the course of psychotherapy (Meyer, 1963). Psychiatric, psychological, and social work approaches to the diagnosis of minimal brain pathology in children were investigated by Mohrbacher (1961). Gunn (1962) studied psychologists and social workers asked to solve problems involving interpersonal conflict. Gunn's study contained an excellent review of clinical judgment literature from the frameworks of medicine, psychiatry, and the Wechsler-Bellevue Intelligence Scale.

Most recently, Rimoldi's technique has been used to investigate the relationship between thinking and language (Rimoldi, 1967), the inter-relationships between logical structure, language, and thinking (Rimoldi, 1969), aging and problem solving (Rimoldi and Vander Woude, 1969), and, a comparison of problem solving processes between hearing and deaf children (Vander Woude, 1969). Rimoldi and his associates consistently have distinguished between the study of "products" and the study of "processes," placing greatest emphasis on a systematic understanding of the latter. More important than inferring how a subject proceeds by study-ing the subject's responses exclusively is the knowledge of how a subject proceeds in order to reach a certain response. A goal-directed approach is assumed in which the subject actively searches for, combines, and checks the information that he considers will lead to the solution.

Some of the pertinent general findings resulting from the studies cited may be listed.

1. Clinical experts selected information items which had highest utility value for the group as a whole.
2. Clinical experts selected a smaller number of information items in answering clinical questions than did less experienced workers.
3. Clinical workers arrived at similar diagnostic conclusions even though they followed different procedures of interpretation.
4. Clinical experts showed a high degree of correspondence in outcome, despite the emergence of greater personal style associated with experi-ence, whether they were physicians solving medical problems or psy-chologists interpreting Rorschach records.
5. Physicians interpreted information in similar ways for a particular case even though their training reflected different schooling.
6. Junior medical students selected information not valued by the general medical group.

7. Senior medical students were more critical in their diagnostic approach than were Juniors, reflecting the influence of increased knowledge and experience.

In Tabor's study, "a definite lawfulness" was found in the sequence in which Rorschach data were accumulated by experienced psychologists. The clinicians generally proceeded from quantitative data to more qualitative, symbolic data. The latter finding was not in agreement with the findings of Symonds (1955), Powers and Hamlin (1957), and Hamlin and Powers (1958), and likely was related to a limitation in Tabor's study having to do with the way in which Rorschach data were made available to the clinicians. That is, the content of the response was available primarily in summary form, under the traditional content categories represented by H, Hd, A, Ad, and so forth.

Tabor's clinicians were highly self-consistent in their information needs, showing little individual variation across the three diagnostic problems. Internal consistency would be expected to be lower were clinicians asked to solve problems which were not all related to diagnosis.

R, F%, and F+% were found to represent the basic orientation data necessary for diagnostic interpretation by the clinicians in Tabor's study. Minor variations peculiar to the individual protocols were noted. For example, the rigidity of the Schizophrenic personality elicited greater concern with Dd, S, and d. The Normal record elicited greater seeking of evidence of normality with regard to FK and Fc. The sterility of the Organic protocol gave rise to suspicions regarding the depression, C', and the basic question of degree of contact with reality, P. While it also was noted that two-thirds of the clinicians were "basically correct" in their diagnostic statements about the three protocols presented to them, diagnostic accuracy showed no relationship to the amount of information from which diagnoses were derived, or to sequential selections of information, or to the efficiency level of selection. Tabor explained these negative observations by indicating that arbitrary and excessive accumulation of information could influence efficiency scores in one direction only, that of reducing efficiency. He suggested that a finer differentiation of Rorschach data in its experimental presentation might result in more positive findings.

> Items might be classified according to types of scoring categories, for example, (1) location scores, (2) determinants, (3) content categories, and (4) numerical ratios. The relative emphasis in these various areas by different analysts might yield some fruitful findings. A tentative exploration of this problem indicates considerable differences among analysts. Some explore one area thoroughly, for example, location scores, before moving on to another, for example, determinants. There appears to be a

quite deliberate, though perhaps unconscious, concentration on one area at a time. Others, on the other hand, transfer continually from one area to another, suggesting a more macroscopic view of the Rorschach (p. 109).

The Rimoldi technique is consonant with the general research findings reported in earlier chapters which survey the literature on clinical judgment with the Rorschach. The technique can allow for the fullest possible operation of *the critical eye of the clinician* (Hertz, 1959) and *the integrating factor of the clinician* (Armitage et al., 1955) in Rorschach interpretation. Fuller freedom of operation could result only by providing the clinician with entire Rorschach protocols. However, experimental control over the process of Rorschach interpretation then would be sacrificed.

Within the limits of Rimoldi's problem solving technique and of "blind" diagnosis, the clinician is free to select as little or as much Rorschach data as he wishes. No restrictions are placed on the order of his selections, although once an information card is selected, its sequential position then is determined. The clinician is allowed to make written notations as he proceeds in his evaluations, constructing psychograms or other formal summaries according to his own preferences or needs. Introspections also may be encouraged in order to provide a running description and explanation of the data selections, limited only by the clinician's personal willingness to verbalize them. Although it is true that clinicians would not be able to gain an immediate holistic overview of the Rorschach record, the possibility of their gaining such an overview nevertheless would be open to them. Clinicians would have only to select all of the data cards. In sum, the clinical interpretation of Rorschach protocols under the Rimoldi conditions could occur in a way which would be as maximally similar to the natural Rorschach setting as possible, limited only by the experimental goal of maintaining step-by-step control over the interpretative process.

The research study to be reported on in the present volume utilized Rimoldi's technique and may be viewed as consonant with Hamlin's (1954) conclusions that outcomes in Rorschach research have been directly related to the simplicity or complexity of the material to be judged and to the adequacy of the experimental conditions in allowing the clinician to derive judgments from the material. The study also may be seen as consistent with Cummings' (1954) conclusion that Rorschach studies most closely approximating the operation of the clinician-in-action most often yielded positive relationships in their outcomes. In the present study, each clinician was able to determine his own limits of simplicity or complexity of the material to be judged. Each clinician was able to determine for himself the amount and type of Rorschach data necessary to arrive at clinical conclusions. He was free to utilize part or all of the available data. He was free to rely on content factors or on traditional determinant scores, according to his own desired emphasis, the latter recognized to be an important variable in Rorschach interpretation (Symonds, 1955).

Success in clinical judgment with the Rorschach has been shown to be more characteristic for some areas of personality than for others (Powers and Hamlin, 1957). In the present study, three different types of clinical problems were presented. One problem was a request for psychiatric diagnosis, another an estimate of severity of anxiety, and the final one an estimate of current intellectual functioning. Lower self-constancy than was found in Tabor's study was predicted for individual clinicians across the three Rorschach protocols.

The present study also attempted to control for possible cues associated with language, behavioral observation, and background data. Rorschach responses *per se* were separated from accompanying verbalizations and examiner observations. Background data, however, were made available to the clinicians in keeping with the design format of separate items of information appearing on separate cards (Sherman, 1952; Chambers and Hamlin, 1957; Bower, Testin, and Roberts, 1960). Each clinician in the study was able to make some relative determination of "adequate time" for his interpretations (Corsini et al., 1955; Richards and Murray, 1958). Finally, combinations of various criteria were used in ascertaining the final accuracy of the clinicians' interpretations, including (a) results from other projective tests, (b) psychiatric judgments, and (c) results from the Stanford-Binet Intelligence Scale.

Chapter 5

Experimental Methodology
and Clinician Sample

Recent surveys have shown Rorschach's technique to be the most widely used psychological test in American clinical settings, the psychological instrument used most often in research, and the clinical tool given greatest emphasis in the American graduate curriculum. Despite wide evidence of Rorschach use, however, the validity of the technique has not been experimentally demonstrated. Interestingly, Rorschach validation research typically has failed to incorporate the critical influence of the clinician, or even to establish experimentally the ways in which clinicians use Rorschach information in actual practice.

In the present study, 36 experienced clinical psychologists practicing in the Chicago area were asked to interpret three Rorschach protocols under the conditions of Rimoldi's data-selection technique. An *experienced clinical psychologist* was defined as a person (a) holding the Ph.D. degree in clinical psychology, (b) having at least four years clinical experience since the time the Ph.D. degree was conferred, (c) having utilized the Rorschach technique in clinical investigation, and (d) willing to participate in the study, which required approximately 1½ hours time, or more (see Table 1).

The purpose of the present research was to clarify the discrepancy found to be existing between Rorschach utility and validity by determining the actual sources of information used in Rorschach interpretation by·

Table 1.   Description of Clinician Sample

Variables	Mean	SD	Range
Age in years	44.7	8.1	32–65
Years since Ph.D.	13.4	7.6	4–30
Rorschachs administered, interpreted, or supervised during past five years	265.6	310.1	25–1500

	Number	Per Cent
APA membership	36	100
Diplomate in clinical psychology	18	50
Rorschach orientation		
Beck	25	69
Klopfer	11	31

Primary Setting of Rorschach Use

Clinic	Hospital	Private Practice	Research	Academic
47%	39%	8%	6%	0%
	Outpatient	Inpatient	Other	
	64%	33%	3%	

Primary Group of Rorschach Use

	Male	Female	Both	
	75%	14%	11%	
Adult	Young Adult	Child	Adolescent	Elderly
56%	22%	14%	8%	0%
Personality Disturbance	Psychotic	Neurotic	Neurological	Mixed	Normal
36%	28%	19%	3%	14%	0%

Value of Rorschach in Clinical Investigation

Attitude Favorable	Attitude Unfavorable
100%	0%

Use of Rorschach in Test Battery

Most of the time	All of the time	Occasionally	Little	None of the time
53%	30%	17%	0%	0%

Table 1. *continued*

Usefulness of Rorschach Ranked for Three Clinical Problems

	First	*Second*	*Third*
Diagnosis	72%	14%	14%
Anxiety	22%	68%	10%
Intelligence	6%	18%	76%

experienced clinical psychologists. Utility was defined in two ways: *what* information clinicians used in interpretation (frequency, consistency), and *how* this information was used (when, for what questions, by which clinicians).

Two general hypotheses were established, combined from observations based on traditional Rorschach theory, literature findings, and clinical practice. The major hypothesis stated that the utility of different sources of information used in Rorschach interpretation would vary primarily as a function of the type of clinical question asked. The second hypothesis indicated that the sources of utility in Rorschach interpretation would vary as a function of the clinician's approach, quantitative or qualitative.

Hypothesis I: The utility of different sources of Rorschach information varies according to the clinical question asked.

Hypothesis II: Clinicians show distinguishable patterns of approach to Rorschach interpretation.

The formulation of the problem reflected a basic conceptual shift which questioned traditional Rorschach assumptions and, correspondingly, the framework from which numerous validation studies have been undertaken and proven unsuccessful. The formulation (a) questioned the assumption that sources of Rorschach utility have been established, (b) directed the focus of Rorschach effectiveness toward the instrument's clinical user, the Rorschach clinician, and (c) asserted that clearer understanding of utility must precede more meaningful evaluation of Rorschach validity.

Clinical and experimental needs were accommodated simultaneously in the study through construction of an apparatus adapted from Rimoldi (1955) which controlled access to the Rorschach information, one item at a time. The apparatus provided nearly all of the information a clinician would require for Rorschach interpretation while permitting a high degree of control over, and quantitative treatment of, this information. The order in which the three Rorschach records were presented was rotated systematically so as to control for potential errors associated with position effects, familiarity with the experimental procedure, and general interpretative context. The design also included both Beck and Klopfer scoring information.

Friedman's two-way analysis of variance test (Siegel, 1956) was used to determine the differential utility of 329 information items for answering the three clinical problems of Diagnosis, Anxiety, and Intelligence.

Two assumptions were made in determining the relative utility value of the information available for Rorschach interpretation in the study. First, items and categories perceived as more useful by clinicians would be *selected more frequently* than those perceived as less useful. Second, more useful items and categories would be *selected earlier* in the interpretation sequence than those perceived as less useful. These two assumptions thus permitted the data to be viewed from the dual perspectives of *what* was used and *how* or when it was used.

The specific measure of *what* information clinicians used was the Utility Index (UI), indicating the frequency with which items were selected. Expressed as a percentage, the UI represented the ratio of the number of times an item was selected to the total number of clinicians doing the selecting. As each of the 36 clinicians in the study was free to select any given card, the maximum UI for an information item would be 100 per cent and the minimum UI would be 0.0 per cent.

In order to provide a general framework for evaluating the relative emphasis given to the information selected by the clinicians, each item also was assigned to one of six Utility Levels (UL), according to the magnitude of the item's Utility Index. The six Utility Levels were based on cumulative percentage divisions of the normal curve, approximating ±3 standard deviations, as illustrated in Figure 1.

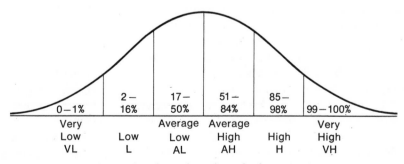

Figure 1. Six levels for classifying the utility of information items.

The principal measure of *how* information was used by the clinicians in the study was the Mean Rank (MR), indicating the average sequential point of selection for each item. As each information card was assigned a rank indicating its ordinal position in the selection sequence on each protocol for each clinician, it was possible to sum the ranks assigned to a given card and divide the resulting figure by the total number of clinicians doing the selecting. Cards which had not been selected by a clinician were assigned the average rank of all remaining cards in the record, on the statistical assumption that each card would have had an equal probability of being selected next. The maximum MR for a given information item would be 1.0 (selected first by all clinicians) and the minimum MR would be 329.0 (selected last by all clinicians).

The attempt to obtain two subgroups of clinicians representing both Beck and Klopfer orientations to Rorschach interpretation was partially successful. Both orientations were represented in the sample, although unequally. The predominant orientation was that of Beck ($N = 25$) and accounted for 69 per cent of the clinicians in the sample. The remaining 31 per cent was comprised of clinicians following Klopfer's orientation ($N = 11$). A single clinician who identified his approach with that of Piotrowski was grouped with the Beck sample on the basis of his greater use of Beck scores than of Klopfer scores in the study. The total clinician sample thus was defined as two-thirds Beck and one-third Klopfer in orientation. The effect of this two-to-one ratio was to limit generalizations of comparative findings between the two major Rorschach approaches commonly used in this country. However, the subgrouping served to control for influences associated with differences in academic training and background experiences.

Clinicians interpreted each Rorschach protocol by selecting whatever information items they considered to be "necessary and sufficient" for answering the clinical problem which accompanied it. For each of the three protocols, information was written on separate $2\frac{1}{2}'' \times 3''$ cards, inserted into pockets on a specially constructed $2' \times 3'$ cardboard folder, and grouped in vertical columns according to traditional Rorschach categories. The cardboard folder was self-supporting when presented in an upright, open-book fashion. The upright presentation facilitated ready access to the information cards, making it possible for the clinicians to view all of the information cards rapidly and comprehensively. Figure 2 provides an illustration of the experimental apparatus used in the study.

Sixteen categories of Rorschach information were available for selection by the clinicians, with some overlap in information items occurring due to separate presentation of Beck and Klopfer scorings.

Information Categories	*Examples*
Personal Data	Sex, Age, Education
Locations Klopfer	W, D%, Succession
Locations Beck	W, D, Z Sum
Determinants Klopfer	M, FM, Fc
Determinants Beck	M, F+, Blend
Content Klopfer	H, AAt, Obj
Content Beck	H, An, Oj
Totals Klopfer	R, FK + F + Fc%, Additionals
Totals Beck	R, Extended F + %, Avg Reaction Time
Individual Scorings Klopfer	W F A P, D KF Cl
Individual Scorings Beck	W F+ A P 1.0, D VF+ Cl
Free Associations	"Bat, wide spread of wings"
Verbalizations and Behavior	"It looks like a (laughter)"
Location Areas	Location chart area, circled
Responses to Cards	Card II: 4 responses, #5–#8
Reaction Times to Cards	Card I: 2"

The separate data cards thus appeared on the information board within the broad categories employed in the study. The traditional Rorschach symbol, word, ratio, or response number was written on the front of each of the data cards in order to indicate the type of information that could be obtained by removing the card from its pocket and reading what was on the reverse side (see Figure 3). There was a total of 329 separate information cards available for selection for each protocol in the study, although some of the cards represented equivalent forms of similar Rorschach data for the Beck and Klopfer scoring methods. The experimenter was present during the interpretations in order to record the sequence of item selections and each clinician's voluntary verbalizations. The experimenter also communicated some of the Rorschach information directly to the clinicians (Reaction Times to Cards and Location Areas). The three Rorschach protocols used in the study were taken from the existing literature, and will be identified and discussed shortly.

As soon as one of the three cardboard folders had been presented to the clinician, the following written instructions were given to him.

> This study is an attempt to determine how the clinician goes about evaluating Rorschach data in answering clinical questions.
>
> In front of you is a cardboard folder into which data cards have been set. Each folder represents an authentic Rorschach protocol. Each data card indicates an item of Rorschach information generally utilized in Rorschach analysis. The information can be obtained by selecting any card, turning it over, and reading what is on the back.
>
> When you select a card, draw it from its pocket, read the information on the reverse side, and lay it on the desk. Do not replace any card in the

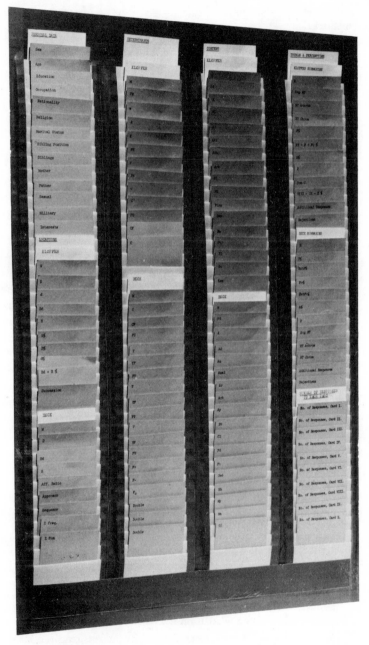

Figure 2. (left and right): *Information board used for Rorschach interpretations.*

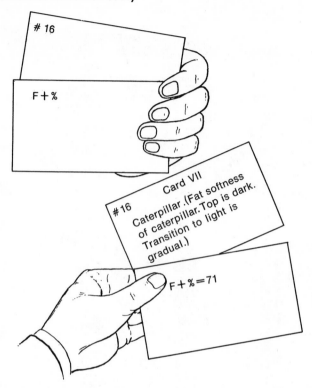

16

F + %

Card VII

16   Caterpillar .(Fat softness
of caterpillar. Top is dark.
Transition to light is
gradual.)

F + % = 71

Figure 3.   Illustrations of information cards used for Rorschach interpretations.

pockets of the board after you have drawn it from its pocket. Proceed in this fashion for all the cards that you find necessary to select. As soon as you feel quite sure of your answer to the clinical question that will be presented to you shortly, write it on the paper. Stop drawing further cards.

You are asked to select those cards you believe to be necessary and sufficient to arrive at answers to the clinical questions.   Avoid selecting a card unless you feel you really need it in order to answer a particular question.   According to your clinical judgment, you may select as few or as many cards as you wish. Not all of the information will be positively given; that is, information may be made available through omission, the reverse side of a selected card being found blank. You are asked to make your data selections in the manner consistent with what you have found to be the most satisfactory, on the basis of your own Rorschach experiences, however personal.

Feel free to reread any card previously drawn. Feel free also to utilize any of the materials that have been placed on the desk in connection with this study. The making of notations is encouraged. You also may wish to make comments as you proceed, perhaps verbalizing your thinking, which would be welcome.

There will be three clinical questions, and protocols, in all. The estimated time is about 1½ hours, total.

You are requested to read all the items on the board, and to familiarize yourself with its format, before selecting any card.

Note: The techniques of both Beck and Klopfer frequently are given separate representations on the board, in order to reflect and make available their different dimensions. Feel free to select any of the cards, at any time in your analysis.

After the clinician had read the instructions and familiarized himself with the data board, the experimenter verbally added the following:

If you would like to know the reaction time to any of the cards, or the specific location for any of the responses, ask me and I will indicate it to you.

Reaction Times were indicated verbally to the clinician, upon request. The Location Areas were indicated graphically by the experimenter who circled appropriate response areas on a standard location chart. These two exceptions to the general cards-in-pockets format of the design were necessitated by the limited board space. The desirability of including all relevant data was weighed against the desirability of maintaining a workable apparatus.

After the clinician indicated his familiarity with the information board and his understanding of the procedure, the experimenter presented him with a written question form containing the clinical question which corresponded with the Rorschach record before him. Each protocol was accompanied by a different type of clinical problem. One Rorschach protocol involved a question of clinical Diagnosis, a second protocol an estimate of severity of Anxiety, and the third protocol an estimate of present level of Intelligence functioning. Examples of the three written question forms appear later in the text, accompanying the process and introspective interpretations made by the clinicians participating in the study.

Two levels of interpretative judgment were requested of the clinicians for each question. The first level was a general one and called for the clinician to make a pencil check next to one of a number of broad categories, such as "Average . . . Below Average . . . Above Average." The second level was a more specific one and called for detailed clarification of the clinician's earlier general conclusion, such as numerical IQ. It was thought that this differentiation between general and specific levels of interpretation would prove useful in evaluating the accuracy of the clinicians' final judgments. The differentiation might indicate points at which clinical agreement remained high or broke down.

As it turned out, the two levels of Rorschach judgment did not fully reflect the degree of accuracy or similarity of the clinicians' interpretative understanding, particularly on the Diagnosis problem. Final Diagnostic judgments were made quite arbitrarily at times, and reluctantly. The complexity of *Gregor's* personality functioning and the hazy areas of overlap between Psychotic-Personality Disturbance and Personality Disturbance-Neurotic were represented inadequately by the judgment categories. The two levels of judgment frequently missed such clinician agreements as "sexual functioning is homosexual . . . affectively hungry" (Diagnosis), and "fears pregnancy . . . not consciously anxious . . . overdefending" (Anxiety). Clinician nonagreements also were missed at the outcome levels, "intellectually bright, the passive homosexual partner . . . below average intellectually, the active homosexual partner" (Diagnosis).

The supplementary "materials" referred to in the instructions were placed on the desk for use by the clinicians if they desired. These materials included blank paper, Klopfer summary and psychogram forms, Beck summary forms, and standard location charts. A complete set of Rorschach inkblots was available upon request.

As the clinicians in the study proceeded in their interpretations, the experimenter made written notations of the sequence in which the information cards were selected. Descriptive and explanatory comments relevant to the interpretative process also were recorded.

This general experimental procedure was maintained for the presentation of the second and third protocol folders. At the end of each session, the clinician was asked to provide information regarding his Rorschach background and experience. The information form used for this purpose followed that outlined earlier in Table 1. Brief discussion then was encouraged by the experimenter, in order to (a) obtain the retrospective comments of the clinician, (b) determine whether any of the protocols had been recognized by the clinician, and (c) provide whatever feedback might be requested by the clinician regarding either the specific Rorschach protocols used or the study in general.

The three protocols employed in the study were selected from existing Rorschach records appearing in the literature. The protocols thus were authentic, obtained by experienced clinicians in actual clinical settings. Some advantages were seen as resulting from this selection procedure. First, potential biases associated with a single examiner's having administered and scored all three Rorschach protocols were lessened. For example, the Anxiety record was scored by Beck, and the Intelligence record by Bochner and Halpern. Second, background and interpretation material were available for all three cases, including psychiatrist reports and, for the Diagnosis and Intelligence records, findings from other psychological tests. Third, as the number of Rorschach responses (R) has been shown to have a significant influence on some of the major Rorschach scoring categories (Fiske and Baughman, 1965), it was thought that desirable control of R would be facilitated by selection of literature protocols. R in the present study ranged from 33 (Intelligence) through 34 (Anxiety) to 37 (Diagnosis).

The Diagnosis protocol was *The Case of Gregor*, a study presented by John Bell at a 1949 APA symposium. *Gregor* appeared in two issues of the *Rorschach Research Exchange* (Bell, 1949) as part of an extensive research project undertaken to investigate interrelationships among multiple projective and objective techniques. Data from 22 different psychological tests were available for *Gregor*, with each test interpreted by a different clinical specialist. The Rorschach was interpreted by Bruno Klopfer who formed the clinical impression of "a highly schizoid personality of long standing with a possible history of psychotic breaks and a general symptomatology compounded of paranoic, depressive and catatonic elements" (p. 460). A psychiatric evaluation also was included in the case material, as was a final integrative diagnostic summary by the symposium's moderator, Frederick Wyatt: "schizophrenia . . . seems to express the most fundamental fact of Gregor's disease. . . . Gregor's fundamental disturbance is a disturbance of thinking" (p. 467).

Although the Rorschach interpretation of *Gregor* was done by Klopfer, the original response scorings were not indicated on the published protocol. The final protocol scorings used in this study were derived from a joint conference of five advanced Veterans Administration interns in clinical psychology. For all protocols, translations of the primary scorings into the alternate Beck or Klopfer scorings generally were direct and literal (e.g., W = W, FY = FC', At = An) with the exception of more unique categories such as FM, m, and F+, where appropriate adjustments among other categories were made. For all protocols, of course, the original scorings were probably more true to their own specific theoretical orientation than were the alternate scorings to theirs. However, it was believed that the alternate scorings would be more meaningful and reliable to the clinician working within the context of his own theoretical framework than would scorings from a framework which, while the original, would be unfamiliar to him.

The Anxiety protocol was taken from Beck (1945), *The Classic Signs*. "The record points to a central anxiety that must be deeply distressing . . . a pervasive emotion in her. Also, it is the more intense in a person as introversive as she is . . . the anxiety from which she suffers deeply" (pp. 244–245). The record was unique in that despite the severe anxiety and the disintegrating effects of the "heavy blacks" of the blots there was no appearance of shading used as a determinant in the record. Beck did not specify events related to the possible heightening of anxiety in *Classic Signs*, apart from affective arousal, but he did mention a number of psychological defenses which were being employed to handle the anxiety: fantasy, disregard of reality, regressive tendencies, resignation, inadequate affective response, autistic solutions, and intellectual contact.

The Intelligence record was of an essentially normal *Adolescent Girl* which was taken from Bochner and Halpern (1942). A Stanford-Binet intelligence test score of 118 was reported for *Adolescent Girl*. A brief amount of case history material accompanied the record, including a psychiatrist's diagnostic note which indicated essentially healthy personality features for the subject. The protocol was scored by Bochner and Halpern from a Klopferian framework.

It was considered unlikely that any of the protocols would be recognized by the clinicians participating in the study. The fragmentation of the Rorschach data under the experimental conditions employed, and the improbability of there being any "set" among the participants toward protocols taken from the literature, were seen as supporting this assumption. Specific response contents would present the most obvious clues to recognition (e.g., the "flying red horse" in the Diagnosis record or the "two seeds . . . carried away on the wind" in the Anxiety record). Determinants and numerical ratios would provide less obvious clues. In order to provide a check on this assumption, however, the clinicians were asked at the end of the experimental session whether the protocols were familiar to them. None of the clinicians in the study indicated that they had recognized any of the three protocols. The closest approach to recognition occurred when one clinician, while interpreting the Intelligence record, stated that he wished he had "Halpern's textbook" at hand.

Chapter 6

Sources of Rorschach Utility

The major hypothesis in the study was confirmed. The utility of different sources of Rorschach information was found to vary according to the clinical question asked, even though there was a general consistency among Rorschach clinicians to value information related to the Free Associations and selected Personal Data of the test subjects, as well as a high degree of interclinician variation. Differential utility was found for 58 of the 329 items across the three clinical problems of Diagnosis, Anxiety, and Intelligence ($p<$ .05). This finding was a conservative one. First, the Klopfer subgroup of clinicians was too limited to contribute statistical significance on the 89 specifically Klopfer scoring items. Greater support for the major hypothesis would be expected were the number of Klopfer clinicians making interpretations to be doubled. Second, over one-half of the Rorschach items were selected too infrequently (0–16%) to contribute significantly to the results. None of the 329 information items available was selected at the Very High or High levels of utility, defined in the study as 85–100% frequency of selection, whereas 185 of the items, or 56%, were selected at the Low or Very Low utility levels, defined as 0–15% frequency of selection. Considering only the 134 most useful items (17–100% selection), differential utility was obtained for 43% of the items (see Table 2).

Table 2.   Utility Indices (UI) and Utility Levels (UL)* for 329 Information
Items by Category

| | Problems | | | | | | |
| | Diagnosis | | Anxiety | | Intelligence | | |
Personal Data Items	UI	UL	UI	UL	UI	UL	p**
Sex	75***	AH	80	AH	69	AH	
Age	78	AH	86	H	78	AH	
Education	69	AH	61	AH	78	AH	
Occupation	61	AH	53	AH	39	AL	.10
Nationality	30	AL	25	AL	19	AL	
Religion	28	AL	22	AL	8	L	.10
Marital Status	50	AL	67	AH	14	L	.001
Sibling Position	33	AL	36	AL	11	L	.05
Sibling Description	30	AL	28	AL	8	L	.10
Mother Description	39	AL	39	AL	14	L	.05
Father Description	39	AL	39	AL	14	L	.05
Sexual History	50	AL	64	AH	22	AL	.01
Military History	30	AL	17	AL	8	L	.10
Interests	36	AL	36	AL	25	AL	

*Refer to Figure 1
**Friedman two-way analysis of variance
***Rounded to nearest whole number
Note: Blank spaces in last column indicate not significant.

Table 2. *continued*

	Problems						
	Diagnosis		Anxiety		Intelligence		
Location Items	UI	UL	UI	UL	UI	UL	p
Klopfer							
W	11	L	11	L	22	AL	
D	11	L	14	L	17	AL	
d	6	L	8	L	11	L	
Dd	8	L	11	L	8	L	
S	6	L	8	L	3	L	
W%	6	L	6	L	14	L	
D%	6	L	3	L	6	L	
d%	3	L	3	L	0	VL	
Dd+S%	6	L	3	L	3	L	
Succession	3	L	6	L	8	L	
Beck							
W	36	AL	30	AL	47	AL	.10
D	25	AL	30	AL	22	AL	
Dd	33	AL	28	AL	19	AL	
S	36	AL	28	AL	14	L	.10
Approach	25	AL	28	AL	33	AL	
Sequence	19	AL	17	AL	19	AL	
Affective Ratio	22	AL	30	AL	8	L	.10
Z Frequency	6	L	6	L	22	AL	.10
Z Sum	8	L	14	L	50	AL	.01

Note: Item abbreviations are defined in Appendix A

Table 2. *continued*

	Problems						
	Diagnosis		Anxiety		Intelligence		
Determinant Items	UI	UL	UI	UL	UI	UL	p
Klopfer							
M	19	AL	14	L	22	AL	
FM	22	AL	19	AL	22	AL	
m	14	L	22	AL	17	AL	
k	8	L	11	L	3	L	
K	8	L	11	L	3	L	
FK	8	L	11	L	3	L	
F	8	L	8	L	6	L	
Fc	11	L	11	L	3	L	
c	6	L	11	L	3	L	
C'	8	L	14	L	3	L	
FC	17	AL	14	L	6	L	
CF	17	AL	11	L	3	L	
C	11	L	6	L	3	L	
Beck							
M	56	AH	53	AH	58	AH	
C	53	AH	42	AL	17	AL	.05
CF	50	AL	44	AL	17	AL	.02
FC	50	AL	42	AL	14	L	.01
Y	36	AL	47	AL	6	L	.01
YF	36	AL	44	AL	6	L	.01
FY	42	AL	44	AL	6	L	.01
T	30	AL	30	AL	3	L	.05
TF	33	AL	25	AL	3	L	.05
FT	36	AL	30	AL	6	L	.05
V	33	AL	33	AL	6	L	.05
VF	33	AL	30	AL	8	L	.05
FV	33	AL	33	AL	8	L	.05
F+	28	AL	25	AL	11	L	.10
F—	30	AL	25	AL	11	L	.10
F_o	22	AL	14	L	8	L	
Blend 1	30	AL	25	AL	11	L	.10
Blend 2	30	AL	0	VL	11	L	.05
Blend 3	30	AL	0	VL	11	L	.05

Table 2. *continued*

Content Items	Problems						
	Diagnosis		Anxiety		Intelligence		
	UI	UL	UI	UL	UI	UL	p
Klopfer							
H	8	L	11	L	11	L	
Hd	6	L	11	L	8	L	
A	11	L	11	L	8	L	
Ad	6	L	8	L	6	L	
At	3	L	8	L	0	VL	
AAt	3	L	3	L	3	L	
AObj	0	VL	0	VL	3	L	
Art	6	L	3	L	3	L	
Cl	0	VL	0	VL	3	L	
Fd	3	L	3	L	3	L	
Fire	6	L	6	L	3	L	
Geo	0	VL	0	VL	0	VL	
Na	3	L	0	VL	3	L	
Obj	3	L	0	VL	3	L	
Pl	0	VL	0	VL	3	L	
Sc	0	VL	0	VL	3	L	
Sex	11	L	6	L	6	L	
Beck							
H	33	AL	30	AL	14	L	.10
Hd	30	AL	30	AL	6	L	.05
A	28	AL	19	AL	19	AL	
Ad	28	AL	22	AL	11	L	.10
An	28	AL	30	AL	6	L	.05
Anal	19	AL	17	AL	6	L	
Ar	8	L	6	L	14	L	
Art	17	AL	6	L	3	L	
Ay	8	L	6	L	3	L	
Bt	14	L	6	L	3	L	
Cl	17	AL	11	L	6	L	
Fd	17	AL	8	L	3	L	
Fi	19	AL	17	AL	8	L	
Ge	8	L	6	L	8	L	
Hh	11	L	6	L	3	L	
My	11	L	8	L	6	L	
Na	14	L	6	L	3	L	
Oj	8	L	6	L	3	L	

Table 2.   continued

Totals Items	Problems						p
	Diagnosis		Anxiety		Intelligence		
	UI	UL	UI	UL	UI	UL	
Klopfer							
R	17	AL	17	AL	25	AL	
Avg Reaction Time	6	L	8	L	8	L	
RT Achromatic	8	L	8	L	3	L	
RT Chromatic	8	L	8	L	3	L	
F%	11	L	14	L	11	L	
FK+%	6	L	8	L	3	L	
A%	11	L	11	L	8	L	
P	11	L	11	L	11	L	
Sum C	22	AL	17	AL	11	L	
8-9-10%	6	L	14	L	8	L	
Additionals	3	L	3	L	0	VL	
Rejections	6	L	8	L	0	VL	
Beck							
R	58	AH	53	AH	56	AH	
F%	36	AL	36	AL	25	AL	
Extended F%	11	L	17	AL	14	L	
F+%	72	AH	58	AH	61	AH	
Extended F+%	30	AL	33	AL	33	AL	
A%	30	AL	36	AL	25	AL	
P	50	AL	44	AL	25	AL	.05
Avg Reaction Time	28	AL	17	AL	6	L	.10
RT Achromatic	19	AL	19	AL	3	L	.10
RT Chromatic	19	AL	19	AL	3	L	.10
Additionals	14	L	11	L	11	L	
Rejections	25	AL	30	AL	8	L	.10

Table 2.   continued

| Individual Scoring Items—Klopfer | Problems | | | | | | p |
| | Diagnosis | | Anxiety | | Intelligence | | |
	UI	UL	UI	UL	UI	UL	
1	3	L	8	L	6	L	
2	3	L	3	L	8	L	
3	3	L	3	L	6	L	
4	3	L	3	L	6	L	
5	3	L	3	L	3	L	
6	3	L	3	L	3	L	
7	6	L	3	L	3	L	
8	6	L	6	L	3	L	
9	3	L	8	L	3	L	
10	3	L	8	L	6	L	
11	6	L	6	L	3	L	
12	3	L	8	L	3	L	
13	3	L	6	L	6	L	
14	3	L	3	L	3	L	
15	3	L	3	L	6	L	
16	3	L	3	L	3	L	
17	3	L	3	L	3	L	
18	3	L	3	L	3	L	
19	3	L	3	L	6	L	
20	6	L	3	L	3	L	
21	6	L	3	L	3	L	
22	6	L	3	L	3	L	
23	8	L	3	L	3	L	
24	3	L	3	L	3	L	
25	3	L	3	L	3	L	
26	3	L	3	L	3	L	
27	3	L	3	L	3	L	
28	3	L	3	L	3	L	
29	3	L	6	L	3	L	
30	3	L	3	L	3	L	
31	3	L	14	L	6	L	
32	3	L	3	L	8	L	
33	3	L	3	L	6	L	
34	0	VL	3	L	6	L	
35	0	VL	0	VL	6	L	
36	0	VL	0	VL	6	L	
37	0	VL	0	VL	6	L	

Table 2. *continued*

Individual Scoring Items—Beck	Problems						
	Diagnosis		Anxiety		Intelligence		
	UI	*UL*	*UI*	*UL*	*UI*	*UL*	*p*
1	19	AL	22	AL	14	L	
2	22	AL	19	AL	17	AL	
3	17	AL	25	AL	17	AL	
4	25	AL	17	AL	22	AL	
5	22	AL	17	AL	19	AL	
6	28	AL	17	AL	19	AL	
7	19	AL	17	AL	17	AL	
8	22	AL	25	AL	17	AL	
9	22	AL	19	AL	19	AL	
10	17	AL	14	L	11	L	
11	14	L	22	AL	14	L	
12	14	L	19	AL	8	L	
13	14	L	25	AL	6	L	.10
14	17	AL	19	AL	8	L	
15	14	L	19	AL	8	L	
16	19	AL	22	AL	8	L	
17	19	AL	14	L	3	L	.10
18	17	AL	19	AL	6	L	
19	17	AL	14	L	6	L	
20	11	L	17	AL	6	L	
21	11	L	17	AL	6	L	
22	11	L	17	AL	6	L	
23	19	AL	8	L	3	L	.10
24	17	AL	14	L	11	L	
25	19	AL	8	L	8	L	
26	17	AL	11	L	6	L	
27	14	L	14	L	6	L	
28	14	L	11	L	11	L	
29	22	AL	14	L	17	AL	
30	17	AL	8	L	11	L	
31	14	L	11	L	14	L	
32	11	L	8	L	19	AL	
33	17	AL	8	L	17	AL	
34	3	L	8	L	14	L	
35	0	VL	3	L	14	L	
36	0	VL	0	VL	14	L	
37	0	VL	0	VL	14	L	

Table 2. *continued*

Free Association Items	Problems						
	Diagnosis		*Anxiety*		*Intelligence*		
	UI	*UL*	*UI*	*UL*	*UI*	*UL*	*p*
1	83	AH	83	AH	61	AH	.05
2	78	AH	80	AH	56	AH	.05
3	69	AH	80	AH	56	AH	.05
4	69	AH	75	AH	56	AH	.10
5	69	AH	72	AH	58	AH	
6	86	H	75	AH	53	AH	.02
7	89	H	72	AH	44	AL	.01
8	72	AH	75	AH	44	AL	.02
9	67	AH	75	AH	56	AH	.10
10	69	AH	69	AH	56	AH	
11	58	AH	78	AH	39	AL	.01
12	53	AH	78	AH	33	AL	.01
13	67	AH	78	AH	30	AL	.01
14	61	AH	67	AH	39	AL	.05
15	67	AH	67	AH	39	AL	.05
16	67	AH	69	AH	36	AL	.02
17	61	AH	53	AH	30	AL	.05
18	61	AH	67	AH	25	AL	.01
19	67	AH	69	AH	25	AL	.01
20	64	AH	75	AH	25	AL	.001
21	67	AH	69	AH	30	AL	.01
22	61	AH	61	AH	30	AL	.02
23	50	AL	56	AH	33	AL	.10
24	69	AH	50	AL	30	AL	.01
25	64	AH	50	AL	33	AL	.05
26	58	AH	53	AH	33	AL	.05
27	61	AH	50	AL	30	AL	.05
28	69	AH	47	AL	47	AL	.05
29	61	AH	56	AH	44	AL	.10
30	56	AH	56	AH	42	AL	
31	56	AH	50	AL	39	AL	.10
32	53	AH	44	AL	47	AL	
33	47	AL	42	AL	39	AL	
34	22	AL	44	AL	42	AL	.10
35	3	L	19	AL	39	AL	.02
36	3	L	0	VL	39	AL	.01
37	0	VL	3	L	42	AL	.01

Table 2.   *continued*

| Verbalization and Behavior Items | Problems | | | | | | p |
| | Diagnosis | | Anxiety | | Intelligence | | |
	UI	UL	UI	UL	UI	UL	
1	33	AL	47	AL	30	AL	.10
2	39	AL	42	AL	30	AL	
3	36	AL	47	AL	25	AL	.10
4	33	AL	28	AL	22	AL	
5	30	AL	28	AL	17	AL	
6	36	AL	22	AL	19	AL	.10
7	30	AL	28	AL	22	AL	
8	22	AL	39	AL	22	AL	.10
9	17	AL	28	AL	25	AL	
10	19	AL	19	AL	22	AL	
11	22	AL	22	AL	17	AL	
12	19	AL	25	AL	14	L	
13	14	L	28	AL	11	L	.10
14	14	L	19	AL	17	AL	
15	14	L	17	AL	14	L	
16	17	AL	25	AL	14	L	
17	19	AL	14	L	11	L	
18	22	AL	28	AL	8	L	.10
19	19	AL	28	AL	8	L	.10
20	17	AL	36	AL	8	L	.05
21	17	AL	25	AL	11	L	
22	17	AL	17	AL	11	L	
23	28	AL	17	AL	11	L	.10
24	19	AL	11	L	14	L	
25	22	AL	11	L	14	L	
26	17	AL	14	L	11	L	
27	19	AL	19	AL	11	L	
28	14	L	11	L	19	AL	
29	22	AL	22	AL	17	AL	
30	14	L	19	AL	14	L	
31	17	AL	11	L	14	L	
32	14	L	8	L	19	AL	
33	14	L	11	L	17	AL	
34	3	L	17	AL	14	L	
35	0	VL	3	L	17	AL	.10
36	0	VL	0	VL	17	AL	.10
37	0	VL	0	VL	17	AL	.10

Table 2. *continued*

Individual Location Items	Problems						
	Diagnosis		*Anxiety*		*Intelligence*		
	UI	*UL*	*UI*	*UL*	*UI*	*UL*	*p*
1	17	AL	8	L	6	L	
2	30	AL	25	AL	6	L	.05
3	19	AL	25	AL	6	L	.10
4	22	AL	22	AL	14	L	
5	19	AL	25	AL	3	L	.10
6	14	L	22	AL	6	L	
7	11	L	22	AL	8	L	
8	8	L	25	AL	8	L	.10
9	17	AL	8	L	17	AL	
10	6	L	14	L	6	L	
11	19	AL	14	L	11	L	
12	17	AL	28	AL	8	L	.10
13	8	L	47	AL	8	L	.01
14	11	L	42	AL	17	AL	.05
15	8	L	22	AL	3	L	.10
16	17	AL	8	L	6	L	
17	19	AL	8	L	8	L	
18	19	AL	11	L	6	L	
19	8	L	17	AL	6	L	
20	11	L	14	L	6	L	
21	11	L	8	L	6	L	
22	8	L	11	L	6	L	
23	14	L	6	L	6	L	
24	8	L	14	L	6	L	
25	17	AL	11	L	6	L	
26	11	L	11	L	6	L	
27	14	L	14	L	6	L	
28	6	L	11	L	6	L	
29	19	AL	8	L	8	L	
30	14	L	8	L	8	L	
31	17	AL	11	L	8	L	
32	6	L	8	L	14	L	
33	8	L	11	L	8	L	
34	0	VL	6	L	14	L	
35	0	VL	0	VL	8	L	
36	0	VL	0	VL	11	L	
37	0	VL	0	VL	8	L	

Table 2. *continued*

| | | Problems | | | | |
| Items | Diagnosis | | Anxiety | | Intelligence | | p |
	UI	UL	UI	UL	UI	UL	
Number of Responses to Each Rorschach Card							
Card I	22	AL	25	AL	17	AL	
Card II	22	AL	25	AL	11	L	
Card III	30	AL	36	AL	22	AL	
Card IV	17	AL	39	AL	8	L	.05
Card V	11	L	19	AL	11	L	
Card VI	22	AL	33	AL	6	L	.05
Card VII	22	AL	33	AL	11	L	.10
Card VIII	22	AL	30	AL	8	L	.10
Card IX	25	AL	22	AL	17	AL	
Card X	22	AL	30	AL	22	AL	
Reaction Time to Each Rorschach Card							
Card I	25	AL	19	AL	8	L	.10
Card II	22	AL	19	AL	8	L	
Card III	19	AL	17	AL	8	L	
Card IV	14	L	14	L	6	L	
Card V	14	L	14	L	6	L	
Card VI	14	L	17	AL	6	L	
Card VII	14	L	17	AL	6	L	
Card VIII	17	AL	19	AL	6	L	
Card IX	11	L	14	L	11	L	
Card X	11	L	17	AL	11	L	

The Intelligence question was most influential in contributing to the differential use of Rorschach information. The Intelligence question also required significantly less information and time to answer (see Table 3), while being the question answered most accurately by the clinicians. Summary results derived from questionnaires presented to the 36 clinicians following their participation in the study indicated that they considered the Rorschach to be least useful for answering Intelligence questions, compared with questions of Diagnosis and Anxiety (see Table 1).

Although none of the Klopfer items contributed significantly to the differential utility hypothesis, Klopfer's determinant FM was used suffici-

Table 3. Summary Results for Items Selected and Time Taken for Three Rorschach Problems

| Measures | Problems | | | | Friedman Two-way Analysis of Variance |
	Diagnosis	Anxiety	Intelligence	Combined	
	Number of Items Selected				
Mean	70.8	71.9	47.9	63.5	22.96*
SD	37.6	35.0	39.0	33.8	
Range	7–157	12–154	5–151	24–431	
	Number of Minutes Taken				
Mean	26.3	29.7	14.9	23.6	31.85*
SD	14.6	20.0	13.0	13.2	
Range	5–67	7–120	2–64	16–238	

*$p < .001$

ently often by Beck-oriented clinicians to have it approach significance. This exception suggested that clinicians interpreting Rorschachs from Beck's orientation may value Klopfer's animal movement score as useful, despite Beck's view of this as "a serious source of error" (1961, p. 74). Klopfer-oriented clinicians found parallel utility in Beck's F+ and F— scores, especially in the absence of Klopfer form-level ratings.

Items selected most often and earliest for interpretation were the Free Association responses, Personal Data, and Beck's F+ %, R, P, M, C, CF, FC, and W scores (see Table 4). Information categories comprised of individual response scorings, graphic locations, content summary scores, and initial reaction times were found to be consistently low in utility. Surprisingly, *no single Rorschach score or variable was found to have outstandingly high utility for any clinical question.* Highest utility (85%–98%) was obtained only for two items representing free associations to Rorschach blots II and III on the Diagnosis question, and to the Age item on Anxiety question. Average High utility (51%–84%) was observed for 27 of the items for the three problems combined, representing only 8 per cent of the total number of items available for selection. In fact, agreement among clinicians was greater concerning information that was less useful than more useful.

Table 4.   Utility Indices and Relative Ranks of Selection of Information Items
for Three Rorschach Problems Combined

Utility Indices*	Items	Relative Ranks	Items
No item was selected at the Very High (99–100%) or High (85–98%) levels of utility			

Average High Utility: 51.0–84.9%

81	Age	1	Age
76	Free Association 1	2	Sex
75	Sex	3	Free Association 1
71	Free Association 2	4	Free Association 2
	Free Association 6	5	Education
69	Education	6	Free Association 6
68	Free Association 7	7	Free Association 3
	Free Association 3	8	Free Association 4
67	Free Association 5	9	Free Association 7
	Free Association 4	10	Free Association 5
66	Free Association 9	11	F+% Beck
65	Free Association 10	12	Free Association 9
64	F+% Beck	13	Free Association 8
	Free Association 8	14	Free Association 10
58	Free Association 11	15	R Beck
	Free Association 13	16	M Beck
57	Free Association 15	17	Free Association 11
	Free Association 16	18	Free Association 13
56	M Beck	19	Free Association 15
	Free Association 21	20	Free Association 16
	Free Association 14	21	Free Association 12
	R Beck	22	Free Association 14
55	Free Association 12	23	Occupation
	Free Association 20	24	Free Association 21
	Free Association 28	25	Free Association 20
54	Free Association 29	26	Free Association 19
	Free Association 19	27	Free Association 28

Average Low Utility: 17.0–50.9%

51	Free Association 22	28	Free Association 18
	Free Association 30	29	Free Association 29
	Occupation	30	Marital Status
	Free Association 18	31	Free Association 22
50	Free Association 24	32	Sexual History
49	Free Association 25	33	Free Association 17

*Rounded to nearest whole number
Note: Item abbreviations are defined in Appendix A

Table 4. *continued*

Utility Indices	Items	Relative Ranks	Items
48	Free Association 17	34	Free Association 24
	Free Association 26	35	Free Association 30
	Free Association 31	36	Free Association 25
	Free Association 32	37	Free Association 26
47	Free Association 27	38	Free Association 23
46	Free Association 23	39	Free Association 31
45	Sexual History	40	W Beck
44	Marital Status	41	Free Association 27
43	Free Association 33	42	Verbalization 1
40	P Beck	43	Free Association 32
38	W Beck	44	P Beck
37	CF Beck	45	Verbalization 2
	Verbalization 2	46	C Beck
	Verbalization 1	47	CF Beck
	C Beck	48	Verbalization 3
36	Free Association 34	49	FC Beck
	Verbalization 3	50	Free Association 33
35	FC Beck	51	F% Beck
32	Extended F+ % Beck	52	Extended F+ % Beck
	F% Beck	53	Interests
	Interests	54	A% Beck
31	Mother Description	55	FY Beck
	FY Beck	56	Father Description
	Father Description	57	Mother Description
	A% Beck	58	Y Beck
30	Responses Card III	59	YF Beck
	Y Beck	60	Approach Beck
29	Approach Beck	61	Free Association 34
	YF Beck	62	Verbalization 4
28	Verbalization 8	63	Dd Beck
	Verbalization 4	64	D Beck
27	Verbalization 7	65	Nationality
	Dd Beck	66	Sibling Position
	Sibling Position	67	Responses Card III
26	Verbalization 6	68	Verbalization 8
	H Beck	69	Verbalization 7
	S Beck	70	S Beck
	D Beck	71	Verbalization 5
25	FV Beck	72	H Beck
	Nationality	73	Verbalization 6
	Verbalization 5	74	FV Beck
	Responses Card X	75	Z Sum Beck
24	Z Sum Beck	76	V Beck
	FT Beck	77	VF Beck

Table 4. *continued*

Utility Indices	*Items*	*Relative Ranks*	*Items*
24	VF Beck	78	FT Beck
	V Beck	79	Sibling Description
23	Location 14	80	Verbalization 9
	Verbalization 9	81	Rejections Beck
22	Sibling Description	82	Hd Beck
	Responses Card VII	83	Responses Card X
	F- Beck	84	Blend 1
	Blend 1	85	Responses Card I
	A Beck	86	T Beck
	Hd Beck	87	Location 2
21	T Beck	88	Location 14
	Responses Card I	89	A Beck
	Location 13	90	Religion
	Rejections Beck	91	F- Beck
	F+ Beck	92	Scoring 4 Beck
	FM Klopfer	93	An Beck
	Responses Card IX	94	Location 4
	Scoring 4 Beck	95	Affective Ratio Beck
	Scoring 8 Beck	96	TF Beck
	Responses Card IV	97	F+ Beck
	Scoring 6 Beck	98	Scoring 6 Beck
	An Beck	99	Responses Card VII
20	Verbalization 29	100	R Klopfer
	Responses Card VI	101	Ad Beck
	Free Association 35	102	Location 13
	Verbalization 11	103	Responses Card IV
	Scoring 9 Beck	104	Sequence Beck
	Verbalization 10	105	Military History
	TF Beck	106	Verbalization 10
	Verbalization 20	107	Scoring 2 Beck
	Location 2	108	FM Klopfer
	Ad Beck	109	Scoring 8 Beck
	Affective Ratio Beck	110	Scoring 3 Beck
	Responses Card VIII	111	Verbalization 11
19	Location 4	112	Responses Card IX
	Scoring 3 Beck	113	Responses Card VIII
	R Klopfer	114	Scoring 1 Beck
	Responses Card II	115	Responses Card II
	Religion	116.5	Scoring 9 Beck
	Verbalization 18	116.5	Responses Card VI
	Scoring 5 Beck	118	Scoring 5 Beck
	Scoring 2 Beck	119	Verbalization 12
	Verbalization 12	120	Reaction Time 1

Table 4. *continued*

Utility Indices	Items	Relative Ranks	Items
18	Verbalization 16	121	Location 3
	Military History	122	M Klopfer
	Sequence Beck	123	Verbalization 20
	Verbalization 19	124	Avg Reaction Time Beck
	Verbalization 23	125	Location 12
	Scoring 1 Beck	126	Verbalization 18
	M Klopfer	127	Verbalization 16
	m Klopfer	128	Verbalization 13
	Reaction Time 1	129	Location 5
	Scoring 7 Beck	130	Scoring 7 Beck
	Verbalization 13	131	Free Association 35
	Verbalization 21	132	Reaction Time 2
	Location 12	133	m Klopfer
	Scoring 29 Beck	134	Verbalization 29

Low Utility: 2.0–16.9%

Utility Indices	Items	Relative Ranks	Items
17	Scoring 16 Beck	135	Verbalization 19
	Avg Reaction Time Beck	136	Verbalization 14
	SumC Klopfer	137	Verbalization 23
	Verbalization 27	138	Scoring 11 Beck
	Scoring 11 Beck	139	Location 6
	Reaction Time 2	140.5	SumC Klopfer
	Location 3	140.5	Verbalization 21
	Verbalization 14	142	Location 7
16	Verbalization 30	143	F_0 Beck
	Location 5	144	Location 11
	Verbalization 25	145	Location 8
15	Verbalization 15	146	Location 9
	Verbalization 22	147	Scoring 16 Beck
	F_0 Beck	148	Scoring 29 Beck
	Location 11	149	Reaction Time 3
	Verbalization 28	150	Extended F% Beck
	Verbalization 17	151	Fi Beck
	W Klopfer	152	Verbalization 15
	Fi Beck	153	W Klopfer
	Verbalization 24	154	RT Achromatic Beck
	Scoring 13 Beck	155	RT Chromatic Beck
	Free Association 37	156.5	Verbalization 17
	Scoring 14 Beck	156.5	Scoring 14 Beck
	Reaction Time 3	158	Verbalization 27
14	Location 7	159	Anal Beck
	RT Achromatic Beck	160	Blend 2
	Responses Card V	161	Scoring 13 Beck

Table 4. *continued*

Utility Indices	Items	Relative Ranks	Items
14	D Klopfer	162	Blend 3
	Verbalization 33	163.5	Verbalization 25
	Verbalization 32	163.5	Responses Card V
	Verbalization 31	165	Reaction Time 8
	Verbalization 26	166	Verbalization 22
	Reaction Time 8	167	Scoring 12 Beck
	RT Chromatic Beck	168	Verbalization 24
	Location 6	169	D Klopfer
	Scoring 10 Beck	170	Scoring 10 Beck
	Blend 3	171	Scoring 15 Beck
	Blend 2	172	Verbalization 28
	Location 8	173	Z Frequency Beck
	Extended F% Beck	174	Free Association 37
	Scoring 24 Beck	175	Verbalization 30
	Scoring 12 Beck	176	Additionals Beck
	Free Association 36	177	Scoring 18 Beck
	Scoring 15 Beck	178.5	Reaction Time 10
	Location 9	178.5	Location 1
	Anal Beck	180	Scoring 24 Beck
	Scoring 33 Beck	181	Verbalization 26
	Scoring 18 Beck	182	Reaction Time 6
13	Scoring 31 Beck	183	Free Association 36
	Scoring 32 Beck	184	Reaction Time 7
	Reaction Time 10	185	Location 18
12	Location 31	186	Location 17
	Scoring 28 Beck	187	Reaction Time 9
	Reaction Time 6	188	Reaction Time 4
	Scoring 30 Beck	189	Cl Beck
	Reaction Time 9	190	Verbalization 31
	Reaction Time 7	191	Reaction Time 5
	Additionals Beck	192	Location 15
	Location 17	193	Scoring 33 Beck
	Scoring 25 Beck	194	FC Klopfer
	F% Klopfer	195	F% Klopfer
	FC Klopfer	196	Verbalization 32
	Location 18	197	Verbalization 33
	Location 29	198	Scoring 17 Beck
	Scoring 17 Beck	199	Scoring 19 Beck
	Scoring 19 Beck	200	Scoring 31 Beck
11	Reaction Time 4	201	P Klopfer
	Reaction Time 5	202	Scoring 32 Beck
	Scoring 21 Beck	203	Scoring 25 Beck
	Scoring 20 Beck	204	Scoring 30 Beck
	Z Frequency Beck	205	Location 16

Table 4. *continued*

Utility Indices	*Items*	*Relative Ranks*	*Items*
11	P Klopfer	206	Scoring 28 Beck
	Location 15	207	Location 25
	Scoring 22 Beck	208	Location 29
	Scoring 26 Beck	209	Location 19
	Verbalization 34	210	Scoring 22 Beck
	Location 27	211	Location 27
	Scoring 27 Beck	212	Ar Beck
	Location 25	213	H Klopfer
	Cl Beck	214	Scoring 20 Beck
10	Location 19	215	Location 31
	A Klopfer	216	CF Klopfer
	CF Klopfer	217	Scoring 26 Beck
	A% Klopfer	218	Location 20
	Scoring 23 Beck	219	Scoring 27 Beck
	H Klopfer	220	Fd Beck
	Location 20	221	Location 10
	Location 16	222	A Klopfer
	Location 1	223	Scoring 21 Beck
	Location 30	224	A% Klopfer
9	Location 32	225	My Beck
	Location 24	226	Scoring 23 Beck
	Location 33	227	Art Beck
	Ar Beck	228	Verbalization 34
	Dd Klopfer	229	Location 24
	8–9–10% Klopfer	230	Location 30
	Fd Beck	231	Dd Klopfer
	Location 26	232	Location 26
8	d Klopfer	233	8–9–10% Klopfer
	Location 23	234	Fc Klopfer
	W% Klopfer	235	Ge Beck
	Art Beck	236	Location 23
	Location 21	237	W% Klopfer
	Location 10	238	Location 21
	C' Klopfer	239	Location 22
	Fc Klopfer	240	C' Klopfer
	My Beck	241	Bt Beck
	Hd Klopfer	242	Na Beck
	Scoring 34 Beck	243	Location 32
	Location 22	244	Hd Klopfer
7	F Klopfer	245	d Klopfer
	Bt Beck	246	K Klopfer
	Sex Klopfer	247	FK Klopfer
	K Klopfer	248	k Klopfer
	Scoring 31 Klopfer	249	F Klopfer

Table 4. *continued*

Utility Indices	Items	Relative Ranks	Items
7	Location 28	250	Scoring 1 Klopfer
	Ge Beck	251	Sex Klopfer
	FK Klopfer	252	Location 33
	k Klopfer	253	Hh Beck
	Avg Reaction Time Klopfer	254	Scoring 34 Beck
	Na Beck	255	Location 28
6	Hh Beck	256	Avg Reaction Time Klopfer
	C Klopfer	257	Scoring 31 Klopfer
	Location 34	258	Ay Beck
	RT Chromatic Klopfer	259	C Klopfer
	RT Achromatic Klopfer	260.5	Oj Beck
	c Klopfer	260.5	Scoring 10 Klopfer
	Ad Klopfer	262	c Klopfer
	Verbalization 35	263	Scoring 2 Klopfer
	Ay Beck	264	Verbalization 35
	FK+% Klopfer	265	Scoring 8 Klopfer
	Oj Beck	266	Scoring 9 Klopfer
	Succession Klopfer	267	Ad Klopfer
	Scoring 1 Klopfer	268	FK+% Klopfer
	Verbalization 36	269	Scoring 13 Klopfer
	S Klopfer	270.5	Scoring 12 Klopfer
	Verbalization 37	270.5	Scoring 11 Klopfer
	Scoring 35 Beck	272	Location 34
	Scoring 10 Klopfer	273	RT Acromatic Klopfer
5	Scoring 23 Klopfer	274	RT Chromatic Klopfer
	Scoring 32 Klopfer	275	Fire Klopfer
	Scoring 36 Beck	276.5	Scoring 35 Beck
	D% Klopfer	276.5	S Klopfer
	Rejections Klopfer	278	Scoring 3 Klopfer
	Scoring 37 Beck	279	Scoring 4 Klopfer
	Scoring 9 Klopfer	280.5	Rejections Klopfer
	Scoring 8 Klopfer	280.5	Verbalization 36
	Scoring 2 Klopfer	282	Scoring 7 Klopfer
	Scoring 11 Klopfer	283	Verbalization 37
	Fi Klopfer	284	Scoring 23 Klopfer
	Scoring 12 Klopfer	285	Succession Klopfer
	Scoring 13 Klopfer	286	Scoring 36 Beck
4	Scoring 33 Klopfer	287.5	Scoring 15 Klopfer
	Art Klopfer	287.5	Scoring 37 Beck
	At Klopfer	289	D% Klopfer
	Scoring 4 Klopfer	290	Art Klopfer
	Scoring 21 Klopfer	291	Scoring 19 Klopfer

Table 4. *continued*

Utility Indices	*Items*	*Relative Ranks*	*Items*
4	Scoring 7 Klopfer	292	Scoring 20 Klopfer
	Location 36	293	Scoring 5 Klopfer
	Scoring 15 Klopfer	294	Scoring 32 Klopfer
	Dd + S% Klopfer	295	Scoring 6 Klopfer
	Scoring 22 Klopfer	296	Scoring 21 Klopfer
	Scoring 29 Klopfer	297.5	At Klopfer
	Scoring 19 Klopfer	297.5	Scoring 22 Klopfer
	Scoring 3 Klopfer	299	Scoring 14 Klopfer
	Scoring 20 Klopfer	300	Scoring 16 Klopfer
3	Scoring 16 Klopfer	301	Scoring 29 Klopfer
	Scoring 28 Klopfer	302	Scoring 17 Klopfer
	Location 35	303	Dd+S% Klopfer
	Scoring 17 Klopfer	304	Fd Klopfer
	Scoring 26 Klopfer	305	Scoring 18 Klopfer
	Scoring 18 Klopfer	306	Scoring 33 Klopfer
	Scoring 34 Klopfer	307	Location 36
	Scoring 6 Klopfer	308	AAt Klopfer
	Scoring 27 Klopfer	309	Scoring 24 Klopfer
	AAt Klopfer	310	Scoring 25 Klopfer
	Fd Klopfer	311	Scoring 26 Klopfer
	Location 37	312	Scoring 27 Klopfer
	Scoring 30 Klopfer	313	Scoring 28 Klopfer
	Scoring 25 Klopfer	314	Scoring 30 Klopfer
	Scoring 14 Klopfer	315	Scoring 34 Klopfer
	Scoring 24 Klopfer	316	Obj Klopfer
	Scoring 5 Klopfer	317	Na Klopfer

Very Low Utility: .0–1.9%

2	Scoring 37 Klopfer	318	Location 35
	Scoring 36 Klopfer	319	Location 37
	Scoring 35 Klopfer	320	d% Klopfer
	Additionals Klopfer	321	Additionals Klopfer
	Obj Klopfer	322	Scoring 35 Klopfer
	Na Klopfer	323	Scoring 36 Klopfer
	d% Klopfer	324	Scoring 37 Klopfer
1	Sc Klopfer	325	Pl Klopfer
	AObj Klopfer	326	Sc Klopfer
	Cl Klopfer	327	AObj Klopfer
	Pl Klopfer	328	Cl Klopfer
	Geo Klopfer	329	Geo Klopfer

Clearly, experienced clinicians as a group found qualitative forms of information to have the greatest utility value for Rorschach interpretation. Ninety per cent of the Rorschach Free Associations also were selected earliest in the combined interpretation sequence, within the first 15 per cent grouping of the 329 items, along with nearly 50 per cent of the Personal Data items. This general finding is an important one because it counters a basic assumption underlying many past Rorschach validation studies that the critical sources of information in Rorschach interpretation are quantitative.

The above finding is not to be intepreted to mean that clinicians found little utility value in the quantitative sources of Rorschach information. A comparative review of the item selections made by clinicians on an individual basis indicated that two-thirds of the clinicians in the sample typically selected some traditional summary scores before proceeding to the Free Association responses, and made intermittent or final returns to quantitative Rorschach scores. Because of the high degree of interclinician variation, however, the consistency of quantitative item selections for the group as a whole was relatively low. It would appear that each clinician had his own preferred quantitative indices for making interpretations, as well as his own sequential timing, different from other clinicians.

The functions of quantitative Rorschach information indeed may be general and secondary ones for experienced clinicians, providing clinicians with some familiar structural orientation concerning the test subject, or a set of expectations to be checked out, or some working model to be matched and supplemented by other information in the record. The function of the quantitative scores may be to provide the loose outline or skeleton of the test subject's personality which later is filled out and shaped by material appearing in the free association responses. The approach verbalized by many of the clinicians in the study in fact was one of "checking out" hypotheses. Clinicians frequently made anticipatory predictions about the type of information a particular item card would contain. Clinicians also expressed confidence or surprise with the selection of a confirming or contraindicating information item.

The importance placed on qualitative aspects of Rorschach responses was emphasized further by some of the verbal reports made by clinicians in connection with certain of the free associations. For example, the descriptions "rear view of a bull . . . legs without toes . . . fat rat . . . conventional rendering" attracted clinician attention on the Diagnosis record because these phrases were viewed as unusual or strange. On the Intelligence record, there were four free associations which attracted clinician attention: "foliage . . . beautifully blue satin pillows . . . delicious orange and strawberry sundaes . . . surrealist painting." Cues related to level of vocabulary and syntax appeared to be most operative in eliciting attention in these latter instances.

A third source of evidence supporting the general finding that qualitative information had greatest utility in Rorschach interpretation for the clinicians sampled may be seen in Table 5. Table 5 summarizes the within-category utility of each of the 16 broad informational sources employed in the study. The Utility Indices (UI) in these instances were derived from the percentage of cards selected within each of the categories, independent of what occurred in other categories. Only the Free Associations had greater than 50 per cent selection as an information category for the three Rorschach problems combined, followed by the Personal Data category at 41 per cent selection. Summation of the percentages for related Beck and

Table 5. Comparative Utility Indices (UI) and Mean Ranks (MR) of Sixteen Information Categories for Three Rorschach Problems*

Information Categories	Problems							
	Diagnosis		Anxiety		Intelligence		Combined	
	UI	MR	UI	MR	UI	MR	UI	MR
Personal Data	46	113	47	119	29	135	41	122
Locations Klopfer	6	190	7	191	9	175	8	186
Locations Beck	23	157	23	158	26	142	24	152
Determinants Klopfer	12	182	13	181	7	178	11	180
Determinants Beck	36	137	31	145	12	170	26	151
Content Klopfer	4	194	4	195	4	182	4	191
Content Beck	18	171	13	178	7	177	13	175
Totals Klopfer	10	186	11	185	8	177	9	183
Totals Beck	33	140	31	146	22	150	29	145
Individual Scorings Klopfer	3	195	4	194	4	183	4	191
Individual Scorings Beck	16	177	15	179	12	171	14	176
Free Associations	59	106	60	105	41	123	53	111
Verbalizations and Behavior	19	170	21	167	16	163	19	167
Location Areas	12	181	15	177	8	176	12	178
Responses to Cards	22	165	29	154	13	167	22	162
Reaction Times to Cards	16	177	17	172	8	176	13	175

*Utility Indices derived from the percentage of cards selected within each category; Mean Ranks derived from the ranks of items within each category
Note: Numbers rounded to nearest whole

Klopfer categories would place the quantitative Totals (38 per cent) and Determinants (37 per cent) categories closely behind Personal Data in utility. Selections within the quantitative Contents (18 per cent) and Individual Scoring (17 per cent) categories were relatively low, superseded slightly by Responses to Cards (22 per cent) and Verbalizations and Behavior (19 per cent). Comparisons of the UI and MR data across the three clinical problems will provide the reader with some idea of the relative variations in category usage according to the clinical question asked. The general similarity of the Diagnosis and Anxiety selections may be noted, in contrast with the Intelligence selections.

Table 6 draws upon the findings of all of the preceding tables in order to provide a summary guide to the influence of the clinical question asked on the utility of various sources of Rorschach information. Assignment of some of the items in the table was made with the recognition that differences between the Diagnosis and Anxiety selections often were not as great as the placements might suggest. A general impression may be gained that clinicians did use Rorschach information in theoretically directed ways. While "traditional" information items were sought by clinicians, it is important to remember that these items may not have been critical sources of information for answering the clinical problems. For example, although the shading determinants were selected by clinicians in a theoretically directed attempt to answer the Anxiety problem, there were no shading scores present in the Anxiety record, necessitating clinician reliance on other sources of anxiety information in the record.

The Diagnosis problem elicited relatively greater use of the Determinant, Content, Totals, Individual Scorings, and Location Areas categories. Differentially high utility was found for color and form-textured determinants, popular response total, and free associations to Rorschach Cards II, III, VII, and IX.

The Anxiety problem elicited relatively greater use of the Personal Data, Free Association responses, Verbalizations, Number of Responses to Cards, and Reaction Time categories. Differentially high utility was found for sexual and interpersonal background information, light and dark shading determinants, pure shading determinants, Hd and Anatomy content scores, and free associations to Cards IV, VI, III, and VIII.

The Intelligence problem elicited relatively greater use only of the Location category. Differentially high utility was found for educational background information, Z Sum, W, M, and F+ % scores, and for free associations to Cards IX and X.

The influence of certain Rorschach Cards in guiding the clinicians' interpretative approaches was discernible. Interest in the color shock (II),

Table 6.   Selected Items Showing Differential Utility Among Three Rorschach
Problems*

	Problems		
	Diagnosis	*Anxiety*	*Intelligence*
Information Categories		*Items*	
Personal Data		Marital Status Sexual History Sib Position	Education
Locations			Z Sum W
Determinants	C CF FC TF FT	Y YF FY T V	
Contents		Hd At	
Totals	P		$F+\%$
Free Associations to Cards	II III VII IX	III IV VI VIII	IX X
Number of Responses to Cards		IV VI	

*$p < .05$, Friedman two-way analysis of variance

interpersonal (III, VII), and most complex (IX) Cards was high for the
Diagnosis problem. The shading and masculine Cards (IV, VI), and color
Cards (III, VIII) guided information selections on the Anxiety problem.
The differential approach to the Intelligence problem was geared to the
two difficult W Cards (IX, X).

The second hypothesis in the study also was confirmed. The hypothesis stated that clinicians would show distinguishable patterns of approach
to Rorschach interpretation. That is, some clinicians would employ a
basically quantitative approach which would emphasize the selection of
summary scores, numerical ratios and percentages, and determinants,
whereas other clinicians would employ a basically qualitative approach
which would be directed toward the free associations, background data,
and accompanying subject verbalizations and examiner observations of
behavior.

Although the majority of clinicians in this study maintained a general balance between qualitative and quantitative sources of information in their interpretations, it was possible to identify a small subgroup of nine clinicians who focused mainly on qualitative data and another small subgroup of four clinicians who focused mainly on quantitative data. These identifications were made by determining the mean per cent usage of the three categories Free Associations, Personal Data, and Verbalizations for the 36 clinicians (Mean usage = 52.8 per cent), and then separating those clinicians falling above and below the first standard deviation (SD = 14.4 per cent). Those clinicians whose qualitative information usage represented at least 67.2 per cent of their total card selections were separated from the group as high qualitative users ($N = 9$). Clinicians whose use of qualitative information represented 38.4 per cent or lower of their total card selections were classified as high quantitative users ($N = 4$). The finding that twice as many clinicians were identified as qualitative rather than quantitative users again may point to the generally high utility value of this information in Rorschach interpretation.

An attempt was made to determine some of the characteristics of the above two subgroups. However, in view of the small number of clinicians represented in the subgroups, generalizations drawn from the following descriptions must be evaluated with caution. The intent of the discussion is to suggest ideas for further consideration and investigation.

Five of the nine high qualitative users and all four of the high quantitative users employed Beck's method. The remaining four qualitative users represented 36 per cent of the Klopfer sample. None of the high users were among the five clinicians who answered all three clinical problems most accurately according to the criteria, although one of the high quantitative users appeared among the top 8 most accurate clinicians. Compared with the total group mean of 266 Rorschachs administered or supervised during the past five years, the mean number for the quantitative users was 244, while that for the qualitative users was 183.

Systematic differences in outcome characterized the two subgroups. Of the 14 clinicians who checked the alternative "Neurotic" on the Diagnostic question, 7 were high qualitative users and 3 were high quantitative users, together accounting for 70 per cent of clinicians responding to this alternative. The fourth quantitative user checked the alternative "Basically Adjusted," while the two remaining qualitative users checked "Personality Disturbance." The criterion answers for the Diagnosis question were "Psychotic" and "Personality Disturbance."

On the Anxiety question, seven of the nine qualitative users and three of the four quantitative users answered by checking either of the acceptable categories "Much" or "Severe" anxiety. The numbers here represented 77 per cent accuracy for the two subgroups combined, which was only slightly below that of the remainder of the clinician group (87 per cent accuracy), and not meaningfully different from the latter.

It was believed that clinicians characterized by a quantitative approach to interpretation would show relatively lower success in estimating the severity of anxiety due to the absence of determinant indicators of anxiety in the protocol (shading scores, m). The hypothesis, not supported by the outcomes of the high quantitative subgroup identified in this study, could not be tested due to the fact that determinants and free associations had been used by nearly every nonqualitative clinician in interpreting this protocol. Suggestive only was the observation that the two clinicians in the high qualitative group who underestimated the severity of anxiety ("Normal") were those who had selected the determinant anxiety indicators. The remaining qualitative clinicians selected almost none of these indicators. Of the 23 clinicians characterized by a more balanced approach in their use of quantitative and qualitative information, only 3 underestimated the criterion level of anxiety. No features common to these latter three clinicians were discernible.

On the Intelligence question, the mean estimation of IQ by the total group was 115.3 (SD = 8.5). This result was less than three points away from the Stanford-Binet criterion IQ of 118. Eight of the total 36 clinicians specified their IQ answer to within ±1 point of 118, with an additional 11 specifying the IQ to within ±5 points. The specific accuracy of these results is especially noteworthy when it is considered, first, that use of the Rorschach for intelligence estimation traditionally has been disadvised, and, second, that nearly 80 per cent of the experienced clinicians in this study rated the Rorschach as having lowest utility for intelligence questions (6 per cent), compared with highest utility for diagnosis (72 per cent). The Diagnosis problem was the one on which the clinicians showed least agreement in outcome.

Comparison of the outcomes of the two subgroups on the Intelligence question showed that their estimates were equivalent to those of the majority group of clinicians who used a balanced approach to interpretation. The mean IQ estimates for the total clinician, high quantitative, and high qualitative groups were 116, 117, and 114, respectively. Differences between these means were not statistically significant. However, of the 8 clinicians who answered with the alternative "Average," 4 were from the high qualitative subgroup, as were two other clinicians whose estimates were the most extreme (IQ = 135, 130).

One conclusion that reasonably may be drawn from the above discussion is that an interpretative approach which was balanced between qualitative and quantitative sources of information generally resulted in greater accuracy of outcome. Although a high quantitative approach tended to be the "safer" of the two extremes, resulting in equivalent accuracy on the Intelligence and Anxiety problems compared with the total group, no clinician in this subgroup appeared among the five clinicians who met the criterion answers for all three problems. A high qualitative approach was by far the most variable and the least accurate approach, although somewhat "safer" in relation to the Anxiety question. A relationship was suggested between high qualitative usage and relatively lower Rorschach administration and supervision by clinicians.

The Intelligence question was answered far more accurately than that of Diagnosis, but slightly less accurately than that of Anxiety estimation (see Table 7). In order to test the significance of the difference between the outcomes on the Anxiety and Intelligence questions, the answer alternatives for both questions were collapsed to two, "right" or "wrong." The acceptable answer for the Intelligence question was "above average" whereas both "much" and "severe" were acceptable for Anxiety estima-

Table 7. Percentage of Clinicians Answering Each Alternative for Three Problems

Diagnosis				
Basically Adjusted	Neurotic	Personality Disturbance*	Psychotic*	Organic
5%	39%	42%	14%	0%
Anxiety				
No	Little	Normal	Much*	Severe*
0%	11%	6%	72%	11%
Intelligence				
Below Average		Average		Above Average*
0%		22%		78%

*Criterion answers

tion, the equivalent of "above average." Computation of chi square in a 2 × 2 contingency table failed to show significance between the accuracy of outcome for the two questions ($\chi^2 = .18$, $df = 1$).

It was thought that clinical accuracy would be higher at the more general levels of interpretation than at more specific levels. The hypothesis was supported by the outcomes to the Anxiety and Intelligence questions, but less so by the outcomes to the Diagnosis question. For example, although only five of the clinicians answered the Diagnosis question with the criterion alternative "Psychotic," five other clinicians who had checked the alternative "Personality Disturbance" specified this general-level conclusion with the statements "Schizoid Personality . . . marginal adjustment . . . incipient schizophrenia." The latter specifications could be viewed as being in the direction of the criterion answer "Schizophrenia," and consistent with Bruno Klopfer's interpretation of the Rorschach record as "schizoid." A number of clinicians in fact questioned the five-category format employed for the Diagnosis question.

A second instance which highlighted the difficulty of determining answers to clinical questions at general levels occurred with the Anxiety problem. Two common reactions were expressed by the clinicians. First, that the line of judgment between the alternatives "Much" and "Severe" anxiety was arbitrary, the determining factor viewed as related to the presence of sufficient evidence of the subject's being totally "overwhelmed" by anxiety or being without adequate defenses. Second, there was a more immediate question concerning what was meant by "anxiety." The latter concern could be reduced to two considerations—manifest anxiety or latent anxiety, i.e., anxiety as conscious or unconscious.

The accuracy of the specific IQ estimates made by the majority of the experienced clinicians in this study (mean estimate = 115.3, criterion IQ = 118) again is noteworthy, especially when consideration is given to the amount of potential information lost in clinical judgment studies which utilize only general levels of interpretation.

It was predicted that clinicians interpreting from either the Beck or Klopfer methods would show similar levels of success in their final conclusions. The hypothesis was supported in all three cases. Again using the dichotomous framework "right" or "wrong," chi squares obtained for accuracy of outcome between Beck and Klopfer orientations on Diagnosis ($\chi^2 = .23$), Anxiety estimation ($\chi^2 = .03$), and Intelligence estimation ($\chi^2 = .30$) all failed to reach significance.

For purposes of statistical analysis, the criterion answers for the Diagnosis and Anxiety problems were collapsed into three categories. On the Anxiety problem, the alternatives Much and Severe were considered to be equivalent to the Above Average category in the Intelligence problem, with Little and No Anxiety the equivalent of Below Average on the Intelligence problem. The Psychotic alternative on the Diagnosis problem was adhered to strictly when determining the five most accurate clinicians in the study, while the Personality Disturbance alternative was viewed to be an acceptable answer when determining the number of clinicians who answered two of the three Rorschach problems accurately. It may be recalled that the Psychotic alternative represented the final integrative diagnosis for *Gregor*, while the Personality Disturbance alternative represented Bruno Klopfer's Rorschach diagnosis of *Gregor*.

Table 8. Summary of Clinician Frequencies for Four
Possible Answer Outcomes

| | *Number of Accurate Outcomes* | | | |
Clinician Frequencies	*None*	*One*	*Two*	*Three*
Expected	10⅔	16	8	1⅓
Observed	2	3	26	5

Table 8 shows the numbers of clinicians that would be expected by chance to answer according to each of the four possible outcomes in the study, as well as the numbers of clinicians actually answering according to the four outcomes. Computation of chi square, corrected for continuity, resulted in a figure which was significant beyond the .001 level (χ_c^2 = 65.11, df = 3). It may be seen that the number of clinicians answering any two of the three problems correctly (and one incorrectly) or all three problems correctly was three to four times greater than would be expected. It would appear that experienced clinicians utilizing Rorschach's inkblot technique were able to demonstrate a substantial degree of agreement in meeting the criterion answers to a variety of clinical problems.

It was anticipated that the clinicians in the present study would show a lower degree of self-constancy across the three Rorschach problems than was shown by the clinicians in Tabor's 1959 study, due to the fact that the problems were not confined to clinical diagnosis. This expectation was confirmed only partially. The mean number of information cards selected by the 30 clinicians in Tabor's study was 22, 20, and 23 (cards available = 52). The mean number of cards selected for the three problems in the present study was 71, 72, and 48 (cards available = 329). The similarity between the means on the Diagnosis and Anxiety problems in the present study supported Tabor's conclusion that the number of cards selected was more a factor of the clinicians' personal needs than of variations in the complexity of the Rorschach problems. However, the clear dissimilarity of the Diagnosis and Anxiety means in comparison with the Intelligence mean supported the prediction of the present study regarding the influence of the type of question asked in Rorschach interpretation.

Two non-Rorschach factors were seen as influencing the utility of information in the study. First was the high degree of variation in interpretative style and data needs among clinicians. For example, although the free association category proved to have highest utility for the clinicians as a group, five clinicians using the Beck method found this category to have Low utility value. Four clinicians used no Personal Data, which represented the second highest utility category for the group as a whole, and nine clinicians used no Verbalization items. Second, placement of information on the experimental apparatus, according to the format of traditional summary sheets, influenced the utility value of information. The fact of certain Rorschach information preceding other information, as with R_1 appearing before R_2 or W prior to D, enhanced the likelihood that the prior item would be selected more frequently and earlier in Rorschach interpretation.

The following comparisons between two of the clinicians in the present study may serve to illustrate the observations of high interclinician and relatively low intraclinician variations. Both clinicians were among the five clinicians who answered the three Rorschach problems most accurately according to the criteria established. Clinician # 25 required an average of 144 items for his interpretations whereas Clinician # 29 required only 8 items (Diagnosis = 138 items:7 items, Anxiety = 142 items:12 items, Intelligence = 151 items:5 items). The Free Association and Verbalization information accounted for an average of nearly 50 per cent of the card selections for Clinician # 25 (48 per cent, 48 per cent, 49 per cent), but only 20 per cent of the items selected by Clinician # 29 (29 per cent, 33 per cent, 0 per cent). The Personal Data items for Clinicians # 25 and # 29 represented the following percentages of their total card selections: Diagnosis = 3 per cent: 0 per cent, Anxiety = 4 per cent:25 per cent, Intelligence = 3 per cent:40 per cent. The Determinant percentages for the two Clinicians were: Diagnosis = 9 per cent:0 per cent, Anxiety = 8 per cent:25 per cent, Intelligence = 9 per cent:20 per cent.

The degree to which the clinicians sampled in this study showed common agreement in their interpretative approaches for each of the clinical problems was determined by computing Kendall coefficients of concordance (W). Table 9 summarizes the results for the clinicians' sequences of card selections. Kendall W's for the selected-not selected dimension were not computed due to the excessive ties which would have been involved. Table 9 shows that the correlations among clinician selections generally ranged in the .20's and low .30's. However, using chi square values and a modification of Fisher's Z distribution, the W's resulting from the total clinician group all were significant at or above the .01 level. Agreement among clinicians interpreting from a single orientation, Beck or Klopfer, would be expected to be higher than when the two orientations were combined. Higher agreement did result when separate W's were computed for the Beck and Klopfer groups, although no clear pattern of significance for the latter W's was obtained. Clinicians of both orientations showed similar degrees of agreement in their approaches to all three problems, with least agreement shown in relation to the Intelligence question.

Table 9.   Kendall Coefficients of Concordance (W) for Three Problems Based on Sequence of Card Selections

		Problems	
Clinicians	Diagnosis	Anxiety	Intelligence
Combined	.27	.27	.20
Beck	.35	.34	.26
Klopfer	.34	.33	.28

The generality of the findings reported for the study may be limited somewhat by the particular conditions imposed by the design of the study —"blind" Rorschach interpretation, atomistic access to the data—and by the moderately unequal representation of the Klopfer and Beck clinician samples.

Chapter 7

Past Failures of
Rorschach Validation

The theoretical aim of the research reported on in this volume was to account for the discrepancy existing between Rorschach utility and validity. The following observations based on the findings of the study are suggested.

First, the large majority of past Rorschach validation studies have focused their attention on quantitative Rorschach scores. Number of Rorschach responses, movement and color scores, number of popular responses, $F+$, $W\%$, frequency of eye and water percepts, and other numerical summaries, percentages, and ratios have been employed in numerous validation studies. These same quantitative scores also have been specially grouped into multiple regression equations, have been reduced by factor analytic techniques into two or three basic dimensions, and otherwise have been weighted statistically to predict one criterian group, while failing on the cross-validation to predict its counterpart. Characteristic of these studies, however, has been the nonincorporation of the actual sources of these quantitative scores, the free associations. In the present study, experienced clinicians found the free associations to have highest utility as a source of information, supported in the greatest number of instances by statistical significance concerning their utility for answering different clinical questions. This finding highlights the need to combine quantitative and qualitative information in Rorschach validation studies.

The failure of past Rorschach validation studies to incorporate free association material in their designs, although unfortunate, likely has had some realistic bases. Quantitative scores lend themselves more naturally to the experimenter's methodological goals of maximum definition and control of the variables he selects. Also, the key elements in verbal responses frequently are difficult to specify. The meaning of a Rorschach association is apt to be ambiguous, surrounded by subtle contextual and grammatical cues and influenced by selective factors in interpretation. "Important" elements may vary from one clinician to another. The dilemma posed by this simultaneous striving for experimental control and Rorschach variables which are representative frequently has failed to reach a balanced resolution. Experimenters more often than not have opted in favor of the methodological consideration.

Continued failure to incorporate free association responses in Rorschach validation studies may require qualification of the findings as involving a distortion of the Rorschach's characteristic pattern of implementation. Conclusions about the "failure" of numerical signs, ratios, and summary scores to validate the Rorschach also may require qualification. Quantitative scores contribute only partially to the data typically used by experienced clinicians in Rorschach interpretation. In addition, quantitative scores serve in a secondary, supportive capacity for some clinicians, as a means of checking-out tentative hypotheses initially established on the basis of free associations or performances on individual Rorschach blots.

Characteristic of the majority of clinicians in the study was a balanced approach to interpretation, with high agreement shown concerning the earlier importance of qualitative information in the interpretation process. Especially did those clinicians who achieved consistently accurate outcomes utilize a balanced approach to interpretation. Clinicians who employed either a qualitative or a quantitative approach proved to be most variable and least accurate in their outcomes.

A second observation may be made with regard to the above. Past validation research has for the most part focused on general sources of Rorschach information, using totaled or summary scores or holistic clinical judgments. However, experienced clinicians in the present study regularly attended to particular responses, especially in the context of a given Rorschach Card. Individual responses showed a capacity for eliciting immediate clinical hypotheses from clinicians and for directing clinicians to other sources of information which might clarify or "check out" a hypothesis. Investigation of individual sources of Rorschach utility, and inclusion of these sources of information in validation studies, also may be viewed as a necessary complement to strictly quantitative approaches typical of past studies.

Third, the results of the present study support the concept of Rorschach-and-clinician as a single working unit. High accuracy of judgment was obtained for the three different clinical questions asked, against a variety of criteria. The experienced clinicians in this study showed 83 per cent accuracy in estimating severity of anxiety, 78 per cent accuracy in estimating level of intelligence—including a mean IQ estimate of 115 ±8 points against a Stanford-Binet IQ of 118, and a likely 56 percent accuracy in diagnosing a difficult psychiatric case. On the Intelligence question, 8 clinicians specified the criterion IQ within ±1 point, and 19 specified it within ±5 points.

The conditions under which the clinicians achieved their high degree of accuracy could not have been less favorable to successful outcome for Rorschach judgments. The interpretations were done "blind." The experimental apparatus allowed information to be known only atomistically, one item at a time. The protocols used in the study were difficult ones, not of the typical "textbook" variety. The protocol employed for the Anxiety question, for example, was unusual in that traditional shading indicators of anxiety were entirely absent. Also, the psychiatric status of *Gregor*, whose Rorschach record was used for the Diagnosis question, was not definitively psychotic. Diagnoses made by 22 different psychological test experts and psychiatrists encompassed not only "Psychotic," but "Personality Disturbance" (Klopfer) and "Neurosis" as well. Finally, the number of Rorschach responses (R) was controlled in the three protocols.

As for Rorschach theory, it was clear that the clinicians in this study were being guided in their data selections by traditional hypotheses about relationships between the data and clinical questions asked. Shading determinants and information on Rorschach Cards IV and VI—the shading Cards—were selected for the Anxiety question. Location, organization (Z), and M scores were selected for the Intelligence question. Contrary to recent conceptualizations of the Rorschach as a disguised interview (Zubin, 1956), clinicians did not rely on secondary verbalizations of test subjects and examiner observations of behavior. The latter information had been separated from the actual free associations.

Fourth, if Rorschach experimenters nevertheless consider it desirable to remain within the framework of quantitative and general sources of Rorschach information, findings of the present study suggest that this framework may prove more successful for some clinical questions than others. For example, a high quantitative approach to interpretation was least successful in relation to the diagnostic question and relatively more successful for the question of intelligence estimation. Use of the quantitative framework for validation of the Rorschach as an intelligence measure likely would meet with greater success, as has been reported in the literature (Bialick and Hamlin, 1954; Sommer, 1958).

Finally, although the Rorschach technique has never been basically intended nor accepted as a measure of intelligence, the consistently successful outcomes which have been obtained in studies employing it for this purpose cannot be ignored. The success conveys importance for Rorschach practice as well as research. First, the criterion measure for the intelligence question, which provided the most specific accuracy of outcome in this study, was itself the most objective of the three criteria employed. Compared with psychological or psychiatric diagnostic judgments and with projective test measures of diagnosis or anxiety, the standard intelligence test repeatedly has been shown to have the highest reliability and validity. Failures in Rorschach validation research may bear a direct relation to the objectivity of the criterion measure used. Second, Bialick and Hamlin's (1954) judgment that intelligence represents the variable that clinicians know best is viewed as sound. Clinicians' concepts about the meaning of "intelligence" evidenced greater clarity and consensual validation than did their concepts of either "anxiety" or "diagnosis." No clinician in the present study asked for clarification of the intelligence question, while clarifications of the diagnosis and anxiety questions were requested frequently. Clinicians evidenced greater agreement in describing what they look for in estimating intelligence, and the operations involved, than in describing similar processes for diagnosis and anxiety estimation. Although intelligence is admittedly less multidimensional than personality, intelligence dimensions have been given more concrete definitions and there are a number of different measures of intelligence available for clinicians to use. More precise definitions and measures of anxiety, along with more reliable ways of describing severities of pathology, would be expected to increase success in outcomes for the latter two questions in studies of clinical judgment with the Rorschach.

In sum, reasons for past Rorschach validation failures may lie less with the Rorschach and more with ambiguities present in experimental situations related to (a) defining the question, (b) specifying the criteria, (c) selecting the Rorschach variables, and (d) applying the technique. Results of the present research question the representativeness of past Rorschach validation studies, whose results largely have been negative. The "failure" of quantitative signs, ratios, and summary scores to validate the Rorschach may be based on a distortion of the technique's typical manner of application. Clinicians used qualitative as well as quantitative sources of information in their Rorschach interpretations and collectively assigned low weightings to many of the variables which have "failed" to predict or differentiate statistically in past studies.

Part II

Interpretations by
Rorschach Clinicians

INTRODUCTION

The material presented in Part II consists of the actual Rorschach interpretations made by the 36 clinicians who participated in the study. There are 108 interpretations in all, distributed equally among the three Rorschach problems of Diagnosis, Anxiety estimation, and Intelligence estimation. All of the interpretations incorporate the item selections, in sequence, made by the clinicians, as well as the final answers given to each of the three problems. It is hoped that the reader will be able to gain understanding of the Rorschach process not only from the standpoint of *what* information was used for interpretation, but also *how* the information was used, i.e., when, for which questions, by which clinicians. Most of the interpretations are accompanied by comments and verbal reports volunteered by the clinicians as they proceeded in their analyses.

The decision to incorporate all of the 108 Rorschach interpretations was guided by two ideas. First, much valuable information would be lost through inclusion only of a few selected or "representative" interpretations. Second, multiple interpretations of single Rorschach records generally have not been available in past Rorschach literature (Hertz and Rubenstein, 1939). It is believed that each of the interpretations presented in Part II conveys something of the wide variety of personal style and interclinician variation observed among the Rorschach clinicians participating in the study. It also is believed that increased appreciation may be gained of the complexities inherent in the processes of Rorschach interpretation and judgment.

Part II is organized into three sections, corresponding with the three different problems posed to the Rorschach clinicians. Thus, there are 36 different interpretations for each problem. The Diagnosis and Anxiety interpretations are presented in order of decreasing approximation of the criterion answers employed in the study. For example, the Diagnosis interpretations begin with those clinicians who checked the strict criterion answer Psychotic, then proceed through the acceptable answer Personality Disturbance, and then through Neurotic and Basically Adjusted. The Anxiety series is ordered from most to least anxiety, with the categories Severe and Much Anxiety representing the criterion answers. It is recognized that some arbitrary placements of the records in a series occurred within answer categories, due to the subjectivity involved in making relative determinations among similar answers. The difficulty of deciding the relative placements of the majority answer Much Anxiety was resolved partially by presenting first the interpretations of those clinicians who were most accurate in their answers to the three problems overall. The Intelligence interpretations are ordered along a continuum of lower-to-higher intelligence, with the criterion IQ of 118 being met midway in the series.

Preceding each series of interpretations is a summary of the actual information made available to the clinicians for selection. The information is presented in a format closely approximating that used in the study. Also included in each of the three sections are the original interpretations of the Rorschach records made by Bruno Klopfer (1949), S. J. Beck (1952), and Bochner and Halpern (1942).

THE CASE OF GREGOR

Rorschach Interpretation by B. Klopfer*

The dominant impression yielded by Gregor's Rorschach record is of a markedly unintegrated and loose-jointed personality organization. In a series of strange contrasts ranging from semi-giftedness to uncontrolled and bizarre confusions he presents the picture of a man whose native capacities are marred and made inefficient by time-hardened cracks and warpings.

The first obvious discrepancy lies in Gregor's semantics. In successive responses he passes from a marked inadequacy in articulation of thought and a misuse of words, as when he repeatedly uses "profile" where he means "relief" or intends to give some impression of depth, to so sophisticated a response as a reference to a Gauguin painting. This contrast between the use of semi-technical language and gross semantic distortion continues throughout the record and makes it very doubtful whether the artistic ambitions of Gregor mentioned in Dr. Bell's introductory remarks could be taken seriously.

On the level of concept formation we find an unevenly used tendency to specify, even to over-specify, combined with vague and almost helpless responses. When Gregor is unable to avoid the problem of holding his thinking together by the usual defense of remaining vague, he tries to protect himself by becoming over-specific in a seemingly over-reacting, quasi-compulsory manner. Often, however, his specifications trail off in a tangential direction. When in the second response to Card X Gregor tries, instead of using the frequently seen concept of a bull, to be more specific and see only the hind end, he is confronted with the necessity of explaining what happened to the rest of the bull, and this gets him into insuperable difficulties. He starts out, "The front of the bull has- -uh- -s-s-s-uh- -surrealistic- -uh- -front half to it." His attempt to be over-specific leads him into a blind alley from which his only weak attempt at escape is the term "surrealism." In the Inquiry he repeats the same vicious circle, starting out by becoming even more specific, pointing out the strain in the legs and the tail, but again he ends up with an inability to pull the whole concept together and says rather vaguely, "It's very fantastic, yet it seems attached."

Instead of solving the problem of integration in such an approach Gregor only highlights his inability to do so. It is in this failure to integrate that his pathetic lack of ego strength becomes most evident. Breaks in reality testing do appear, but they are overshadowed by such blatant inadequacy in configurational thinking.

The contrast between Gregor's naive sensuousness and infantile need for affection and his pseudo-sophisticated and rather morbid preoccupation with sexual concepts is only thinkable in a highly schizoid personality of long standing. The openness to shading and the naivete which Gregor shows in its use would usually be combined with a young, budding reaction to sexual con-

*B. Klopfer, in J. E. Bell, 1949, pp. 458–460.

cepts that is far from the overt expression engaged in this record. Or, conversely, the sophisticated level of sexual expression which Gregor shows is usually combined with a use of shading cautiously limited to sexual symbolism. Only a genuinely mature person can combine a genital interest in sex with a tenderness in his use of shading, and that Gregor is not mature is betrayed by the lack of emotional depth and control in his reaction to color. In the flatness of his color response he betrays that his pretense of a mature integration of sexual interest and tenderness in affection has no foundation.

Where his sexual interest becomes overt or transparent, it deals predominantly with two content elements. One is with the seemingly mutilated parts of the female body, as "the lower half of a woman's body—rear view" in Card I, response 3, or the pair of woman's legs without toes and the manikin's leg without feet in Card V. The second concern is with the rear ends of humans and animals, for example, the woman's torso from the rear just mentioned and the hind end of the bull in Card X. This choice of concepts might be accidental in some instances—the lower half of the woman's body in Card I is usually seen from the rear—but in this record we have an unmistakable barometer or tension-indicator that Gregor's preoccupation with these content elements is not accidental but obviously connected with panic-like tension. This indicator is his peculiar use of the word "profile" mentioned previously. It occurs six times and is usually followed by the tangential trailing off of his thinking described earlier.

The first misuse of "profile" is in the inquiry to Card I, response 2, where Gregor mentions it in connection with "the distance from the back" of the flying horse, and this is followed by the first of his vapid explanations that the "distance is in proportion to what this horse might have." It appears the second time in the next response when he tries to explain the rear view of the woman's body. The third instance is in Card V, response 2, where, after having mutilated one woman's leg in the previous response, he struggles with the manikin's leg. In Card VII, response 2, where he associates "profile" with a strangely mutilated face consisting of a shriveled-up mouth and chin and the back of a head, the response is again followed by a vapid explanation that "it's a man's face that you see in illustrations ...uh... famous legends, famous stories, I should say, that dates back some time." As further evidence of Gregor's state of excitement the examiner observes for the first time his tortured blowing. Final appearance of the profile concept occurs on Card X after the strange preoccupation with the hind end of the bull described previously. Here Gregor seems to be so close to a homosexual panic that he has to repeat the word "profile" like a magic formula in the two subsequent responses, and he concludes this disturbed card with his most confused geographical concept.

It seems fair to assume that Gregor's psychosexual development never exceeded the stage described as pre-phallic in Freudian terminology. His behavior is subject to shifting without any marked transition from the expressions of infantile dependency symbolized by the naive pleasure with which he enjoys all the soft warm objects seen frequently in the shaded portions, such as "the fat softness of the caterpillar" in Card VII, to polymorphous perverse experimentation with partners of either sex. The gloved hands reaching out in Card I reappear in Card II with swords!

The final test for the consistency of the previous deductions about Gregor's thinking, affectivity, and psychosexual development would have to be found in his response to emotionally charged stimuli. The absence of even the slightest discomfort in his dealing with color and shading shows more clearly than anything else the pathetic lack of ego-defensiveness which has been his undoing. Even when, under the impact of accumulating color stimuli in the last three cards, his conceptualization becomes increasingly bizarre, he is not in the least disturbed or, apparently, even very conscious of what is happening. His use of color is limited to the "ice" in Card VIII, the "St. Bernard" in Card X (which, upon inquiry, he feels is "orangy"), and his strange concluding response of aerial photography to a blue area. Throughout the record, instead of showing any subjective discomfort, Gregor produces a concentrated dose of his peculiar semantics and vapid explanations. His personal dissociation has reached a point where the danger of being emotionally involved without having means of handling this involvement fails to ring any warning bell of anxiety to call forth some form of defense.

Gregor's record gives the clinical impression of a highly schizoid personality of long standing with a possible history of psychotic breaks and a general symptomatology compounded of paranoic, depressive and catatonic elements. His recent course in therapy has had very limited therapeutic success, as one would expect where there is no ego strength to effect integration in the therapeutic situation.

At the time the record was taken Gregor was not psychotic but had made what might be called a social recovery. Whenever he is supported by a strong analyst who can act as a sort of integrating figure, Gregor is able to function without too evident ineffectiveness. It is clear, however, that when such support is removed—and with it the pseudo-integration—the frail links in his personality are in danger of breaking and precipitating him into a psychotic condition.

Answer form presented to clinicians at the beginning of Diagnosis interpretation.

Question: Determine the *clinical diagnosis* of this individual, on the basis of the Rorschach data available.

As soon as you feel quite sure of the diagnosis, check one of the five diagnostic categories below and write your own more specific clinical impression.

Basically Adjusted   _____
Neurotic   _____
Personality Disturbance _____
Organic   _____
Psychotic   _____

Specific Clinical Impression _____

DIAGNOSIS

Listing of cards available for selection (*Items*) by clinicians and information contained on reverse side of cards (*Information*) for the Diagnosis question. (Refer to Chapter 5 for detailed explanation of method used for presenting information to clinicians.)

Personal Data

Items	*Information*
Sex	Male
Age	30 years
Education	10 years. Vocational High School. Some art school.
Occupation	Unskilled laborer. Work in textile mill planned.
Nationality	Eastern European. Came to U.S. at age 7.
Religion	
Marital Status	Single
Sibling Position	½
Siblings	Sister. Left home at age 20 to escape father's physical abuse.
Mother	Died when S age 9. S raised in foster home.
Father	Unwilling to support S from childhood. Remarried when S age 23. Works in textile mill. S closer to father than to mother.
Sexual	Many homosexual experiences.
Military	WW II veteran. Marine Corps.
Interests	Commercial art.

Locations—Klopfer

W	$W = 3$
D	$D = 25$
d	$d = 0$
Dd	$Dd = 5$
S	$S = +1$
W%	$W\% = 9$ (expect 20–30%)
D%	$D\% = 76$ (expect 45–55%)
d%	$d\% = 0$ (expect 5–15%)
Dd + S %	$Dd + S \% = 15$ (expect $< 10\%$) $+ 1S$
Succession	Succession = orderly

Locations—Beck

W	$W = 2$
D	$D = 26$
Dd	$Dd = 5$
S	$S = +1$
Approach	Approach $= ((W))$ D! Dd!
Sequence	Sequence = occasionally confused
Aff. Ratio	Aff. Ratio = .74
Z freq.	Z freq. = 7
Z Sum	Z Sum = 21.5

Determinants—Klopfer

Items	Information
M	M = 2
FM	FM = 2
m	m = 0
k	k = 0
K	K = 0
FK	FK = +1
F	F = 23
Fc	Fc = 1 + 2
c	c = 1
C′	C′ = 1 + 2
FC	FC = 2
CF	CF = 1
C	C = 0

Content—Klopfer

Items	Information
H	H = 2
Hd	Hd = 8
A	A = 10
Ad	Ad = 1
At	At = 3
AAt	AAt = 1
AObj	AObj = 3 + 3
Art	Art = + 1
Cl	Cl = 0
Fd	Fd = 1
Fire	Fire = 0
Geo	Geo = 3
Na	Na = 1
Obj	Obj = 2
Pl	Pl = 0
Sc	Sc = 0
Sex	Sex = + 1

Determinants—Beck

M	M = 2
C	C = 0
CF	CF = 0
FC	FC = 1
Y	Y = 0
YF	YF = 0
FY	FY = 2
T	T = 0
TF	TF = 1
FT	FT = 0
V	V = 0
VF	VF = 0
FV	FV = 0
F+	F+ = 17
F—	F— = 7
F_0	F_0 = 0
Double	Double = FT·Y+
Double	Double = FC·Y—
Double	Double = CF·VF—

Content—Beck

H	H = 2
Hd	Hd = 8
A	A𝟙= 8
Ad	Ad = 1
An	An = 4
Anal	Anal = +1
Ar	Ar = 0
Art	Art = +1
Ay	Ay = 3
Bt	Bt = 0
Cl	Cl = +3
Fd	Fd = 1
Fi	Fi = 0
Geo	Geo = 3
Hh	Hh = 0
My	My = +1
Na	Na = 1
Oj	Oj = 0

Totals and Percentages—Klopfer Summaries

Items	*Information*
R	R = 33
Avg RT	Avg RT = 28″
RT Achrom	RT Achrom = 29″
RT Chrom	RT Chrom = 27″
F%	F% = 70
FK + F + Fc %	FK + F + Fc % = 73
A%	A% = 27
P	P = 3 (10 possible)
Sum C	Sum C = 2.0
VIII–IX–X%	VIII–IX–X % = 42
Additional Responses	Additional Responses = 0
Rejections	Rejections = 0

Totals and Percentages—Beck Summaries

R	R = 33
F%	F% = 73
ExtF%	ExtF% = 94
F+%	F+% = 71
ExtF+%	ExtF+% = 74
A%	A% = 33
P	P = 11 (21 possible)
Avg RT	Avg RT = 28″
RT Achrom	RT Achrom = 29″
RT Chrom	RT Chrom = 27″
Additional Responses	Additional Responses = 0
Rejections	Rejections = 0

Number of Responses to Each Card

Card I.	Card I.	5	(#1–#5)
Card II.	Card II.	1	(#6)
Card III.	Card III.	1	(#7)
Card IV.	Card IV.	3	(#8–#10)
Card V.	Card V.	2	(#11–#12)
Card VI.	Card VI.	3	(#13–#15)
Card VII.	Card VII.	4	(#16–#19)
Card VIII	Card VIII.	4	(#20–#23)
Card IX.	Card IX.	4	(#24–#27)
Card X.	Card X.	6	(#28–#33)

Reaction Times to Each Card

Items	*Information*	
Card I.	Card I.	20″
Card II.	Card II.	46″
Card III.	Card III.	25″
Card IV.	Card IV.	23″
Card V.	Card V.	57″
Card VI.	Card VI.	20″
Card VII.	Card VII.	27″
Card VIII.	Card VIII.	27″
Card IX.	Card IX.	21″
Card X.	Card X.	17″

Individual Response Scorings—Klopfer

# 1	# 1 Card I.	W	F	A
# 2	# 2 Card I.	Dd	FM	(A)
# 3	# 3 Card I.	D	F	Hd
# 4	# 4 Card I.	D	F	Hd, Obj
# 5	# 5 Card I.	Dd	F	Hd
# 6	# 6 Card II.	W	M	H,Obj
# 7	# 7 Card III.	D	M	H P
# 8	# 8 Card IV.	W	cF	AObj
# 9	# 9 Card IV.	D	F	Ad
#10	#10 Card IV.	D	F	Hd,Obj
#11	#11 Card V.	D	F	Hd
#12	#12 Card V.	D	F	(Hd)
#13	#13 Card VI.	D	F	Obj
#14	#14 Card VI.	D	FC′	AObj
#15	#15 Card VI.	D	F→Fc	Obj,Art
#16	#16 Card VII.	D	Fc, FC′	A
#17	#17 Card VII.	D	F	(Hd)
#18	#18 Card VII.	D	F	AAt
#19	#19 Card VII.	Dd	F	Geo
#20	#20 Card VIII.	D	F	At
#21	#21 Card VIII.	D	F	At
#22	#22 Card VIII.	D	F	A P
#23	#23 Card VIII.	D	F	Na
#24	#24 Card IX.	D	FC,FC′	Geo
#25	#25 Card IX.	Dd,s	F	AObj
#26	#26 Card IX.	D	F→Fc	Hd
#27	#27 Card IX.	Dd	F	At
#28	#28 Card X.	D	F	A P
#29	#29 Card X.	D	FM	A,Sex
#30	#30 Card X.	D	F	A
#31	#31 Card X.	D	FC	A
#32	#32 Card X.	D	F	Fd

Individual Response Scorings—Klopfer—Continued

Items	Information			
#33	#33 Card X.	D	CF→FK	Geo
#34				
#35				
#36				
#37				

Individual Response Scorings—Beck

# 1	# 1 Card I.	W	F+	A	1.0
# 2	# 2 Card I.	Dd	F—	A,My	
# 3	# 3 Card I.	D	F+	Hd	P
# 4	# 4 Card I.	D	F+	Hd,Cl	
# 5	# 5 Card I.	Dd	F+	Hd	
# 6	# 6 Card II.	D	M+	H,Cl P	4.5
# 7	# 7 Card III.	D	M+	H P	3.0
# 8	# 8 Card IV.	W	TF+	A P	2.0
# 9	# 9 Card IV.	D	F+	Ad	
#10	#10 Card IV.	D	F+	Hd,Cl P	
#11	#11 Card V.	D	F+	Hd	
#12	#12 Card V.	D	F+	Hd P	
#13	#13 Card VI.	D	F+	Ay	
#14	#14 Card VI.	D	FY+	Ay	
#15	#15 Card VI	D	FY+	Ay, Art	
#16	#16 Card VII.	D	FT·Y+	A	
#17	#17 Card VII.	D	F+	Hd P	
#18	#18 Card VII.	D	F—	An	
#19	#19 Card VII.	Dd	F—	Ge	1.0
#20	#20 Card VIII.	D	F+	An	
#21	#21 Card VIII.	D	F—	An	
#22	#22 Card VIII.	D	F+	A P	
#23	#23 Card VIII.	D	F+	Na	
#24	#24 Card IX.	D	FC·Y—	Ge	
#25	#25 Card IX.	Dds	F—	A 5.0	
#26	#26 Card IX.	D	F+	Hd P	
#27	#27 Card IX.	Dd	F—	An 5.0	
#28	#28 Card X.	D	F+	A P	
#29	#29 Card X.	D	F—	A,Anal	
#30	#30 Card X.	D	F+	A P	
#31	#31 Card X.	D	FC+	A	
#32	#32 Card X.	D	F+	Fd	
#33	#33 Card X.	D	CF·VF—	Ge	
#34					
#35					
#36					
#37					

Location Areas

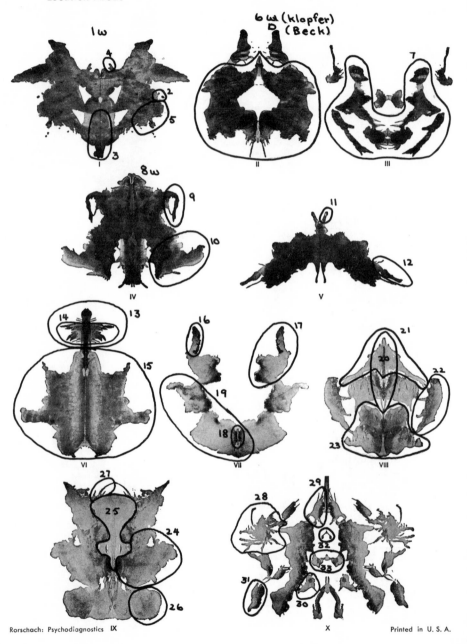

Free Associations

Items		*Information*
# 1	# 1 Card I.	Bug.
# 2	# 2 Card I.	Large pair of wings. Of flying red horse. (On trademark. Wings attached to horse. Profile. Outline of back and belly.)
# 3	# 3 Card I.	Lower half of woman's body. Rear view. (Hip. Profile. Like painting by Gaughin.)
# 4	# 4 Card I.	Hands. Gloves on them. (Thumb. Fingers. Smooth outlines.)
# 5	# 5 Card I.	Profile of funny-paper face. Man. (Nose. Like end of broomstick. Mouth.)
# 6	# 6 Card II.	People. Dancing. About to duel. (Duelling. Gloves on. Points of swords. Weapons.)
# 7	# 7 Card III.	Man. With spats. Has got basket of coal. Reflection in mirror. (Positions. Pulling something heavy. Legs done up in leggings. Legs thin.)
# 8	# 8 Card IV.	Hide of large animal. (Texture leathery. Middle where body was stripped. Suggestion of where vertebrae had been.)
# 9	# 9 Card IV.	Horns. From steer.
#10	#10 Card IV.	Feet. With boots on. (Heel. Toes. Part where lacings come.)
#11	#11 Card V.	Woman's legs. Without toes. (Calf. Heel. Knee.)
#12	#12 Card V.	Manikin's leg. Without Feet. (Profile. Woman's leg.)
#13	#13 Card VI.	Indian totem pole. (Decorations on it. Outline. Long and narrow. Like tree trunk.)
#14	#14 Card VI.	Colored feathers. (Ends of feathers. Light. Lines delicate. Designs painted on. As Indians do.)
#15	#15 Card VI.	Indian rug. (Center of rug. Haven't completed outside the main design.)
#16	#16 Card VII.	Caterpillar. (Fat softness of caterpillar. Top is dark. Transition to light is gradual.)
#17	#17 Card VII.	Profile of man's face. In illustrations of famous legends, stories. (Nose. Old shriveled up mouth and chin. Back of head.)
#18	#18 Card VII.	Vertebrae. Of small animal. (Symmetry.)
#19	#19 Card VII.	Map of Spain and Germany. (Outline accurate.)
#20	#20 Card VIII.	Vertebrae. (Down through center. Symmetry.)
#21	#21 Card VIII.	Three ribs. (Little lines coming out from center bone. In symmetrical way.)
#22	#22 Card VIII.	Fat rat. (Head. Back. Fore legs. Full around shoulders.)
#23	#23 Card VIII.	Ice. (Conventional rendition. Smeared. Large chunks. Casualness of rendering.)
#24	#24 Card IX.	Map of Norway and Sweden. (Outline. Color. Like in geography books. Graduation of dark and light. Soft way it's done.)

Free Associations—Continued

Items		*Information*
#25	#25 Card IX.	Animal hide. Where strip it around the vertebrae. (Symmetry.)
#26	#26 Card IX.	Profile of Chinaman's head. (Bald. Moustache that Chinese have. Smoothness of head.)
#27	#27 Card IX.	Ribs. (Symmetrical. Repetitious. Spaced like bones).
#28	#28 Card X.	Spider. (Number of thin legs. Length of legs.)
#29	#29 Card X.	Hind end of bull. Kind used in bull fighting. Abstract. Surrealistic front to it. (Legs have great strain. From weight of body. Tail. Hind legs with hoof.)
#30	#30 Card X.	Modern design of dog. Profile. (Nose. Head. Paws. Outline suggests fur around neck.)
#31	#31 Card X.	Profile of shepherd dog. (Bushy outline. Color. Head. St. Bernard. Orangy. Or Collie.)
#32	#32 Card X.	Wishbone. (Symmetrical. General shape.)
#33	#33 Card X.	Aerial photograph. Of globe. (Photographs in books. Color. Mountains. Level surfaces. Land. Earth's surface.)
#34		
#35		
#36		
#37		

Verbalizations and Behavioral Observations

Items		*Information*
# 1	# 1 Card I.	Well, I make out a_____. INQ: Uh, let's see, gee I don't remember. I don't see the_____.
# 2	# 2 Card I.	Uh - - make out - - uh . . . Reminds me of_____. INQ: (*S outlines.*)
# 3	# 3 Card I.	Then - - uh - - make out the_____. INQ: I've seen something like that.
# 4	# 4 Card I.	And - - uh - - make out a_____. Those are the things that - - uh - - is that enough? I mean did you expect me to go much further - - to go on longer? INQ: Well, could make out a_____.
# 5	# 5 Card I.	Well, the last thing I see is_____. INQ: Well, yes, right here.
# 6	# 6 Card II.	Well I see_____. First I thought they were_____. Then it looks as though they were_____. - - uh - - that's about all on that. INQ: Well, that - - uh - - I can't explain for - - but_____.

Verbalizations and Behavioral Observations—Continued

Items		*Information*
# 7	# 7 Card III.	Uh - - I see a_____. - - uh - - and then - - uh - - then I see - - uh_____. That's all. INQ: Right here.
# 8	# 8 Card IV.	(*Turns head aside, moves mouth.*) Well I make out a_____. INQ: I could make out the_____.
# 9	# 9 Card IV.	I make out a_____. INQ: Well, no it—no that's all.
#10	#10 Card IV.	Then I make out - - uh - - a_____. That's all. INQ: Yes, right here.
#11	#11 Card V.	I can make out a_____. (*Head aside, slight sigh.*) INQ: Right here.
#12	#12 Card V.	Uh - - I make out - - uh - - uh a_____. Uh - - that's all. INQ: Right here.
#13	#13 Card VI.	Well, I make out a_____. INQ: (*Looks up at E, smiles, looks back at card.*) uh - - uh - - well . . . that's all - - 'cept_____.
#14	#14 Card VI.	That's uh_____. INQ: Uh - - well, you can make out_____. You can make out_____.
#15	#15 Card VI.	And_____. That's all. INQ: Well, you know they____.
#16	#16 Card VII.	I make out - - uh_____. INQ: Right here. Well_____.
#17	#17 Card VII.	Uh - - make out a_____. I should say. (*Blew.*) INQ: (*Tilts head and studies card.*) Oh right here. Can make out the_____.
#18	#18 Card VII.	Uh - - I make out a_____. (*Looks up questioningly at E.*) INQ: Right in here.
#19	#19 Card VII.	That's all. When I first looked at it the_____. When I went back to it, I couldn't see those_____ any more. That's all. INQ: In here.
#20	#20 Card VIII.	Well, I make out some more_____. INQ: Yeah.
#21	#21 Card VIII.	Uh - - see . . . uh - - . . . uh_____. INQ: Right in here.
#22	#22 Card VIII.	Uh - - see - - uh - - see - - uh_____. INQ: (*Points*).
#23	#23 Card VIII.	See some - - uh - - some_____. Uh - - that's all (*Holds card for 40″.*) INQ: I can't describe it very well. - - of course I realize it's an accidental thing.
#24	#24 Card IX.	(*Tilts head.*) Well I see the_____. (*Yawns.*) Excuse me. INQ: Right in here.
#25	#25 Card IX.	An' I see - - uh_____. INQ: Well there you have this_____.
#26	#26 Card IX.	(*Tilts head.*) Uh - - if I look at it sideways, see - - uh - - see - - uh_____. INQ: Yeah, right here.
#27	#27 Card IX.	And I see a_____. That's all. INQ: Up in here. And well they suggest_____. They're repetitious.
#28	#28 Card X.	(*Smiles.*) Last one, eh? Well I make out a_____. INQ: Yes, right here.
#29	#29 Card X.	Make the_____. INQ: (*Indicates details.*) It's very fantastic, yet it seems_____.
#30	#30 Card X.	Uh_____. (*Turns head, coughs.*) INQ: That was here.
#31	#31 Card X.	Make out_____. INQ: Right here. Well, you _____.

Verbalizations and Behavioral Observations—Continued

Items		Information
#32	#32 Card X.	Hunh - - see a_____. (*Head aside, blows out.*) INQ: Right here.
#33	#33 Card X	See - - uh_____. That's all. (*Sighs.*) INQ: Right in here, this_____. Well, it reminds me of the_____. I've seen in books.
#34		
#35		
#36		
#37		

Clinician #29	Diagnosis problem	7 cards
Beck orientation	Interpreted third	5 minutes

(R, F #1–2, L #2) That's the response? Large pair of wings? And it includes the horse? Well, we have just eliminated Basically Adjusted and Personality Disturbance, unless this guy is some kind of manipulative, basically angry guy. And rule out Neurotic. The question then is between Organic and Psychotic. (Anal, Sex Content) I suspect I'm gonna call him psychotic, but I'll take one more card to make sure. (F + %) That doesn't help much. I'm gonna call him psychotic. Don't ask me what type because I don't believe in "types."

Answer: Psychotic. Schizophrenia, paranoid, chronic.

Clinician #25	Diagnosis problem	138 cards
Klopfer orientation	Interpreted first	24 minutes

(R, Sex, Age, Education, Nationality, F-V #1, Reaction Time Card I, F-V-L #2-33, W, D, d, Dd, W%, D%, Dd + S%, M, FM, m, k, K, FK, F, Fc, c, C', FC, CF, C, Avg Reaction Time, RT Achromatic, RT Chromatic, F%, FK + %, A%, P, Sum C, 8–9–10%, H, Hd, A, Ad, Succession) I would diagnose him as

Note: Material contained within parentheses refers to the actual data card selections made by the clinician in obtaining Rorschach information item-by-item. Abbreviations are listed and defined in Appendix A.

Clinician #25—Continued   Diagnosis problem   138 cards
Klopfer orientation   Interpreted first   24 minutes

psychotic. The content of the responses more than anything else, and the way he goes about dealing with the blots. He evades the central blot, he edges, goes around. The oral responses. Also, response #29 "the rear end of a bull." The hands that were gloved or sheathed, indicating trouble coming to terms with aggressive impulses. It indicates pressure to act out. Primitive material of a tactual nature. Hands would fit in that too. He's disturbed. He probably has much greater potential intellectually. He can't organize himself. He has a low number of W's. I have difficulty deciding about psychosis. The paranoid aspect is not difficult, but there's a large amount of perseveration in the record. Still it's a sterile record, with guarding of responses. Another thing is the many attempts to show an obsessive-compulsive organization in this situation. The order of the cards, unable to carry through completely. It's an orderly record despite the amount of disturbance. At one time he was organized in an obsessive fashion.

Answer: Psychotic. Schizophrenic reaction, paranoid type, possibly decompensating from an obsessive-compulsive personality structure.

Clinician #7   Diagnosis problem   87 cards
Beck orientation   Interpreted first   59 minutes

There are no more than 37 responses? (That's right) OK. (Sex, Age, R) That gives me some information right away. (F + %, A%, P, Education) I'm now concerned with a stereotype here. This person has finished only tenth grade and is going into art, yet his P is very high. Why is he relying on this? How is he using it? In lieu of what? High P in H and FC. (FC, H, Hd) This guy's awfully anxious. His Hd:H proportion is high. Yet essentially he's under adequate control. His F+ is at an adequate level. Now if I had all of the Rorschach material I'd be able to scan it in different directions for relevant questions. (A, Ad) With the Ad:A I look for the same information as H:Hd, at a more dynamic or perceptual level. Oh the preponderance is psychogenic anxiety, concern over relatedness, specifically in the area of human relations. Let me follow up. How much anxiety is he expressing? (An) OK. This goes along with the hypothesis of a pretty high level. Now I have two directions. I want to know about M and Approach. Maybe an exaggerated D or Dd. (Approach) OK. This is consistent. He has difficulty organizing his thinking. This goes along with his educational level and helps confirm the stereotype. He's dealing with the here and now, concretely. How are his inner resources? (M) I want to find out the whole Experience Balance. (C, CF) Not particularly surprising. F% eliminates the need to investigate the determinants as closely. You know, you're asking me to do this interpretation blind. His artistic background should make

Clinician #7—Continued   Diagnosis problem   87 cards
Beck orientation   Interpreted first   59 minutes

him sensitive to nuances, the Y shading, but my feeling is that he's not free enough to express this. The F% then should be relatively high. (F%) It's not very high. That means he has a fair amount of Y. (Y, YF, FY) Two FY— where's the rest of it? Now to determine whether he's a dependent, clean type or—I'm working on summary first but my usual approach is to look at the responses—I want to duplicate my clinical approach as much as possible. A T-type or a V-type? (V, VF, FV, T, TF, FT) He's a guy who's affectively hungry. Let's see how responsive he is and if he can use it. (Affective Ratio) A fair number of responses but he can't integrate. He's stimulated by feelings, maintains adequate control, but is not able to use it constructively. I want to get a lever on that F%, to see if he's getting into unusual areas that are hard to score (F₀, Extended F+%) No problem here. So, when he gets a minus he gets a minus. What's the nature of his minus responses? Here's what I have at this point. He could be a relatively well defended psychotic or some sort of character disorder. The difference would be in the quality of his responses. Let me check. (F—) I have to know how bad these minuses are, whether they are minor, where they occur. (FM) That doesn't have any minus indication. I'll eventually have to go through the cards. I've been working on an assumption: I didn't pull out some of the cards because I didn't think he was as well organized. This has been a subjective pulling, which I'm willing to bank on at this point. I have to go to the protocol. (S-F-V #1–2) What's the pattern of this guy? The pattern of rejection. I wonder about this rejection of the original percept. Some loosening of association here. (Location #2) Oh, at this point the response moves me in the direction of psychotic thinking. If he had used the D2 area there would not be so much concern. He has associated to the D2 area and then constricted it to a dd. Some loosening of thinking. Another thing here is "outline of back and belly." (S-F-V #3) Oh good recoverability. But it takes him some time to mobilize it, to get a P. He's a high P person. He may come up with the popular butterfly. (S-F-V #4) A loose association. How much of a problem does he have with masturbation? The hand and glove response. (S-F-V #5) He answers my question in part. This guy's thinking is not systematic. It vacillates back and forth. It's irregular to confused. Let's check on it. (Sequence, L #5) OK. He shows a Klopferian sort of F+ that deflates F₀ and inflates F+. I wish I had Beck's Volume I and Small's location guide. (S-F-V #6) He doesn't remobilize enough to reintegrate the popular—"the last thing, I'm through with this damn card." Conventional. He will go along with prescribed activities. He probably was deferential toward the examiner. I now have one of my F—'s. He's not really sure in his relations whether they're friendly or dangerous. This explains the preponderance of Hd over H. He's threatened. At the same time he wants some closeness. He's sort of mixed up. (S-F-V #7) Well this is the only response on Card II, after five responses on Card I. But the response he comes up with is a P, an M, but a threatening M. Reaction Time Card II) It took him a long time and a lot of censoring. But he's able to do it and to maintain it. My guess is at this point that he's a schizophrenic, in partial remission. This will have to be supported or refuted. (Number

Clinician #7—Continued   Diagnosis problem   87 cards
Beck orientation   Interpreted first   59 minutes

of Responses Card III) By his verbalizations he's also indicating that he's got only one response to Card III. These are his two M's. That's all he's got. (Reaction Time Card III and I, Avg Reaction Time) He's spending a lot of time defending himself, mobilizing himself. He has no free energy left anymore. It exhausts him. I have some reflections at this point concerning the problem of narcissism, possibly as a V-type of thing that is not scored. There is adequacy, tentativeness. What time is it? (Individual Scorings #8–17) Totem poles. He's going way back to antiquity, isn't he? I don't know if I'd score the blend this way. (S-F-V-L #18–21) OK. I'll stick to my notion of this guy as a schizophrenic, in partial remission. There is a cognitive disturbance, in check.

Answer: Psychotic. Schizophrenic reaction, partial remission.

Clinician #21   Diagnosis problem   157 cards
Beck orientation   Interpreted third   22 minutes

(Sex, Age, Education, Marital Status, Occupation, Nationality, Religion, Sibling Position, Sibling Description, Mother Description, Father Description, Sexual History, Military History, Interests) On the basis of the personal data my first hypothesis would be that if there were a disorder, and there probably is, it would be a personality disturbance type of disorder. Important here would be the father, the kind of father he is, the sister leaving, the father's unwillingness to provide support. Deprivation is suggested. The homosexuality suggests difficulty in identifying with the father. The mother died so early. The fact that he was a World War II veteran in the Marine Corps would suggest that more severe organic and psychotic processes would be less likely. (R, F%, F+%, A%, P, Avg Reaction Time, RT Achromatic, RT Chromatic, W, D, Dd, S, Sequence, Approach, Affective Ratio, Z Sum, F-V-S #1) "Bug" in association with the brutalizing father reminds me of *Copis Metamorphosis* where the person wakes up one morning and finds he can turn into a bug. It's a short study. (F-V-S #2–5) The bug, flying red horse, woman's body, a nose like a broomstick all suggest some kind of sexual problem. (F-V-S #6–7) People dancing and about to duel also suggests conflict, sexual conflict. (F-V-S #8) Interesting fact that he gave two M and P responses to Cards II and III. I'm not sure what significance it has. (F-V-S #9–10) Card IV is somehow better than one would expect from the personal data references to the father. (F-V-S #11–12, L #11) I would expect more anxiety to be evident. The texture would suggest a seeking of affection from the father, as in homosexual experiences. But Card IV still is better than I thought it would be. This kind of thing where the person turns away from the P response and gives it somewhere else suggests anxiety. (F-V-S #13–16, L #16)

Clinician #21—Continued   Diagnosis problem   157 cards
Beck orientation   Interpreted third   22 minutes

He has an unusual amount of affect available to him, the Y and T responses.
But it's nicely used in many cases. Overall he appears in better shape than I
would have expected. (F-V-S #17–18, L #18) Again some suggestion of sexual
apprehension and confusion. (F-V-S #19) This Card VII female structure is by
far his worst card, his lousy card. A little anxiety I think in response to women.
(F-V-S #20, Reaction Time Card VIII) On Card VIII he comes back. I have
a fairly specific diagnosis now. I would go through the remainder of the cards
to see if he falls apart badly, in those cards that were left. I'd want to see if
there would be evidence that the ego functions would break down on the last
three cards. It would be a check rather than a seeking of any new type of interpretation. (F-V-S #21) Actually he says so little on inquiry, the verbalizations,
that I haven't been looking at this information very much. (F-V-S #22–24) This
is the second geography response. He's had two anatomy responses. It suggests
he's a little sicker than I thought he was. (F-V-S #25–29, L #25, 27, 29) That
response #29 is a pretty overtly homosexual response. (F-V-S #30–33, L #31,
33) That's the end. Whew! The last three cards have been sufficiently chaotic
to make me feel that there's a good chance of his being psychotic. (M, C, CF,
FC, Y, YF, FY) I'll just go down the list here. (T, TF, FT, V, VF, FV, Blend
#1–3, F+, F—, F₀) It's a very tough one: the blends, the number of chromatic
responses, where the guy fell apart on the last three cards, especially the geography
responses and aerial photography of the globe. It makes me feel that although he
held together until Card VII he's probably quite disturbed. It makes me charac-
terize him as psychotic. Probably manic-depressive or schizo-affective.

Answer: Psychotic. Schizo-affective psychosis.

Clinician #36   Diagnosis problem   82 cards
Beck orientation   Interpreted third   60 minutes

(Sex, Age, Education, F-L #1–2, S #2) My immediate impression is that this
is either an organic or a psychotic. Pegasus you get certainly, the red horse.
(F-L #3–5) I begin to get a feel of a paranoid psychotic. Somebody who's
running away from homosexuality. (F-L #6–14, L #14) A rather intelligent
person. Almost picks out the same detail as in responses #11 and #16. (F-L
#15–21) A lot of somatic preoccupation. (F-L-V-S #22–23) A very cold,
fearful man. He's preoccupied with his own anatomical functioning. (F-L
#24–33, F #34) I expected to see much more disturbance. I get the feeling of a
very well-compensated paranoid. His intelligence has enabled him to manage
his world, like he says "with gloves." He's very much aloof, distant. There's no

| Clinician # 36—Continued | Diagnosis problem | 82 cards |
| Beck orientation | Interpreted third | 60 minutes |

picture of systematized delusions. But homsoexual—the rear view of things, from which he's fleeing. He's preoccupied with his own somatic functioning, with spines and vertebrae. He has suffered a good deal of dehumanization, alienation in his life. He's quite capable of being fairly brutal. I haven't got a slot for what I want to say here. He's not Basically Adjusted and not Neurotic. I would say pseudo-psychoneurotic schizophrenic. The neurosis is used as a defense against the psychotic process. I expect to find him in an occupation that doesn't involve people too much, with figures or machines or something like that. I don't know why but I get a feeling that he might be an oldest son, with an overbearing mother, and a rather weak, passive father. (Education, Occupation, Marital Status, Sibling Position, Mother Description, Father Description, Sexual History) He's too cold to be a Don Juan. There's autoerotic activity on his part.

Answer: Psychotic. Pseudo-psychoneurotic schizophrenic with strong paranoid component.

| Clinician # 10 | Diagnosis problem | 63 cards |
| Klopfer orientation | Interpreted first | 53 minutes |

(Age) I'll cross over on the Beck. (F+ % Beck, F%, R, M, W, FM, P) Only three P out of 33 responses? Where are the DW? There's no indication here of contamination or confabulation. (FC) On the basis of the F%, the patient wouldn't be psychotic. There are too few W also. I would anticipate more W in a psychotic record. The few P's and high F suggest a neurotic disturbance at this time. It's a fairly high number of responses for a neurotic, though, and would counter-indicate a depressive reaction. I would like to get the flavor of his responses now. The M's probably came from Cards III and VII. (Number of Responses Card III, F #7) There are four responses unaccounted for. (CF) My wild guess now is Neurotic, with possibly obsessive-compulsive tendencies. There's no definite evidence yet. (Dd) That's not so much. (D) It's different working the interpretation this way. It's hard. You have to know what you're looking for. (Avg Reaction Time, Rejections, Education, Number of Responses Card I, F #1–5, L #4) I'd better try to work from the psychogram. (C') I know there are only a few responses left. I've already zeroed in on them. They're all in the center of this board. (A%) This wouldn't make much difference in the interpretation. (Obj) Only 27%? Most of the responses should be Objects. (Art) Are they art responses? (AAt, At, Na, A, Sex, Number of Responses Card VIII, F #20–23) Is that a W Response? (L #23, Sexual History, Marital Status, Occupation) He's pretty smart to be unskilled labor. (Military History,

| Clinician #10—Continued | Diagnosis problem | 63 cards |
| Klopfer orientation | Interpreted first | 53 minutes |

V #23) The first response to Card II would be #6. I want to see what his response is to color. (F-L #6, Fc, Additionals) The psychogram is very constricted, but it certainly doesn't look schizophrenic. (F-S #8, Number of Responses Card X, F #28–32, L #30) I haven't got a real good picture at all. Something's disturbing him, but his record is not bad. Yet he's this highly constricted personality, without loss of contact. He's unconventional, afraid to let loose, and not an obsessive-compulsive pattern, which you would expect in a person like this. Maybe he's schizoid? I don't know. It can't be Organic, and not Basically Adjusted. The anxiety is not open but pretty well bound. It's not hysteria. (Extended F+%) I want to see Card IV. (F #9–11) Now this is Card V. Let's see what reactions he makes to color. (V #29, #31) I'd just go on and pick everything. Right now I'd have to guess Personality Disturbance.

Answer: Personality Disturbance. Schizoid personality.

| Clinician #2 | Diagnosis problem | 116 cards |
| Beck orientation | Interpreted third | 30 minutes |

I'm afraid that for this one I'll need all of the data. (Age, Sex, Education, Occupation, Nationality, Religion, Marital Status) The assumption here is that he has never been married. (Sexual History) Aha. (Interests) Of course the question is whether homosexuality is a neurosis or a personality disturbance. I guess it depends on whether he worries about it. (F, R, Military History, Sibling Position, Sibling Description) Oh, let's see what we can find about the way he approaches things. (W, D, Dd, S, Affective Ratio) This affective ratio, now what is this? I don't remember that. This is something that Beck added after I took the course. (Z Frequency) His organization is pretty damn poor. Is he Personality Disturbance or Psychotic? (M, C, CF, FC, Y, YF, FY, T, TF, FT, V, VF, FV, F+, F—) Well I think here I would also take a sequence analysis of the responses. (F-V #1–2) Already puts him in the category of the slightly maladjusted. I suppose it's the flying red horse. (F-V #3–6) I suppose these are the usual locations. (F #7) He's hung up on hands with gloves on them. Gloves on the hands and spats on the feet. (V #7, F-V #8–12) Woman's legs without toes, and a manikin's legs without feet. (V-F #13–22) Not only a rat but a "fat" rat. (V-F #23–33) Well, this guy is definitely neurotic. Neurotic in the sense that he has a good deal of anxiety and confusion. He's not a well

| Clinician #2—Continued | Diagnosis problem | 116 cards |
| Beck orientation | Interpreted third | 30 minutes |

adjusted homosexual. I might place him in the Neurotic category. (V-F #34) Except that there are a few indications that he might even be worse than that. (F+ %, A %) I don't suppose that in these cases a testing of the limits was done, was there? What were the response times on these cards? (Reaction Time Card I–X) You know, I think if I had a guy like this I'd give a test of the limits with the notion of ruling out ambulatory schizophrenia. There isn't quite enough here to diagnose that. But there are no indications of any specific neurosis as I can see. Just on the basis of what you see there I would think a neurotic disturbance. But I couldn't say what type. Still I have a feeling it's more than that. OK. My guess is ambulatory schizophrenia. Borderline. Schizoid. How's that. (P) With a testing of the limits I would check out sexual responses, the things that he didn't get. You certainly don't get the feeling of populars when you look through them. I'd inquire for more M and more color. There's only one little measly FC. What I usually do in dealing with these is to give them the feeling that they don't have to be so careful about what they see, kind of anything goes, including responses they might have given before but were too far out. The sexual responses kind of give a feeling about the degree of control.

Answer: Personality Disturbance. Schizoid personality.

| Clinician #23 | Diagnosis problem | 9 cards |
| Beck orientation | Interpreted third | 5 minutes |

(F #6–8, 20–21, 31–32, 27–28) High average intelligence, perhaps more. Introversive tendencies as indicated by the high M, and elaboration of the M. Severe anxiety. Self-devaluation. With intact F+ relatively high. High W. Low C. Some anatomical preoccupation, reflecting a sexual problem, a problem of anxiety. Variable moods and anxiety and introspection would make him moody. Sometimes there is inappropriate laughter. Edging. Reflects again the high tension. Low F—. The difficulty here is between Personality Disturbance and Neurotic—severe. Only one other possibility exists, i.e., the high M, edging, and anatomy suggests the possibility of having had an earlier psychotic episode.

Answer: Personality Disturbance. Schizoid personality structure, with variable mood reactions.

Clinician #14   Diagnosis problem   118 cards
Beck orientation   Interpreted first   30 minutes

(Sex, Age, Occupation, Education, Marital Status, Sexual History, Military
History, Religion, Mother Description, Father Description, Sibling Description,
Sibling Position, M, C, CF, FC, F+, F+%, R, Affective Ratio, F%, P) The
F% and Affective Ratio are high. I'm not sure whether it's a character disorder,
a personality disturbance. There's little to indicate Organic or Psychotic, and
he's certainly not Basically Adjusted, especially in view of his family background. His mother is dead and his father rejected him, and he lived in a foster
home. (Approach, YF, Y, FY) Let's see how anxious he is. It's kind of ego-
syntonic. (TF, FT, T, VF, FV, V, Blend #1, A, Ad) I could calculate the A%.
(A%, H, Hd) There are 10 H out of 33 and 9 A responses. (Avg Reaction Time,
RT Achromatic, RT Chromatic) That doesn't help. (Additionals, Rejections)
Typically this is the way I would approach the Rorschach, maybe taking more
content. (An, Anal, Ar, Art, Ay, Bt, Cl, Fd, Fi, Geo) I would guess that he's
fairly bright, at least average intellectually and probably higher. (Hh, My, Na,
Oj, Blend #2–3, S) I do have to realize that there is some anxiety here. (F–S #1–
5, F #6) He gave five responses to Card I. (L #2–5, S #6) Some of these H
responses he saw in clouds. (F-L #7, F-S #8, F-L #9, F #10–12, L #11–12,
F #13) Ha, he missed the popular on Card V. I'll have to revise my thinking.
Beck holds that if the person misses the popular on Card V you have to think
about psychosis. There's a possibility of his being a paranoid schizophrenic,
in a reasonable state of integration. (F #14–17, L #16–17) A man's face.
(F #18) There's a sexual identity question here which, of course, fits from the
history. (F #19–23, V #23) He called it "an accidental thing." (F #24–33,
L #26, 29, 31, S #33, Interests, Nationality) This task is not as easy as I thought
it would be. There's no information about lapsed time per card. (Extended
F+%)

Answer: Personality Disturbance. Passive-aggressive personality with a probability of incipient schizophrenia.

Clinician #35   Diagnosis problem   96 cards
Beck orientation   Interpreted first   43 minutes

I usually orient myself with these. (Sex, Age, Education, Occupation, F #1–11)
There were four responses on the first card with a qualitative richness which
I hadn't anticipated on the basis of education and occupation. Response #7
was suggestive of some unexpected richness. There were five responses to Card I
and one each to Cards II and III, and a jump again to three responses on Card
IV. I'll probably check the Verbalizations on Cards II and III to see how the
encouragement was given. I hold vigorously to Beck's method of encouraging

Clinician # 35—Continued   Diagnosis problem   96 cards
Beck orientation   Interpreted first   43 minutes

responses. (F # 12–20) The variation of the responsiveness I note. The constriction down to one response on Cards II and III makes me wonder about color shock, emotional constriction. There's a feeling on the acromatic cards that his sensitivity to shading and texture suggests, along with his education, that this man has art interests. His sensitivities are incongruent with his classification as an unskilled laborer. (F # 21–34) There's constriction on Cards II and III but the jump on Cards VIII–X indicate responsiveness. His card-by-card productivity is 5-1-1-4-2-3-4-4-4-5. Whatever color shock I inferred from Cards II and III certainly was followed by a recovery. (V # 6–7) Encouragement was not given, otherwise it would say "Most people usually see more than one thing." (R, F%, Extended F%, F+%, Extended F+%, A%, P, Avg Reaction Time, Additionals) I'm struck by the high P value. At the same time A% is only one-third. I ask myself why there are no additional responses. There seems to be a very high F% value here. The Avg Reaction Time is acceptable. (W, D, Dd, S) I'm struck by the low W, and the disproportionately high D. (M, C, CF, FC, Blend # 1–3) The Experience Balance is constricted, coarctated, balanced. I'm confronted with a discrepancy between the richness of the responses versus the determinants as they are formally scored. There's a continuing discrepancy between social class and occupation. It fits the determinant picture but not the 33 responses, seemingly as good as they were. Then the high number of P, one-third of the total responses, and relatively high F%. He's making a very strong effort at control, avoiding being abstract, unable to be. An emphasis on intellectualization is implied. We'll have to check for other determinants. (Y, YF) I would not expect high Y, T, or V. (FY, T, TF, FT, V, VF, FV) I'm surprised that he has no vista responses, also that there are so few shading responses, except in the blends. There seems to be a depressive trend here. I'm trying to evaluate how extensive it is. It seems more extensive, crudely, than the affective determinants of color would show. (F+, F—, F₀) The F—'s are higher than I would have anticipated. There are slight inroads as far as ego processes are concerned, coupled with that balanced Experience Balance. It makes me worry that this man is having more difficulties than I was initially considering. I would eliminate three categories here: Basically Adjusted, Psychotic, and Organic. That leaves two at this point, so I'll take a look at more personal data. (Nationality, Religion, Marital Status, Sibling Position, Sibling Description, Mother Description, Father Description, Sexual History) Note that the patient evidenced some wish to work in a textile mill, which may indicate interest in trying to relate to the father. Homosexuality relates to the R being high and to the artistic trends. It seems to give an account for some of the richness. (Military History, Interests) On the basis of the personal data material, I'm inclined to turn to the Personality Disturbance as the most likely diagnostic category. Think back to the high P and look back at the statements regarding the father. I get the picture of a man trying to present a facade of normalcy, trying to minimize the inroads of his abandonment by his father when the mother died when he was nine years old. He's trying to maintain a close relationship to the father. It suggests some feeling that he was trying to seek more positive affective experiences

Clinician #35—Continued   Diagnosis problem   96 cards
Beck orientation   Interpreted first   43 minutes

with males than with females. One wonders when you look at the facts that he
was a Marine, and interested in commercial art. It sort of epitomizes his turning
to sexuality in an overcoming way, while succumbing to a more passive pattern.
(m, FM) Both of these are surprising. (H, Hd) Very high. (An, Sex, Bt, Art, Fi,
Hh, Na, Fd, A, Ad) We note the reversal direction between A:Ad to H:Hd,
the anxiety associated with humans after reaching out for them. One-third H is
pretty high. I'm going to skim back through the response sequence, looking for
expressions of aggressiveness. There's not too much as I recall. He's more
frozen, under intellectual control. I would think of this individual as having a
character disturbance, as having a passive-aggressive character structure. I
assume that the passive aspect is most clinically observable. There is some
erosion of the ego. F+% is low, relative to the overall record. That, with the
mild depressive reactions and the high P, would suggest some persistent guilt
about his sexual adjustment. His level of aspiration has been low, for the level
of intellectual potential he has. The IQ estimate probably would be 115–120.
But his occupational level is below that level. He didn't pursue the artistic area.
I wonder what would have happened if the GI Bill had been available to him?

Answer: Personality Disturbance. Passive-aggressive reaction, passive em-
             phasis with mild depressive trends and some weakening of ego controls.

Clinician #6   Diagnosis problem   98 cards
Beck orientation   Interpreted second   67 minutes

(Sex, Age, Education, Occupation, Nationality, Religion, Marital Status) Now
so far this is the best bit of information relative to the question. He's 30 years
old and single. There's something wrong with his interpersonal relationships.
(Sibling Position, Sibling Description) He's the second child. Evidently he was
raised in a traumatic early environment. The father left and the mother died.
(Mother Description, Father Description) The father was also rejecting. (Sexual
History) That ipso facto would indicate some definite neurotic manifestation.
In my theoretical orientation it is a definite neurotic adjustment pattern. (Military History, Interests) OK, so I've already decided he's neurotic. Now the
problem is how sick he is? I'm first and foremost interested in the free associations. The way I would go about doing it would be to look at all the free associations. So I'll take them all out. Actually you begin to interpret the Rorschach
as you give it, not with any hard and fast conclusions until the scoring. (F #1–34,
Reaction Time Card I) Now equally I want to know the scoring. So I'm going to
do the same for all the scoring quantities. It's much more important to look
at the responses in sequence for diagnosis than for the intelligence question.

Clinician #6—Continued   Diagnosis problem   98 cards
Beck orientation   Interpreted second   67 minutes

For this kind of a question the sequential analysis is my basic approach, generally. (S #1–33, Reaction Time Card II–X) I divide the Cards into three groups:
I–III, the achromatic IV–VII, and the chromatics VIII–X. There's a big jump in
reaction time on Card II, giving some evidence of color shock. But on Card III
there's some recovery, which indicates to me that he can pull himself together.
He doesn't get worse. Next, his reaction times remain somewhat slow, 17
seconds or more. I'll be looking for some explanation as to why he's so slow.
There's particular difficulty on Card V. Knowing what I know about him, the
homosexual adjustment, I wouldn't have expected it on Card V. Maybe on
Card VI or VII, but I'm curious as to what may explain this. The next thing
I notice is the similarity of progression between Cards II–III, and VIII–IX–X.
There's a lessening of anxiety over associations here. He has initial difficulty
with color but a capacity to gather himself together. I would say neurotic, and
I haven't even looked at the free associations very closely. There's an ego-vulner-
ability, but the ego is not completely shot. These are just hunches. Now I'm
simply looking at the free associations and the accompanying scorings for each
of the cards. OK, I look at Card I. The first thing is a bug response. Uncannily
the first response has to do with self-concept. Don't ask me why. There's a definite
lowering of self-concept here. His responses are an attempt to compensate for
this. It's colorful, associated with the Texaco sign. The flying red horse is quite
opposite from a bug, showing masculinity, forcefulness, and mastery. The
wings give a means of mobility and escape, enabling him to lift himself above
things. He pays particular attention to the back and belly. It may provide some
screen for a sexual preoccupation. The next response is typical of homosexual
responses, a rear view. It's also an indication of a higher level of intellectual
functioning or striving, like a Gaughin painting. The hands and gloves are a
source of immediate contact with people but with ambivalence. The hands are
covered. The thumb would make me wonder whether he ever sucked his thumb.
I'll be looking for orality. His last response on Card I is similar to the first response, bug, and caricatures the vulnerability of his self-esteem. He attempts to
overcompensate and to pursue masculine kinds of strivings while showing ambivalence about relationships with people and sexual anxiety. His heterosexual
anxiety is reacted to probably by homosexual impulses. He sees a woman's
lower half but from the rear view, attempting to turn her around. His basic
strivings are heterosexual but he has a reactive homosexual adjustment to
heterosexual anxiety. There's only one response to Card II, a sloughing off of
productivity. His interpersonal anxiety is fairly intense. There's an upsurge of
reaction time. It's definitely neurotic and ambivalent interpersonally. The
dancing which is something pleasant deteriorates into something unpleasant,
a duel. There's a polarity of impulse, with approach opposed by aggressive
moving against, a kind of impulse talked about by Horney. Again, it's definitely
neurotic. Again hands, gloved hands. Now for Card III. This is a fairly old
Rorschach. People don't wear spats now. He's sort of a dude of a man, exces-
sively concerned about personal appearance, a dandy. This is characteristic of a
homosexual pattern. What's interesting is that it's followed by a basket of coal.

Clinician # 6—Continued   Diagnosis problem   98 cards
Beck orientation   Interpreted second   67 minutes

The ambivalence here is whether he's a dandy or a coal man. Again there's interpersonal anxiety, a reflection instead of two men. Narcissism may be some solution to the anxiety that he has developed. It's an indication of emotional immaturity. All of this correlates highly with his background of homosexuality. I haven't found anything to contraindicate it. There's a reduction of productivity here, too, as he limits himself to one response. So far everything contraindicates Psychosis and Organicity. So I've practically forgotten about that, unless something drastic comes up. He's not Basically Adjusted. I've ruled out three diagnoses. On Card IV his productivity goes up. On Card I he had five responses and now he has three. Both cards have no color. I would guess there's some kind of affective disturbance, particularly with lively affect. Again he's concerned with contact, with a great deal of anxiety about it. His impulse is primarily homosexual, with males. There's leathery texture, vertebrae where they "had" been, then horns. There's considerable anxiety. The horns are phallic and the steer is male. The lacings may mean he has to keep himself protected, covered up, covers and boot lacings. On Card V we need an explanation for the increased reaction time. He sees a woman's legs without toes, castrated. And a manikin's legs, again without toes. He has castration fantasies associated with female appendages. The explanation may be, first, that there's some exacerbation of castration anxiety and/or, second, some covert expression of hostility toward females. I would think both of these possibilities would apply. There's tremendous hostility toward females, as would be characteristic of homosexuals. There's something interesting with Card VI. It tends to conjure up fantasies about masculinity and masculine sex. I want also now to look at Card VII, which conjures up femininity and responsiveness to female sex. We already know what he did on Card V. Women really do seem to give him difficulty. The extent of the disturbance here with the totem is minimal. It's also the second time that he has made reference to color on a noncolor card. It might mean a counterphobic reaction to dysphoric associations. He in turn diverts this and puts color into this reaction, against tendencies toward depression and dysphoria. He even talks about designs that are "painted on" as Indians do. Even though there's no evidence for T, he is preoccupied with contact—feathers, "painted on," rug to walk on or lie on. His covert concern with contact is handled neatly; it's intellectualized. Card VII is a different story. There's a phallic extension described as "fat" and "soft" with a shading quality to it. Then he sees instead of a woman's face, a man's face. There's a progressive deterioration in dealing with woman percepts, the rear view and turning away. He *has* to deal with a man, converting the face into a man's face. The distancing geographical response indicates that this is a disturbing card. He again uses intellectual defenses, quite well, converting to a homosexual situation. Well this Card VIII is a little bit too much. The color is very, very difficult for him to handle. The quality of his responses tends to deteriorate, but not to psychotic proportions, and that is important. The first human response is of a Chinaman's head, which is masculine and a foreign thing. There's anxiety and distancing with the anatomical responses. The hind end of a bull is a very masculine thing but with homosexual

Clinician #6—Continued   Diagnosis problem   98 cards
Beck orientation   Interpreted second   67 minutes

indications. I would guess that this man in his homosexual behavior is inclined to play an aggressive role. For the question at hand I don't really have to look at these but I'm going to. (F+%, M, C, CF, FC) Wow. He certainly can't deal with color actually. But where there is no color he can put it into his responses. It's a defensive facility. Again, it would contraindicate a psychotic process. He's a well-defended neurotic. (P, S) I find the P:S ratio very important. He's not psychopathic and he has impulse control. This is really a character disorder, in that this is a characteristic characterological process. It's not basically acute or reactive. Most helpful in my formulation was the information on his homosexual experiences which made the interpretation very easy. If the evidence had not been given I would have arrived at the same conclusion anyway. I wouldn't ordinarily pigeonhole a guy with the psychiatric nomenclature. The only question is on Cards VIII–X where his performance does deteriorate. In the clinical situation I would have one other piece of information that would help me, namely the reason for referral. I can interpret best in the context of the immediate situation. So, in summary, he's essentially a character disorder. He's unable to make a satisfactory heterosexual adjustment. He's struggling against a defensive reaction. He has real difficulty in handling stimulating affect, one of the most pathological behavioral manifestations that he gives in the whole record.

Answer: Personality Disturbance. Character disorder, homosexual adjustment, with strong depressive trends.

Clinician #11   Diagnosis problem   124 cards
Beck orientation   Interpreted second   51 minutes

(R, F%, Extended F%, F+%, Extended F+%) That's too bad. I had an obsessive-compulsive hypothesis going and 71 doesn't fit that. (A%, P) These are saying that there's fairly heavy control. There are too many responses for a good clinical depression. I'm nowhere right now, just a state of confusion. (Avg Reaction Time) That fits in a sense, it's slow. (Additionals, Rejections) I'm not a color shock man, so I'll skip that. (W Klopfer, Beck) So, Beck only scores two W. Klopfer has cut-off W's. (D, Dd, S, Approach) Another indication of restriction would be the low W and high D and Dd, which fits with the F% and the slow reaction time. (Sequence, Z Frequency, Z Sum) I wouldn't make a diagnosis without going through the content. (M, C, CF, FC) This adds to the picture of constriction. (Y, YF, FY, T, TF, FT, V, VF, FV, F₀, H, Hd) Beck says that more Hd than H signifies interpersonal anxiety. (A, Ad, An, Anal, Ar, Art, Ay, Bt, Cl, Fd, Fi) That should be zero. It's for some sort of a volatile.

Clinician #11—Continued   Diagnosis problem   124 cards
Beck orientation   Interpreted second   51 minutes

(Geo, Hh, My, Na, Oj) I was zeroing in on the anatomy. I was thinking of a
neurasthenic. It fits constriction but not the F+. Maybe it's a very bright
neurasthenic. I would look at the F-'s. (S #1) It's not popular, so it must be
a bird or something. (S-L-F #2, F-V #1) I wanted to see what response #2
is following. Phillips and Smith give some nice hypotheses about this. Bug is
the same as bird, a punitive, rejecting mother figure, as if he'd like to fly away
from a rejecting, punitive mother. This would fit with constriction, but not
productivity. Maybe that's how he doesn't get rejected. (S #3–6) He seems to
handle Card II pretty well. I'll assume some delayed reaction. Cards II and III
come through nicely. (S #7–8) There's not very much on Card IV. (S #9–11)
Card V is a little unusual. There's no bat, but I don't know what to make of that.
(S #12–14) There are 3 Ay in the first responses to Card VI. (S #15–16) Card
VII starts out with an FT. (Blend #1–3) There's a little affect breaking through
and it's not handled particularly well. (S #17–18) A symmetry verbalization.
(F-V #18) Hard anatomy. That would be potentially fear of anger or emotional responses. There's not much likelihood of acting-out. It could indicate
what all of the constriction is aimed at. The hypothesis for Card VII is that of a
rejecting, punitive mother. There's fear of acting-out. (S-F-V #19) Aha, followed
by the urge to get far away again. I'm willing to assume Card VII shock.
The mother's ungiving and demanding but not cruel nor abusive, powerful
but not rejecting. However, this doesn't fit with my notions about the mother
being hostile and punitive. With Card I shock you have potential acting-out,
which may be represented by a poor work record. I'll buy Card VII as being
the more pervasive card. Also, I've been assuming that this is a male (Sex) I
assume that he's not married, that he hasn't got very close to women. (Marital
Status, Age, Education, Occupation, Nationality, Religion, Sibling Position,
Sibling Description, Mother Description, Father Description) OK now. That
father description fouls the picture, the whole picture gets confused. The foster
parents may have carried weight. There's no identification with the father in
terms of hostile acting-out. I doubt that he's cruel and abusive like his father.
(Sexual History) That fits with Card VII. I assume he would be the more passive
partner. (Military History, Interests, S #20, S-F-V #21) Another anatomy
minus, which has to do with the control of hostile impulses. (S-F-V #22) A
"fat rat" is interesting in view of the known history of sexuality. The vocal
gestures like "uhs" also are interesting. He's pressed to say something, without
content, as if he's trying to work up to talk about it. (S #23, S-F-V # 24–25)
Aha, two minuses in a row, and the second symmetry statement. Does it have
something to do with control? Phillips and Smith might consider this to be
related to unacceptable wishes. (S #26, S-F-V #27) Another anatomy F-.
(S #28, S-F-V #29) Now, bulls are father figures or some such jazz. Phillips
and Smith would view bulls the same as apes, a partriarchal father figure.
Fathers are threatening or potentially destructive. That fits with the sister's
view of the father. (S #30–33) The geography response points to strong fellings
of inadequacy. (S #34, F-V #33) I suppose he's sort of schizoid, and from something else too—the poor vocational adjustment and poor sexual adjustment, in

| Clinician #11—Continued | Diagnosis problem | 124 cards |
| Beck orientation | Interpreted second | 51 minutes |

terms of societal norms. It's obvious that he's sort of marginal in many ways. There was the bad flying red horse response, with the notion of flight and getting distance. There were all kinds of geography responses, minus responses, and one other emphasis on bony anatomy. I would exclude Basically Adjusted, Organic, and Psychotic. I would call it a Personality Disturbance. I would not expect much acting-out with hostility.

Answer: Personality Disturbance. Inadequate personality. Marginal adjustment socially, economically, and sexually. Excessive emotional constriction probably with a passive orientation and defenses against hostile impulses. Suspect hypochondriacal or at least excessive somatic concerns. Poor self-concept, strong feelings of inadequacy, and a generally depressive orientation.

| Clinician #8 | Diagnosis problem | 50 cards |
| Beck orientation | Interpreted second | 29 minutes |

(Sex, Age, Education, Occupation, Marital Status, Sibling Description, Mother Description, Father Description, Sexual History, Interests) I'm trying to get background about the person, and then some indicators of diagnosis. (R, F+%, A%, P, Avg Reaction Time) That's upsetting, which is slow, which adds to the dimension of organicity. With the number of P at eleven we'd better find out more details here. (M, FC, CF, C, FY, YF, F+, F-) The idea of accuracy, in terms of F, is what I'm thinking about now. Anxiety and affectivity. I've accounted for 29 of the 33 responses. To this point there's no other evidence of organicity. I kind of doubt if he's psychotic, with the F+% of 71. Let's see what he does on the content. (FT, TF, V, VF) I don't think that's VF. (W, D, Dd) Not bad. (Sequence) At the present time it's a process of elimination, leading more to Neurotic or to Personality Disturbance, with Organicity as an outside possibility. I doubt Basically Adjusted, but with this kind of background. . . . (H, Hd) That's good, relatively higher Hd than H. This narrows it down to Personality Disturbance or Neurotic. One-third of the responses are in the H area. (An, My) The My content frequently is a good indicator of distancing oneself from the present, a good neurotic indicator. But this doesn't add much. I want to know more about his content. (A, Ad, Fi, Bt, Na) He's probably somewhat innocuous, so let's look at our innocuous cards. I tend to use content a good deal for diagnosis, especially in the absence of personal contact. (Anal) That's homosexual, so that's obvious. (Art) He likes art. (Cl) There's a little anxiety here, adding to the neurotic element. (Fd) What was that? OK, so 31. Let's see, he's somewhat identified with the father, working in the same place,

Clinician #8—Continued   Diagnosis problem   50 cards
Beck orientation   Interpreted second   29 minutes

and he has had homosexual expreiences. I have pretty much ruled out here that
this person is Psychotic. There's not much to rule out Organicity, but not much
to rule it in either. This is not a Basically Adjusted individual. I feel some over-
lapping here, probably some sexual problem. A personality disturbance, but
neurotic in nature. So, let's go to Card VI, as it's primarily sexual in nature.
(Number of Responses Card VI, F #13–15) I'm looking for more interpersonal
relations. (Number of Responses Card III, F #7) OK. I would call this a
Personality Disturbance, and specifically a sexual deviation. I don't know if
I could say whether the sexual deviation was primary or secondary from the
data, but my guess would be more primary.

Answer: Personality Disturbance. Sexual deviation.

Clinician #16   Diagnosis problem   83 cards
Beck orientation   Interpreted first   18 minutes

(Sex, Age, Marital Status, Mother Description, Father Description, Sexual
History, Interests, Education) From the information, I'm operating on the
assumption that he is a homosexual, but that he's insecure and intelligent.
(W, D, Dd, S, M, C, CF) But my assumptions aren't coming out on these
determinants. (Y, FC, YF, FY, T, TF, FT, V, VF, FV, F+ %, P, Anal, An, H,
Hd, Cl, Fi, Art, Number of Responses Card VI–VII, R, F #1–36, V #29, 25,
27, 23, 11–12, 2, Rejections, RT Achromatic, RT Chromatic)

Answer: Personality Disturbance. Personality pattern disturbance, constricted
intellect, insecure, with strong homosexual trends.

Clinician #18   Diagnosis problem   58 cards
Klopfer orientation   Interpreted second   20 minutes

With this format you can pick anything in any order. I think I'll expedite this.
(Sex, Age, Marital Status, Education, Religion, Sibling Position, Sibling De-
scription, Sexual History, Mother Description, Military History, Occupation)
Now I'll play around with this thing systematically. (W, D, d, Dd, S, W%, D%,
d%, Dd%, M, FM, m, k, FK, K, C, CF, C', c, F, H, A, Sex, Fire, FC, Fc, Art,
Number of Responses Card II–III, F #6–7, V #6, Number of Responses

Clinician # 18—Continued   Diagnosis problem   58 cards
Klopfer orientation   Interpreted second   20 minutes

Card IV, F #8, 10, Number of Responses Card VII, F #16, 19, Number of Responses Card VI, F #13, 15, Number of Responses Card IX, F #24, 27) This gives it away on his homosexuality. He's kind of a cold guy. He's not Organic and not Psychotic. I think he's accepting his homosexuality pretty well. He's not particularly bright. He does a lot of household chores. There's a certain amount of compulsivity and tension. He's an art student but there's not enough color or imagination for art. (Number of Responses Card X, F #28, 33) He covers his homosexuality well. He doesn't get too near to people. There's some element of protest. He joined the Marines, his mother died when he was young, and his father is a despot.

Answer: Personality Disturbance. Sociopathic personality disturbance, sexual invert.

Clinician #31   Diagnosis problem   37 cards
Beck orientation   Interpreted first   40 minutes

(Sex, Age, Education, Occupation) I would normally look at the summary, and since I'm mostly Beckian I'll go to that. (R, F%, F+ %, P) My first hypothesis is whether he's homosexual. I would have expected R to be somewhat higher. F% is higher than I expected. I began to think about homosexual and hysterical together. The art school and laborer suggests he's underachieving in a way, yet he's working in a textile mill. The content of the material he chose to work with suggests a feminine interest. He may have come out of the Oedipal struggle not bearing to succeed or accomplish and he still may be struggling as a way of resolving this. Part of the problem is that he did go to vocational high school which might make him a trifle sociopathic or psychopathic, or out of the mainstream of things. The 11 P looks hysterical to me, or psychopathic. (M, Sum C) Personality Disturbance, that's what it is. I've eliminated Basically Adjusted because he's a dropout and, second, the P that's elevated. If P had been 6 or 7 I would have been happier. It smacks of defensiveness. Maybe he's not very bright. I get thrown off that lead by the art school information, which maybe is a bias of mine. I want to know how he got that Sum C. (C, CF, FC) I would look for what were his M responses. I'd want to know the quality. It's a good guess that he's got M on Card III. (Number of Responses Card III, F #7) He's a narcissist. What else he is I don't know. There's Art, textile mill, P, and the mirror. He's either got the other M on Card II or Card VII. He really ought to have it on both. (Number of Responses Card VII, F #16–17) He is narcissistic. (F #18–19) He didn't give the M. He sees it first or not at all. That's the female card. (L #17) He's seeing it as a man where most people see it as a woman.

Clinician #31—Continued   Diagnosis problem   37 cards
Beck orientation   Interpreted first   40 minutes

(Number of Responses Card II) I seem to be finding all sorts of evidence to support the first hunch I got about him. I always distrust that. I feel quite sure that this guy is a Personality Disturbance at this point. I'm pursuing it to determine what kind. (F #1–6) The other thing I would normally do is look at Card I. Another bias I have is that there are very few neurotics anymore. There are some areas of conflict, but he's not dys-syntonic. If he were more anxious and less comfortable with himself—he's narcissistic, and consciously afraid of what he was like—his P wouldn't be that high. There are three cards for M. Card I is for his first view or structuring of himself, so I should expect a high H from that. (A, Ad) Not bad. One-quarter A%. I want to know about his blends. (Blend #1–3) I feel I can describe the guy, but not give the "gray book" diagnosis. There's a warding off of depression, the fundamental issue being narcissistic. His latent homosexuality is a defensive tactic. I don't ordinarily think of it as a primary one. I ordinarily might look at W-D-Dd but I've formed the impression that he's not a Dd, and his W's are lazy ones. (W, Dd) Now I want to know where all his Dd's are. Unusual large detail throws a whole new wrinkle on it for me. I'd scan the scoring columns for the Dd's and see what they were. (L-S #5) Now I feel better. He's gotten that Dd by using a fairly prominent edge detail. He hasn't arbitrarily carved something out of the blot. It's a fairly large Dd. The arbitrary Dd would make him rather sicker than I view him at the moment, indicating desperate straits as far as his defenses would be concerned. I see him with a set of characterological defenses which aren't keeping out him of trouble but which are keeping him working. I don't know what I would have done with d if it had been there. It would be totally inconsistent with the impression I've formed of him. I'd have to see if it were a rare event or if I missed the boat on him. He is not schizoid. I think he is not passive-aggressive. I think probably I would call him a narcissistic character disorder. It doesn't do him justice, that's why I never do Diagnostic Manual diagnoses. As it's often used, the narcissistic disorder is a very primitive type, more primitive than this guy. It's Oedipal. I think narcissistic is just one step removed from schizoid, schizophrenic.

Answer: Personality Disturbance. Narcissistic Character.

Clinician #34   Diagnosis problem   72 cards
Klopfer orientation   Interpreted third   18 minutes

(Age, Sex, R, M, FM, m, FK, FC, CF, F, Fc, k, K, C, F+%, Extended F+%, A%, P) I can't make any strong case for pathology at this point. It looks kind of within normal limits, what one would expect. (Number of Responses Card I,

| Clinician #34—Continued | Diagnosis problem | 72 cards |
| Klopfer orientation | Interpreted third | 18 minutes |

F #1–5, S Beck #4, Number of Responses Card II, F #6, V #3, Number of Responses Card III, F–V #7, Number of Responses Card IV, F #8–10, Number of Responses Card VI, F #13–15, V #5–4, Number of Responses Card VII, F #16–19, Number of Responses Card VIII, F #20–23, V #23) What is "conventional rendering"? (Number of Responses Card IX, F #24–27, Number of Responses Card X, F #28–33) He must be a Personality Disturbance. There are a lot of healthy things about him. (RT Achromatic, RT Chromatic, S Beck #29, 23, 17, 5, 33, 30).

Answer: Personality Disturbance. Passive-aggressive personality, passive type.

| Clinician #26 | Diagnosis problem | 25 cards |
| Klopfer orientation | Interpreted first | 31 minutes |

(Age, Sex, Marital Status) The M:C ratio is not available? (M, R, Sum C, Extended F+%, H, Hd, A, Ad, Sexual History, Dd, Mother Description) I wonder what she died of? (Father Description) At this point I would check the Personality Disturbance category. I ruled out the Basically Adjusted because of the low M, Sum C, and H, and the high A. (P) P also is low. I'm tending to rule out the Psychotic category. The Extended F+% is all right, there are three populars, and there is evidence of his having some relationship with people, from the information on his homosexual experience. I ruled psychosis out because the Sum C is low and the Dd is pretty good. The Neurotic category is being fairly well ruled out, being a more general sort of problem. His early childhood was not too good, with his mother dying when he was nine years old and his having a foster home placement. His father relationship probably was not too good and I would view as suspect the information that he was closer to father than mother. This is what leads me to the Personality Disturbance diagnosis. I'm just trying to figure out how to get it down more specifically here. (Fd, Fire, D, FK+%, F #7, F+%, F #1, 8–9–10%, S) Remarkable here is the degree of inhibition, the whole denial. I would suspect here a good deal of aggression which is bottled up, a good deal of anger. He's quite an intelligent individual. He has difficulty with women, which is one of the reasons why he is homosexual.

Answer: Personality Disturbance. Passive-dependent, passive-aggressive personality.

Clinician #3   Diagnosis problem   81 cards
Beck orientation   Interpreted third   35 minutes

I'm not going to get stung again. (Sex, Age, Education, Occupation) What more do I need? Ambulatory schizophrenia. I suspected that but don't ask me why. (Sexual History, F+ %) Well he isn't very well adjusted. (P) I really don't know about this. He's a P person with homosexuality. I should figure this one to be low. (A %) Ha, it's 33. This is working out pretty good. Did I get the F%? (F%, M, C, CF) I was going to say one CF. What is the FC? (FC, m, FM) That would go along with practicing his homosexuality. (H, Hd) What am I trying to decide between, Personality Disturbance or Psychotic? (Blend #1–3) Oh I jumped too fast. The 2:2 is interesting. (R, F#30–33, Ad) The emphasis is on the Hd and on the A. Of course what I really want to know is does he have any evidence of a thought disorder. I'll have to go through all of these. (F #1) Personality Disturbance so far. (F #2–7) He's a little narcissistic isn't he? (F #8–10) Here comes some more populars. (F #11) Woman's legs without toes. (F #12) He's kind of perseverative isn't he. (F #13–14) Uh oh, abortive sublimation we call that. (F #15–16) But there's no thought disorder, at least I don't see any yet. (F #17–20, S #19) Vertebrae. He has some characterological hostility, with the An and Hd. (S, W, D, Dd) He's not a compulsive neurotic. (F #21–23) There's no thought disorder. (F #24) Now we're on Card IX. (S #24, 33) I've got to find his color responses. (F #25–26) I suppose that's the V. (F #27–29) So, what I haven't found is the FC. (S #23) No, it's not the ice. (S #25–27) I've got to find that FC. (S #28–31) There it is, the color. Well, It's a Personality Disturbance as far as I'm concerned. What does homosexuality come under in personality disturbance? He's not one of the personality pattern disorders. I never did look and see if he was married. Would he be an emotionally unstable personality? He's not that unstable. (Affective Ratio)He's excitable, but he doesn't get the pleasure out of it. He's sure as hell not a compulsive personality, or hysterical. He's either passive-aggressive with a—wait a minute. He's not in conflict about his homosexuality. He's expressing hostility by this. I should follow one of my supervision ideas on this and call him schizophrenic, because he didn't give the popular "bat" response on Card V. His color responses are all minus in quality but one, as are all the blends but one. (Interests) I should have known. Any additionals? (Additionals) None. (RT Achromatic, RT Chromatic, Avg Reaction Time) Very good. He's not depressed. I didn't look at the shading in detail, but he has a high F% (FY, TF, FT, VF, FV) It's kind of six of one and uh it depends on your own point of view I guess. What are the M? All right. I'll stay, but I'm not satisfied. He's also passive-aggressive, and shows sexual deviation. The diagnosis here is difficult. Usually when I do this I spend more time getting ready than a lot of people do. I do the scoring, summarizing, the sums card by card, the first sum through the end response, and notations on the side. What I really should have done would have been to take these two columns all the way down.

Answer: Personality Disturbance. Emotionally unstable, passive-aggressive, sexual deviation.

| Clinician #33 | Diagnosis problem | 44 cards |
| Klopfer orientation | Interpreted second | 25 minutes |

(Sex, Age, F+%, R, Number of Responses Card I, F #1, 6, Number of Responses Card II) I don't know what I'm dealing with here. The F+% was to see about possible psychosis. I'm confused by Card II, the indecision. First, people are cooperating and dancing, then the duel. I have an idea about how this guy really feels about people. He's suspicious, not able to get close without feeling upset or frightened. (F #7) This is a guy who's got himself pretty well protected. I wonder what he's frightened of. The thinking is irregular, confused. There's a man dressed in spats but he's carrying coal. There are people dancing and dueling. (Number of Responses Card III, F #8) There's no direct perseveration. Let's see some of the things he said during the test. (V #1–4) I get a feeling that he feels very unsure and indecisive, very unsure of himself. This could be a product of neurosis or organicity. I don't get any feel of psychosis in this guy. F+ isn't too high. That could be a product of organicity also. (Rejections) I want to see more of what this guy said. (F #9–10), Number of Responses Card IV–V) I'm not particularly interested in what he said to Card V. (F #13–15, Interests, Occupation) He's an unskilled laborer and he's interested in commercial art? We don't have his intellectual level, do we? (Education) So, he never graduated high school. Presumably we may have an intelligence of between 80 and 100. That could account for some of the indecisiveness. (V #10–11, 20, Number of Responses Card VII, F #16–17, 19) This guy is not unintelligent. The vocabulary gives me that idea, the "illustrations of famous legends . . . vertebrae . . . symmetry." I don't have a feel for this guy yet. I feel a need to know more of what he said as responses. (Number of Responses Card VIII, F #24–25) I don't see anything wrong with this guy, particularly. (Number of Responses Card IX, F #26, 28) He's not Organic. There's too much of a variety of response. I'm somewhat confused by the F+ of only 71, which seems to be pretty good. There's no perseveration that I've seen, with regard to any area. There haven't been any rejections. You didn't do a testing of the limits on him. (F #29–31) Right now, I would say he's Basically Adjusted. Let's see if this personal data information will give some clues. (Marital Status, Sexual History) That certainly gives some clues. This really is a clue, response #29, which may have led to my pulling of the Sexual History item, which I hadn't planned to do. The "hind end" always makes me think twice in terms of homosexuality. His indecisiveness, unsureness, yet some of the responses. . . . I don't feel strongly inclined toward one direction or the other. Maybe there's some compulsiveness.

Answer: Personality Disturbance, Emotionally unstable.

Clinician #12   Diagnosis problem   101 cards
Beck orientation   Interpreted third   19 minutes

To rule out organicity you could use the R. (Sex, Age, Education, Occupation, Nationality, Religion, Marital Status, Sibling Position, Sexual History) You can rule out Basically Adjusted purely on the basis of his sexual history. (Military History, Sibling Description, Mother Description, Father Description, Interests) He isn't Basically Adjusted. (W, R, Approach) There's a tremendous emphasis on W. (Sequence, F+ %) That's getting low. (Extended F+ %, F%) That's fairly high. I still don't know whether or not he's organic. (M, C, CF, FC, Y, YF, FY, T, TF, FT, V, VF, FV, F+, F-, F₀) I want to determine how wide a range of content he has. (Oj, Na, My, Hh, Ge, Fi, Fd, Cl, Anal, Bt, Ay, Art, Ar, An, Ad, A, Hd, H, P) The eleven populars, plus the control he has, would lead me to rule out psychosis. It boils down to Personality Disturbance or Neurotic. This is partly a matter of definition. (Number of Responses Card I–X, Reaction Time Card II, III, I) It is disturbed. (S–F #6–7, V #1–7, S-F-V #8–10, 16–19) What was the number of M again? There's a tremendous amount of neurotic stuff. Not psychosis. If you call a guy with this disturbance in the sexual area a Personality Disturbance it isn't meaningful. He may be a dependent character. There's no evidence of more difficulties in his sexual behavior.

Answer: Neurotic. Between neurotic and personality disturbance.

Clinician #20   Diagnosis problem   54 cards
Klopfer orientation   Interpreted third   38 minutes

(Sex, Age, Education, Occupation) We can't assume he's white. (Religion, Marital Status) Oh, he's schizophrenic. (Sibling Position, Mother Description, Father Description) Now we want to find out how retarded he is, how much below his potential he is functioning. His well-adjusted IQ might be around 80? He has a fashionable age and socioeconomic level for schizophrenia. (F+ %) That's schizophrenia. (R) Thirty-three responses? He's probably low in IQ level, working as an unskilled laborer. Closer to his father in his relationships sounds rough. How undernourished is his Rorschach? (F-V-L #1–6) Good for him (F #7) Fascinating, for a guy who's an unskilled laborer. He's a fooler. He starts out very much underperforming, suggesting a depreciated self. He starts into the little details, the "flying red horse." The red is accurate on this. He gets up his courage and goes to the woman, with gloves on them. He has a real high IQ, "How much do I have to do for you?" Is this guy a ringer? I suspect a patient but the Rorschach is of a person with a large hidden talent. He's an underachiever. He struggles through expressing himself, in subtle hidden ways. "Gloves on," like don't handle the merchandise. He responds beautifully to color, with dancing. But the competitiveness comes through. I'd call him a

Clinician #20—Continued   Diagnosis problem   54 cards
Klopfer orientation   Interpreted third   38 minutes

neurotic underachiever. The spats, coal, and "load he has to carry" sound a little depressive. It's solitary. It shows narcissism. Suicidal? No. Organic? No. Psychotic? I don't think so. Personality Disturbance? He might be a homosexual—the gloves and spats. I could answer that question by going to the color cards. (Number of Responses Card X, IX, VIII) He's got lots of color responses. Almost half are on the last three cards. (F #19–26, L #23) He's bright. (F #27-28) He sure responded to color. He goes for bones and ribs. He can't be too depressed with all those color responses. OK, I should have played it conservative. (Sum C, M, FC, CF, C) I see. Colorless use of color. (F #29–33) He's self-centered, egocentric. How much is he fighting himself? I can't be sure if he's an acting-out homosexual. He sure has strong tendencies. I wouldn't expect much neurotic symptomatology. But he's underachieving. He has to be neurotic. There's conflict over self-assertion and a symptomatic problem with homosexuality.

Answer: Neurotic. Obsessive-compulsive, manifested in self-depreciation, underachievement, with strong tendencies toward homosexuality.

Clinician #1   Diagnosis problem   64 cards
Beck orientation   Interpreted first   20 minutes

(R, F%, F+%, Extended F+%, Extended F%, Rejections, Additionals, S #34, F #1–34) I can't do a Rorschach without knowing the actual responses. (S #29, 25, 23) This is obsessive, the "hind end" and the "ice" over here. (V #23, 17, L #22–23, 18, S #8, 4) I wonder, did he say anything about that ice business? (V #23, Sex, Age, Education, Affective Ratio, S, Dd, Approach, M, C, CF, FC) Is there information for the Experience Balance? (F−, F+)

Answer: Neurotic. Mixed neurotic with some obsessive features (rigidity, anxiety, concern over detail) and some hysterical features (potential for somatizing is conspicuous).

Clinician #27   Diagnosis problem   19 cards
Klopfer orientation   Interpreted second   13 minutes

(F-V #1) She doesn't remember. (F-V #2–4) It doesn't matter whether it's the Free Association or the accompanying Verbalization, one way or the other. (V-F #5–6) Let's see what we've got here first. I know the diagnosis, tentatively.

Clinician #27—Continued   Diagnosis problem   19 cards
Klopfer orientation   Interpreted second   13 minutes

It's obsessive and compulsive. It's clearly an anal character that you're dealing with. There's some slipperiness in one aspect of the ego. She has some difficulty— or he has—in keeping things separate, and I don't know how serious that is. You want a differential diagnosis between Neurotic and Personality Disturbance. This will require looking at the information a little more closely. (F-V #7–8, F #9–11) Well, I don't see where I'm going to make any change. The whole approach is an obsessive one. His perceptual processes are obsessive.

Answer: Neurotic. Obsessive-compulsive.

Clinician #28   Diagnosis problem   54 cards
Beck orientation   Interpreted second   22 minutes

(F+%, M, C, CF, FC, R, Y, YF, FY, F+, F−, FT, FV, F_0, Blend #1–3, P, F-V #1–5, F # 6–25, F%, F # 26–28, Approach, Dd) I'm somewhat inclined to classify this case as adjusted, Basically Adjusted. I saw it as a choice between Neurotic and Basically Adjusted. The somewhat low F+% swayed me toward a more pathological label, although I wasn't comfortable with any specific kind of Neurotic reaction. I labeled it finally obsessive-compulsive, partly on the basis of the Approach, which wasn't too impressive support for this notion. Also important was some of the attention to detail in the verbalizations of the responses.

Answer: Neurotic. Obsessive-compulsive.

Clinician #24   Diagnosis problem   59 cards
Beck orientation   Interpreted third   19 minutes

(Sex, Age, R, F+%, Extended F+%, W, Avg Reaction Time, RT Achromatic, RT Chromatic) There are fairly long delays. (Sum C, M) These give me some idea of the quality of intellectual functioning, blocking, Experience Balance. (F #1–2) Why a flying red horse? (V #2, L #2–1) The flying red horse is a deviant response. Applebaum finds this type of thing in suicidal responses, color in a noncolor area. It's carved out, peculiar. It makes me worry about something more deviantly pathological. (F #3–6) Aside from that, the record

Clinician #24—Continued   Diagnosis problem   59 cards
Beck orientation   Interpreted third   19 minutes

is in an intellectualizing, obsessive direction, I'll keep that in mind. (F #7–14) Colored feathers. (F #15–28) There's an awful lot of emphasis on anatomy. In order to understand that I'd need to know his occupation. If he were a doctor it would be all right. (Occupation, F #29–32, Education) Another unusual thing is that for somebody who is an unskilled laborer and has ten years of school, this is not a bad record, intellectually speaking. Wait a minute, the flying red horse is a trademark, and it is red. I can scuttle that idea then. The rest of the record is not psychosis. (Reaction Time Card I–IV) I'm trying to get at neurotic qualities in the record. (Reaction Time Card V–VIII) That Card V is bad. It's the easiest card so what you have to wonder about is some delayed reaction to Card IV, or whether you have a man who's psychotic. He's not Organic, as he has only two W's. (L #16–17) I was moving in the direction of a psychosomatic disturbance, because of the four anatomy responses. The other possibility is depression, the heavy shading of Card V that throws him. Let's look at what other evidence we have for that. There are long delays for responses, reaction time delay, and the limited amount of color. I think that there's a fair amount of FY. (FY) Yeah. He's either a neurotic depression or a psychosomatic.

Answer: Neurotic. Neurotic depression.

Clinician #5   Diagnosis problem   135 cards
Klopfer orientation   Interpreted second   30 minutes

Diagnosis, hm? Oh I don't like that. (Sex, Age, Education) I need the person here. The personal data will take the place of the person. (Occupation, Nationality, Religion, Marital Status) I expected that, single. (Sibling Position, Sibling Description, Mother Description) He's deprived of many things right off. (Father Description, Sexual History) He gets relief from his friends, hm? (Military History) He proved his masculinity. (Interests) That's all we can get (F-S-V #1–2, L #2) That's no horse at all. (F-S-V-L #3) That's where I'd expect it to be. (F-S-V-L #4, F-S-V #5) Elongations and projections. (F-S-V #6) He doesn't know whether to fight or screw. If I didn't know he was a homosexual or not I don't know whether I'd be looking in that direction; I guess so. (F-S-V #7) Effeminate, clothing, preoccupied with legs. Usually you get breasts, etc. (F-S-V #8–9, L #9) Are these horns the lateral? (F-S-V #10) I would have expected him to show more anxiety. (F-S-V-L #11) Which are the woman's legs? That's hot. (F-S-V-L #12) Legs, legs, legs. (F-S-V #13) That's all he gives on Card V. It emphasizes the degree of preoccupation. Maybe he has a fetish for legs because he didn't have his own to stand on. (F-S-L-V #14) Expected. He's not showing any psychotic manifestations. (F-S-V #15–16)

Clinician #5—Continued   Diagnosis problem   135 cards
Klopfer orientation   Interpreted second   30 minutes

Here he's interested in the sensual needs, which is a real need for him. It ties in with the biographical data. (F-S-L-V #17–18) This is idiosyncratic. That's unusual to have that described as anatomy. He avoids the phallic connotation. Maybe it's nothing for him to get involved in. (F-S-V #19) Maybe it frightened the hell out of him. He's pushing it away, depersonalizing it. (F-S-V #20–22) He's interested in bodies in a sense. He dwelled on legs and on whether a rat has full round shoulders. (F-S-V #23) Listen to the vocabulary of this, and still he works as an unskilled laborer. He's really frightened. There's a textural thing here that hasn't been scored but he shows a concern with it. (F-S-V #24) Dark and light, which should have a c scoring. (F-S-V #25) A preoccupation with geography, maps. He's kind of evasive and insecure. Things don't mean much, except as a defensive thing. (F-S-V #26–27) He controls his emotions and is not impulsive. He stays with it. (F-S-V #28) Spider. Here we go with legs and thin legs. Now there's relief here. Card IX bothered the hell out of him. (F-V-L-S #29) This is curious symbolism. A bull is masculine. I wonder what his general physical status is. He is concerned with his body and his general self-image. The normal way to approach a bull is head on I suppose, rather than from the rear. It's scored as sex? Yeah, I guess. (F-S-V-L #30–31) There's color on that too. It's respectable. (F-S-V #32–33) Are we gonna run out of cards? No, still going. I wonder if his only real approach is to see it from the air, from a distance. (F #34, R) We're out of business. (Sum C, F%) There it is, he's constricted. (A%) Only 27. (RT Chromatic, RT Achromatic, M, FM, CF, FC) Oh we had that before, really. He's not Psychotic, not Organic, but he's somewhere in between. Neurotic-Personality Disturbance, but not Basically Adjusted. He's not going anywhere.

Answer: Neurotic. A somewhat immature, constricted individual who has strong unmet affectional needs but who is in fair control. The adjustment appears stalled in the sense of being relatively chronic. He is insecure but has reduced stimulation to tolerable levels.

Clinician #32   Diagnosis problem   65 cards
Beck orientation   Interpreted second   16 minutes

(R) That's quite a few. (Sex, Age, Education, Occupation, Nationality, Marital Status, Sibling Position, Sibling Description, Mother Description, Father Description, Sexual History, Reaction Time Card I–X) Doesn't give you much information on that. (F+, F−, F #1, Number of Responses Card I, L-S #1, F-S #2, F-L #3, F-S-L #4, F #5, Number of Responses Card II, F-S #6, F #7, Number of Responses Card III–X, F #8) That's not psychotic. (F-S-L #9, F #10–11) Why does he take such a long response time there? Ah, yes, the woman explains that. (F #13) That's all right. (F #15–16, 20–22, 24, 28, F-S-L #29) He's dependent in the sense of being dependent on the female,

Clinician #32—Continued   Diagnosis problem   65 cards
Beck orientation   Interpreted second   16 minutes

that which is soft, warm, and so on. There are strong hositilities toward the female also. He shows an anal response. You would expect that part of his difficulty would be in assuming the masculine role. The neurotic part can be seen on the first two color cards, which he tended to reject. Then, on the other color cards, he gave many responses. He's unable to control his emotions in any consistent way. I would want to see if there were a paranoid element. He's hysterical, as indicated by the fluctuating way in which he handles his emotional feeling.

Answer: Neurotic. Hysterical.

Clinician #19   Diagnosis problem   45 cards
Beck orientation   Interpreted second   21 minutes

(F+%, M, R) Already I'm thinking it's a minimally disturbed record. It's an average record already. It's got the right number of M's, R, and F+%. (F%, P) There's something. He's got everything else right. He won't have any of these. (S, Extended F%, C, CF, FC) He's not smart enough for blends. (Blend #1) Oh, that's good. He's Neurotic, still inhibited. Or a Personality Disturbance. (Y, YF, FY) I doubt that he has any rejections. (Rejections) I haven't settled in my mind whether he's Neurotic or Personality Disturbance. (T, TF, FT) There's a surprise, a little bit of T. (V, VF, FV) Who would have thought that? That's a little better, actually. I should really check those blends. (Blend #2-3) It's clear that he's a neurotic. He's very inhibited about impulse expression. Now, what's the problem of impulse expression, sex or aggression? (Number of Responses Card I–II) Oh, what happened. There's a smaller number of responses on Card I, and only one response to Card II. He's blocked. (Reaction Time Card II–I, S-F-V #6) So, he'll be blocked on Card IX. (Number of Responses Card IX, S-F-V #24) That's a nice evasive response. He's made anxious. I would say a neurosis, like hysteria. (S-F-V-L #25) See, it's really a stressful card for him. (S-F-V #26) I know what I'll do to decide. I'll see if there's any obsessive-compulsive aspect to it. However, I already know that. I don't really want to go that much further. I'm sure he's neurotic. The neurosis has to do with sexual regression. I have a second thought now. (Number of Responses Card III, S-F-V #7) A symptom for him might be a little bit of homosexuality. He's passive and not sexually aggressive, and it would not be satisfactory for him. It primarily would be a perversion. There would be repression. Stimulation by withdrawal from heterosexual sex.

Answer: Neurotic. Hysterical neurosis, e.g., regressive adaptation to Oedipal anxiety.

Clinician #17   Diagnosis problem   47 cards
Klopfer orientation Interpreted second   12 minutes

(Sex, Age, Education, Occupation, Nationality) I usually work from the pre-senting problem and symptoms, and you have no information on that. (F #1–34) With regard to most of them I sort of know where they are. (L #1–2, 18, 25, 27, 29–31) Mostly I'm considering the kind and sequence of the responses. He can engage in conforming thinking but before a popular response he has to deal with a lot of anxiety. He cuts down on his responses to the color cards. There's a lot of phobic material, e.g. "fox."

Answer: Neurotic. Anxiety hysteria.

Clinician #9   Diagnosis problem   77 cards
Beck orientation   Interpreted third   17 minutes

(W, D, Dd, S, M, C, CF, FC, Y, YF, FY, T, TF, FT, V, VF, FV, F+, F−, F_0, Blend #1–3, F%, F+%, Extended F+%, A%, P, H, Hd, A, Ad, An, Rejec-tions, F #1–2, Sex, Age, Education, F #3–9) The qualitative business is in-teresting. A 30-year-old man shouldn't know about the Mobile task force. A man with spats is a similar kind of thing. There are contradictory things going together. (F #10) Feet with boots on is a strange kind of thinking. (F #11–12, L #11–12, F #13–18) I think he's homosexual. But wait, I'm not finished. The kinds of concerns he has with males and females are hypersexual, veiled sexuality, with a lot of aggression that he then sexualizes. The legs, a woman's leg on a card where it's popular but in a different area. And a manikin's leg. He depersonalizes women. On Card VII, there is the caterpillar followed by men, a phallic significance on a generally female card. (F #19–21) He's also a little crazy, the three ribs. (F #22–33, Sexual History, Occupation, Marital Status, Military History, Interests) He's anxious, fallen apart right now. But I don't think he's Psychotic. The content and lower F+% are important but not of psychotic proportions. I don't want to call him Neurotic. He's a very upset guy right now. He must be Neurotic, anxiety reaction or phobic.

Answer: Neurotic. Anxiety or phobic reaction in a homosexual male.

Clinician #4   Diagnosis problem   30 cards
Klopfer orientation Interpreted first   20 minutes

(Number of Responses Card I, F #1–2, Number of Responses Card II, S #6) That last one was a mistake. (F #6, Number of Responses Card VI, F #13–15, Number of Responses Card IX, F #24–25, Number of Responses Card X,

Clinician #4—Continued   Diagnosis problem   30 cards
Klopfer orientation   Interpreted first   20 minutes

F #28–30, F%, Sum C, Number of Responses Card V, F #11–12) With the responses themselves you can see the impressionistic way he goes about it. If you gave me another test it would be a different matter. (Number of Responses Card III, F #7, Number of Responses Card VIII, F #20–23, V #23) I think he's a man.

Answer: Neurotic. Anxiety neurosis, fairly well controlled neurotic person with a hint of sexual anxiety, male.

Clinician #22   Diagnosis problem   24 cards
Beck orientation   Interpreted first   6 minutes

(F #1–17, S #9, 16) I could make a guess now. I'll take a few more but I feel fairly sure. (F #18–22) I think this is a neurotic individual. An anxiety reaction. There are some phobic features. The cards that I went through contained the strongest evidence of a neurotic response, and evidence of traumatic experience as inducing the anxiety. I found no evidence of Organicity, Psychosis, or Personality Disturbance. I drew impressions as to which cards more nearly fitted these categories. Eliminations came after seeing where the evidence piled up most strongly.

Answer: Neurotic. Anxiety reaction, with phobic features.

Clinician #15   Diagnosis problem   33 cards
Beck orientation   Interpreted second   22 minutes

(Sex, Age, Occupation, F+%, P) I want some overview. (A%, R, M, Sum C, Approach, Sequence, Affective Ratio, Z Sum, S, F%, H, Hd) That's OK. (A, Ad) That's reversed. (An, Blend #1–3, Rejections) Now I want to see if there are any undiluted responses (C, Y, T, V) No, there aren't (Cl, F−) Now I want to go to the timing of responses. (Avg Reaction Time, RT Achromatic, RT Chromatic) I don't think this is a Psychotic. I doubt very seriously that he can be Organic. I think he's pretty well adjusted. I don't know where to go to decide. I'll check Neurotic. The response time is longer than I would have expected, the blends, and it looks like that in the H:Hd but not in the A:Ad. Not too badly adjusted in the blends, the response time Achromatic: Chromatic, the spread of interests in the content categories. There's a pretty high F+%, and a substantial number of populars. But then there's the pretty low A%. I'm im-

Clinician #15—Continued   Diagnosis problem   33 cards
Beck orientation   Interpreted second   22 minutes

pressed by that. I get away from some compulsive type of thing. A character trait disturbance doesn't go with Neurotic. There's a lack of impulsiveness in the reaction time, with a propensity for being confused in the sequence.

Answer: Neurotic. Adjustment reaction.

Clinician #30   Diagnosis problem   116 cards
Beck orientation   Interpreted third   25 minutes

(R, F+%, P, Rejections, W, D, Approach, Sequence, Affective Ratio, M, C, CF, FC, Blend #1–3, Y, YF, FY, F_0, Avg Reaction Time, RT Achromatic, RT Chromatic, Number of Responses Card IX, IV, I, VI, F-V-S #1–15, #24–27, Number of Responses Card VII, F-V-S #16–18, Number of Responses Card X, F-V-S #28–32, H, A, Anal, Fi, An, Fd) The Experience Balance is fairly coarctated. He's Basically Adjusted. He is apprehending reality certainly adequately. He tends to show some compulsive trends and a good deal of constriction. There's not enough to categorize him as maladjusted. He's responsive to emotional stimuli and he's giving expression to emotional feeling and behavior, as well as being cut off from his fantasy. He's able to cope with his impulses and to engage in problem solving. His V's provide me primarily the clue to being somewhat compulsive. His F% and P provide me with the soundness of his reality testing. His Experience Balance is quite constricted and evenly matched, it's balanced perfectly. If there would be some symptomatic development, it would be some type of compulsive individual, an obsessive-compulsive personality structure.

Answer: Basically Adjusted. There is slight personality construction, especially with reference to emotional expression and the utilization of fantasy at an adjustive level. If he were not adjusted, his symptom manifestations would probably be categorized as obsessive-compulsive, with depressive undertones.

Clinician #13   Diagnosis problem   81 cards
Beck orientation   Interpreted first   29 minutes

(R, F+%, W, M, CF, FC, A%, P, C, Rejections, H, Hd, Number of Responses Card VIII, Sex, Age, Education, F-L #1, Reaction Time Card I, F-L #2–6, Reaction Time Card II, F-L #7, Reaction Time Card III, F-L #8, Reaction

Clinician #13—Continued   Diagnosis problem   81 cards
Beck orientation   Interpreted first   29 minutes

Time Card IV, F-L #9, F #10–11, Reaction Time Card V, F #12–13, L #11–13, Reaction Time Card VI, F-L #14–16, Reaction Time Card VII, F-L #17, 20, Reaction Time Card VIII, F-L #21, F #22, Reaction Time Card IX, F-L #24–27, F #28, Reaction Time Card X, V #2–3, S, V #6, 8, 11–12, Occupation)

Answer: Basically Adjusted. There is some anxiety. However, the overall responses do not seem to show sufficient anxiety and related defenses to indicate a neurotic process of substantial magnitude. Neurotic, reactive depression, constriction, some compulsivity.

THE CASE OF THE CLASSIC SIGNS

Rorschach Interpretation by S. J. Beck*

This woman makes virtually no affective contact with the world. Her fantasy, on the contrary, is very free. It is a refuge in which she escapes the anxiety from which she suffers deeply. She frequently disregards reality. The condition shows a mixture of trends within a schizophrenic reaction pattern.

In a record productive above the mean for the average, S only once responds directly with feeling experiences. This association is in the last figure, and its quality is that of the least saturated of the affect-toned reactions (FC). Its content savors strongly of personal determination— 'two seeds . . . which have been carried away from the plant . . . some things that are carried away on the wind'—i.e., it takes a topic that is heavily feeling-laden to stimulate S to this one emotional reaction. She manifests therefore a disorder of the feelings, consisting of inadequate response to the events in life that normally excite affect.

In the other sphere that enters into determination of her inner balance (Exp), namely, the fantasy world, she is liberated to the point of prodigality, in quality and in quantity. Her total of eight fantasy associations is at the high end of the range of superior and creative persons and thus higher than the normal finding in individuals whose productivity is correctly represented by this woman's score (R total, 34). She lives to an abnormal extent, therefore, in a created world. The content of her fantasy projects one or the other of two themes—the one reflecting a child's play and recreational interests, the other embodying material of apprehension-laden character. Examples of the first are: 'a body of a child . . . a stork . . . two storks . . . carrying it' (R 3, R 7); 'a very small figure of two dolls . . . their heads drooping' (R 15); 'two little fairies . . . flitting around . . . like brownies' (R 33). The other theme appears in 'a little devil . . . horns' (R 2), 'a big gorilla . . . a big shape . . . heavy through the shoulders, and has great big legs' (R 16). In two other examples (R 13, R 14) she achieves an odd structural deviation. The fact is that the details in question are usually seen as standing humans; when the card is held upside down, another pair of humans, also standing, emerges. S, when turning the card, sees each pair of humans, but as though in reversed orientation, i.e., she effects a double reversal of perspective in a single percept—"neatest trick of the week," in fact one of the neatest that I have ever seen performed with the test, and requiring a mentality capable of alien concepts.

As regards the stance of the fantasy associations, the human actor is entirely passive in one instance (R 3); the movement is clearly flector in two others (R 15, R 16), and centripetal in another two (R 21, R 33), but with an aggressive aspect in R 21. The odd reversed humans (R 13, R 14) are inactive. But here S elaborates with extensor fantasy— 'two arms and a hand extending from each arm.' In her fantasy world she more frequently takes a bowed pose.

*Beck, S. J., 1945, pp. 244-248.

To a degree this is normal for her, as conforming with the feminine role. But her commitment to it is too complete, even for a woman. Thus in her unconscious living she (a) plays with regressive content (child interests, motifs of inner uneasiness) and (b) shows a too submissive structure.

What is she dodging by means of all this fantasy living? The record points to a central anxiety that must be deeply distressing. The heavy blacks of the test create for her a disintegrating situation. Her associative energy, as represented by productivity, contracts (as shown by an average of 1.5 responses in figures IV, V, VI, VII as compared with an average of 4.67 for the other six cards). First response time slows in figures VI, VII. Her attention, never well controlled, wanders apparently pilotless in figure VI. In figures V, VI (though also in fig. IX), she verbalizes the resignation formula: 'That's all.' She carries this impotence further in figure IV, actually to the point of nihilism, i.e., complete self-negation: 'I wouldn't say that was a gorilla either, I can't determine anything.' Then she accepts (though she also rejects) this response by describing its aspects—'a big shape,' etc. In this figure too she breaks out into laughter quite dissociated from any associational context. The evidence is thus that she breaks when confronted with oppressive stimuli. Anxiety is therefore a pervasive emotion in her. Also, it is the more intense in a person as introversive as she is (Exp shows $M > C$) because it is a characteristic of deeply inward turning individuals that whatever they feel, they feel acutely. A one-sided, El Greco character is thus limned out by the test.

An apparently atypical finding amid this is something that looks like neurotic shock: there is long first reaction time in figure IX, and her attention wanders; here, too, she uses the resignation formula. The only two cards in which she fails to achieve difficult relation (Z) are figures II, IX, in which color shock is most common. Thus she is thrown out of gear also by exciting stimuli, though not as much as by oppressive ones. To the extent to which she does react to affect-toned events, the finding may be favorable, as evincing sensitivity to precipitating factors. But in the light of this whole personality structure, it is not neurotic shock that we have here: it is instability under affective stimulation. This woman demonstrates that not all color shock is neurotic shock; within such a framework, it is not surprising to find disturbed intellectual functioning and deviating control of thinking.

This weak grip makes itself manifest in the anomalous ebb and flow of the psychic energy, in the lengths of the intervals between responses (figs. II, IV, X), and in the wandering of attention noted in figures VI, IX; there is also slow turning of the cards, and in the inquiry S was exceedingly slow in finding many of the details and in answering E. All these reaction modes are in sharp contrast with her rapid-fire tempo in figure VIII, in which all associations were given, as noted, in practically a single breath. This was an isolated phenomenon quite out of line with her regular tempo. She reveals this maldistribution of energy also in her variable productivity from figure to figure: from eight percepts in figure I she drops to two in figure II and expands to five in figure III. Then follow the four inhibiting cards and their reduction of her productivity; but in the all-color figures also she is uneven, though somewhat less seriously so. Through the record as a whole she clearly fluctuates in energy output: she intersperses (a) brief intervals of activity amid (b) longer periods in which her drive is very low and in which (comparably with what was seen at its best in record 24, although her attitude more nearly resembles that seen in record 20) she maintains apathetic unconcern regarding her world.

S shows this flux in another way, i.e., in her quick transformation of one percept into another. The 'old Mother Goose' of R 4 is in the next breath 'a fox.' The 'two little rabbits' of R 20 may also be 'two people making faces at each other.' Of similar import is the abrupt intrusion of entirely alien thinking, e.g., in R 8. Here S first tears out of the blot figure certain portions seldom selected; then she sees quite strange content in them—'mouse-shaped things that are piercing the central body of a bat . . . biting into it.'

Thus we have so far an uneven personality—a woman who sometimes manifests complete disinterest regarding her environment, who sometimes displays unpredictable activity, who makes essentially no affective contact with her real world, and who easily retires into a private one of her own creating. The picture is one of schizophrenia.

The pattern is filled out with signs of aberration in thought processes. 'Mouse-shaped things . . . piercing . . . the bat' is an expample of archaic thinking, although this is S's furthest departure from normal. The others reflect thinking somewhat less off center: e.g., the 'body of a child' with the 'storks . . . carrying it' may be less personally meaningful in so far as the percept reproduces a well known fiction of our culture; the 'picture of a little animal' (R 12) with 'something blinding it . . . something with wool over it' is an odd percept though not an impossible one. S gratuitously attests to its personal force by immediately following it with "My eyes are cloudy" and remembering that she uses glasses for reading. The odd inversions of R 13, R 14 have already been reported.

In the intellectual sphere generally, the construction of accuracy is high to the point of excessiveness. In adaptivity and conformity of thought processes, S rates higher than is expected in view of her uneven functioning. All this points to the rigidity produced by the anxiety, which is reflected also in a functioning intelligence (Z) rather low for a woman who shows such ability as S reveals in her fantasy and in some of her content. This reduction of ability appears also in the low amount of conceptual thinking (W). R 29, R 30 represent one instance of failure to integrate, the more notable in view of the fact that the association is of a kind that lends itself to integration, and that, when it is produced by a person in good health, it is more commonly a large concept (W). The fact remains, however, that at the periphery of the personality, in the intellectual sphere, S remains in touch with the world (A and P). She gives evidence therefore of a capacity for contact with reality. The ego is holding. Furthermore, in her imaginative living she uses good form quality (M+), and otherwise also control persists during her excursions into fantasy.

The errors she commits are in the main personally determined ones. It takes some need to make her distort—e.g., R 22, R 30. These associations are suggestive of an ambition for or interest in a cultivation that may have been beyond her reach. In 'rabbits running in the wrong direction' (R 20) she introduces a personal twist that is highly individualized and therefore requires further study as to its meaning. Concerning the 'face . . . of a little brown bear' (R 6) she gives us no clue, and this may be an impersonal error. Almost certainly under the influence of a personal dynamism are the recurring percepts involving 'two,' e.g., 'two . . . rabbits,' 'two people making faces,' 'two dogs,' one of which is 'a collie' and the other 'a puppy,' 'two . . . fairies,' and 'two seeds.' This last percept is the more remarkable as 'two' because it requires an effort to see it as anything but three (R 31); it is a triple-formed detail most commonly seen as a 'pawnbroker's sign.' The inference is that this accent on 'two' is a lead to some important interrelation in S. In what way and to what extent these personality-dictated eccentric forms are related to the deep anxiety, only further study of the patient can determine.

In summary, the irregular psychic functioning and the large amount of living in a dream world present the configuration of a schizophrenia in which the patient utilizes autistic solutions of her wants. It constitutes her adaptation to her distress, which is consequent on the anxiety, and which appears to be at the core of the personality. The color shock is atypical in this record; also, the patient shows sufficient respect for reality and excessive adaptivity and conformity in thinking, indicating that she is capable of intellectual contact. But the contact is peripheral only. She is out of touch emotionally and lives too completely in her imagination. Perhaps she can be maintained at the level of realistic living peripherally. This record as a whole uncovers enough good material to make one wish that this woman had got some "breaks" in her earlier years.

Answer form presented to clinicians at the beginning of Anxiety interpretation.

Question: Estimate the *severity of anxiety* in this individual, name the types of events likely to heighten it, and name the defenses likely to be utilized in lowering it.

As soon as you feel quite sure of the estimated severity of anxiety, check one of the five categories below, and write down the heightening events and the defenses.

No Anxiety   _____
Little Anxiety   _____
Normal Anxiety _____
Much Anxiety   _____
Severe Anxiety _____

Heightening Events   _____

                                     _____

                                     _____

Defenses Against   _____

                                 _____

                                 _____

ANXIETY

Listing of cards available for selection (*Items*) by clinicians and information contained on reverse side of cards (*Information*) for the Anxiety question. (Refer to Chapter 5 for detailed explanation of method used for presenting information to clinicians.)

Personal Data

Items	*Information*
Sex	Female
Age	26 years.
Education	15 years.
Occupation	Maid
Nationality	
Religion	
Marital Status	Single
Sibling Position	
Siblings	
Mother	Died when S age 2. S reared by paternal grandparents.
Father	Remarried.
Sexual	Little interest in men.
Military	
Interests	Writing

Locations—Klopfer

W	W = 7
D	D = 22
d	d = 4
Dd	Dd = 1
S	S = 0
W%	W% = 21 (expect 20–30%)
D%	D% = 65 (expect 45–55%)
d%	d% = 12 (expect 5–15%)
Dd + S %	Dd + S % = 3 (expect <10%)
Succession	Succession = orderly

Locations—Beck

W	W = 4
D	D = 26
Dd	Dd = 4
S	S = 0
Approach	Approach = (W) D! Dd
Sequence	Sequence = ?
Aff. ratio	Aff. ratio = .62
Z freq.	Z freq. = 9
Z Sum	Z Sum = 25.5

Determinants—Klopfer

Items	Information
M	M = 7
FM	FM = 4
m	m = 1
k	k = 0
K	K = 0
FK	FK = 0
F	F = 22
Fc	Fc = 0
c	c = 0
C'	C' = 0
FC	FC = 0
CF	CF = 0
C	C = 0

Content—Klopfer

Items	Information
H	H = 8
Hd	Hd = 3
A	A = 17
Ad	Ad = 2
At	At = 1
AAt	AAt = 0
AObj	AObj = 0
Art	Art = 0
Cl	Cl = 0
Fd	Fd = 0
Fire	Fire = 0
Geo	Geo = 0
Na	Na = 1
Obj	Obj = 2
Pl	Pl = 0
Sc	Sc = +3
Sex	Sex = 0

Determinants—Beck

M	M = 8
C	C = 0
CF	CF = 0
FC	FC = 1
Y	Y = 0
YF	YF = 0
FY	FY = 0
T	T = 0
TF	TF = 0
FT	FT = 0
V	V = 0
VF	VF = 0
FV	FV = 0
F+	F+ = 19
F−	F− = 5
F_0	$F_0 = 1$
Double	Double = 0
Double	Double = 0
Double	Double = 0

Content—Beck

H	H = 8
Hd	Hd = 3
A	A = 17
Ad	Ad = 2
An	An = 1
Anal	Anal = 0
Ar	Ar = 0
Art	Art = 0
Ay	Ay = 0
Bt	Bt = 0
Cl	Cl = 0
Fd	Fd = 0
Fi	Fi = 0
Ge	Ge = 0
Hh	Hh = 0
My	My = 0
Na	Na = 1
Oj	Oj = 2

Totals and Percentages—Klopfer Summaries

Items	*Information*
R	R = 34
Avg RT	Avg RT = 28″
RT Achrom	RT Achrom = 22″
RT Chrom	RT Chrom = 39″
F%	F% = 65
FK + F + Fc %	FK + F + Fc % = 65
A%	A% = 56
P	P = 6 (10 possible)
Sum C	Sum C = 0
VIII–IX–X %	VIII–IX–X % = 38
Additional Responses	Additional Responses = 0
Rejections	Rejections = 0

Totals and Percentages—Beck Summaries

R	R = 34
F%	F% = 74
Ext. F%	Ext. F% = 100
F+%	F+% = 79
Ext.F+%	Ext.F+% = 85
A%	A% = 56
P	P = 10 (21 possible)
Avg RT	Avg RT = 28″
RT Achrom	RT Achrom = 22″
RT Chrom	RT Chrom = 39″
Additional Responses	Additional Responses = 0
Rejections	Rejections = 0

Number of Responses to Each Card

Card I.	Card I.	8	(#1–#8)
Card II.	Card II.	2	(#9–#10)
Card III.	Card III.	5	(#11–15)
Card IV.	Card IV.	1	(#16)
Card V.	Card V.	1	(#17)
Card VI.	Card VI.	2	(#18–#19)
Card VII.	Card VII.	2	(#20–#21)
Card VIII.	Card VIII.	4	(#22–#25)
Card IX.	Card IX.	3	(#26–#28)
Card X.	Card X.	6	(#29–#34)

Reaction Times to Each Card

Items	*Information*	
Card I.	Card I.	8″
Card II.	Card II.	14″
Card III.	Card III.	8″
Card IV.	Card IV.	14″
Card V.	Card V.	3″
Card VI.	Card VI.	36″
Card VII.	Card VII.	48″
Card VIII.	Card VIII.	—
Card IX.	Card IX.	95″
Card X.	Card X.	—

Individual Response Scorings—Klopfer

# 1	# 1 Card I.	W	F	A	P
# 2	# 2 Card I.	D	M	(H)	
# 3	# 3 Card I.	D	M	H	
# 4	# 4 Card I.	D	F	(H)	
# 5	# 5 Card I.	Dd	F	Hd	
# 6	# 6 Card I.	Dd	F	Ad	
# 7	# 7 Card I.	D	FM	A	
# 8	# 8 Card I.	D	FM	A	
# 9	# 9 Card II.	W	F	A	P
#10	#10 Card II.	D	F	A	
#11	#11 Card III.	D	F	A	P
#12	#12 Card III.	D	F	A	
#13	#13 Card III	W	M	H	P
#14	#14 Card III.	W	M	H	
#15	#15 Card III.	D	M	H	
#16	#16 Card IV.	W	FM	A	
#17	#17 Card V.	W	F	A	P
#18	#18 Card VI.	D	F	A	
#19	#19 Card VI.	D	F	Obj	
#20	#20 Card VII.	D	FM	A	
#21	#21 Card VII.	D	M	H	
#22	#22 Card VIII.	W	F	A,Sc	
#23	#23 Card VIII.	D	F	A	P
#24	#24 Card VIII.	D	F	(Hd)	
#25	#25 Card VIII.	D	F	At	
#26	#26 Card IX.	d	F	Ad	
#27	#27 Card IX.	D	F	Hd	
#28	#28 Card IX.	D	F	A	
#29	#29 Card X.	D	F	A,Sc	
#30	#30 Card X.	D	F	A,Sc	
#31	#31 Card X.	D	Fm	Na	
#32	#32 Card X.	Dd	F	A	

Individual Response Scorings—Klopfer—Continued

Items	Information			
#33	#33 Card X.	D	M	(H)
#34	#34 Card X.	Dd	F	Obj
#35				
#36				
#37				

Individual Response Scorings—Beck

# 1	# 1 Card I.	W	F+	A	P	1.0
# 2	# 2 Card I.	D	M+	H		
# 3	# 3 Card I.	D	M+	H	P	
# 4	# 4 Card I.	D	F+	H		
# 5	# 5 Card I.	Dd	F	Hd		
# 6	# 6 Card I.	Dd	F−	Ad		
# 7	# 7 Card I.	D	F+	A	4.0	
# 8	# 8 Card I.	D	F−	A	3.0	
# 9	# 9 Card II.	D	F+	A	P	
#10	#10 Card II.	D	F+	A		
#11	#11 Card III.	D	F+	A	P	
#12	#12 Card III.	D	F+	A		
#13	#13 Card III.	D	M+	H	P	3.0
#14	#14 Card III.	D	M+	H		
#15	#15 Card III.	D	M+	H		
#16	#16 Card IV.	W	M+	A	2.0	
#17	#17 Card V.	W	F+	A	P	1.0
#18	#18 Card VI.	D	F+	A		
#19	#19 Card VI.	D	F+	Oj		
#20	#20 Card VII.	D	F−	A		
#21	#21 Card VII.	D	M+	H	P	3.0
#22	#22 Card VIII.	W	F−	A,Sc	4.5	
#23	#23 Card VIII.	D	F+	A	P	
#24	#24 Card VIII.	D	F+	Hd,Rc		
#25	#25 Card VIII.	D	F+	An	P	
#26	#26 Card IX.	D	F+	Ad		
#27	#27 Card IX.	D	F+	Hd	P	
#28	#28 Card IX.	D	F+	A		
#29	#29 Card X.	D	F+	A,Sc		
#30	#30 Card X.	D	F−	A,Sc		
#31	#31 Card X.	D	FC+	Na		
#32	#32 Card X.	Dd	F+	A		
#33	#33 Card X.	D	M+	H		
#34	#34 Card X.	Dd	F+	Oj	4.0	
#35						
#36						
#37						

Location Areas

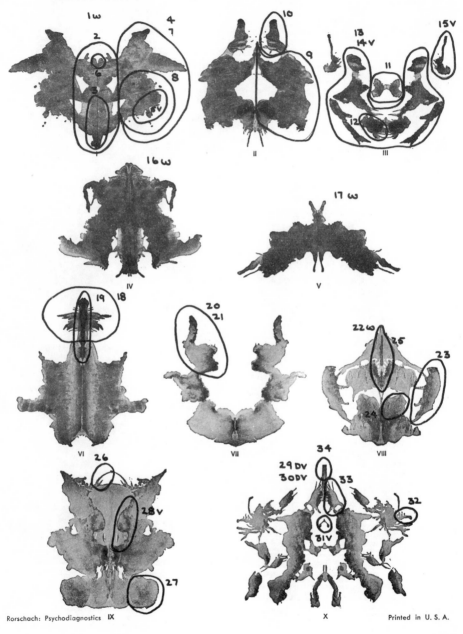

Free Associations

Items		*Information*
# 1	# 1 Card I.	Bat.
# 2	# 2 Card I.	Little devil. (Horns. It's standing up. Straight up.)
# 3	# 3 Card I.	Body of a child.
# 4	# 4 Card I.	Old Mother Goose. (Long nose. Or a fox.)
# 5	# 5 Card I.	Face of a person. Cap on it.
# 6	# 6 Card I.	Face of a little brown bear.
# 7	# 7 Card I.	Stork. (Odd positions. Carrying [central figure].)
# 8	# 8 Card I.	Mouse-shaped things. Piercing the central body of a bat. (Biting.)
# 9	# 9 Card II.	Little puppies.
#10	#10 Card II.	Seals. Heads and body.
#11	#11 Card III.	Butterfly.
#12	#12 Card III.	Little animal. Something blinding it. Something with wool over it.
#13	#13 Card III.	People standing on their heads. Arms. Hand extending from each arm.
#14	#14 Card III.	People standing on their heads. Arms. Hand extending from each arm.
#15	#15 Card III.	Dolls. Small. Heads drooping. Figures of people. Arms.
#16	#16 Card IV.	Big gorilla. (Arms. Heavy through shoulders. Big legs. Head. Sitting on stump.)
#17	#17 Card V.	Butterfly.
#18	#18 Card VI.	Bird.
#19	#19 Card VI.	Pole.
#20	#20 Card VII.	Little rabbits. Running in wrong direction.
#21	#21 Card VII.	People. Making faces at each other.
#22	#22 Card VIII.	Outline of animal. Ameba.
#23	#23 Card VIII.	Bears.
#24	#24 Card VIII.	Heads of doll.
#25	#25 Card VIII.	Backbone.
#26	#26 Card IX.	Horns of deer . . . antelope . . . moose.
#27	#27 Card IX.	People. Faces.
#28	#28 Card IX.	Billy goats.
#29	#29 Card X.	Primitive animals. Beginning animal life. Amebas. Parasitic. Enlarged bacterial cells.
#30	#30 Card X.	Primitive animals. Beginning animal life. Amebas. Parasitic. Enlarged bacterial cells.
#31	#31 Card X.	Seeds. Carried away from the plant, on the wind. Like some trees have.
#32	#32 Card X.	Dogs. Collie. Small. (Puppy.)
#33	#33 Card X.	Little fairies. Flitting around. Like brownies.
#34	#34 Card X.	Post.
#35		
#36		
#37		

Verbalizations and Behavioral Observations

Items		*Information*
# 1	# 1 Card I.	Looks like_____.
# 2	# 2 Card I.	Looks as_____.
# 3	# 3 Card I.	Also there's_____. There are any number of objects that I can see.
# 4	# 4 Card I.	_____, it can be.
# 5	# 5 Card I.	Just an ordinary_____. (*Turns card very slowly.*)
# 6	# 6 Card I.	Also_____.
# 7	# 7 Card I.	
# 8	# 8 Card I.	Also_____. (*Throughout inquiry S is exceedingly slow in locating areas of the percepts. All answers to E are greatly delayed.*)
# 9	# 9 Card II.	
#10	#10 Card II.	(*90″ before this response follows #9.*)_____, perhaps.
#11	#11 Card III.	(*Turns card. Edging.*)
#12	#12 Card III.	(*Card turning.*) My eyes are cloudy. (*S explains about glasses for reading but that they would not help in this.*)
#13	#13 Card III.	
#14	#14 Card III.	
#15	#15 Card III.	. . . wouldn't say they're_____.
#16	#16 Card IV.	(*Continuing laughter. 135″ between initial response and elaboration of it*). I wouldn't say that . . . either. I can't determine anything. It seems to be just_____. (*Sudden laughter quite out of a clear sky.*)
#17	#17 Card V.	. . . That's all that is.
#18	#18 Card VI.	(*Attention wanders from figure.*) Looks like_____.
#19	#19 Card VI.	That's all I can make of it.
#20	#20 Card VII.	
#21	#21 Card VII.	Can also be determined as_____. (*Studies obverse of card.*)
#22	#22 Card VIII.	This is_____.
#23	#23 Card VIII.	(*Response given without pause.*)
#24	#24 Card VIII.	(*Response given without pause.*)
#25	#25 Card VIII.	(*Response given without pause.*)
#26	#26 Card IX.	(*Attention wanders. S just stares into space. E: You're not looking at the figure. S: That's so. Excuse me.*) Looks like_____.
#27	#27 Card IX.	
#28	#28 Card IX.	That's all I can interpret from here.
#29	#29 Card X.	These are_____. What I said before. (*All locations indiscriminately given. No integration.*) Also could be_____.
#30	#30 Card X.	These are_____. What I said before. (*All locations indiscriminately given. No integration.*) Also could be_____.
#31	#31 Card X.	(*Turns card. Long silence.*)
#32	#32 Card X.	Looks like a_____.
#33	#33 Card X.	
#34	#34 Card X.	
#35		

Verbalizations and Behavioral Observations—Continued

Items	*Information*
#36	
#37	

| Clinician #19 | Anxiety problem | 81 cards |
| Beck orientation | Interpreted third | 13 minutes |

(F+ %, Extended F+ %) None of your subjects have any difficulty with F+ %. The Extended F+ % is good because it could include form failure more meaningfully, like an affective plus percent. (M) Hey, that's wonderful. (C, CF, FC, Y, YF, FY, T, TF, FT, V, VF, FV) No anxiety? What kind of a person is this? (F+, F−, F₀) We know what kind of person this is. (Blend #1) That's something. How anxious is he, and what makes him anxious, are the questions to be answered? Dumb he's not. (Rejections) I would make a little psychogram which helps to see the data. (Number of Responses Card I–X, R, Affective Ratio) There's a big burst on Cards I and III. They should be full of M's. (S-F-V #1–3) Body of a child? Devil? That's crazy. (L #3–2, S-F-V #4–8) It turns out to be the abandoned son. You don't want the diagnosis on this one. This response #8 could be misscored. It's certainly a fabulized combination. In Jungian terms there's a big complex. Whether he's schizophrenic or schizoid, I don't know. The question of how anxious he is also is tough. Do we want the manifest anxiety? He wouldn't report much anxiety. There's central anxiety, but he could be drenched in sweat and wouldn't admit it. (S-F-V #11–12) With wool over its eyes? That's schizophrenic. (S-F-V-L #13–14) He is a little perseverative. (S-F-V #15) Referring to the number of responses on Card VIII, it's strange that he didn't get more anxious. There's much more response to people there. (S-F-V #20–21) Birth is certainly all over the place, isn't it?

Answer: Severe anxiety. *Heightening Events:* interpersonal stimulation, unconscious concerns regarding birth and babies (his own birth?), unconscious fantasies symbolic of oral aggression. *Defenses:* fantasy leading to obsessive rumination, regression (childish), thought disorder which interferes with the clear perception of threatening stimuli. I would diagnosis him as schizophrenic.

| Clinician #32 | Anxiety problem | 62 cards |
| Beck orientation | Interpreted third | 13 minutes |

(Reaction Time Card I–X, Number of Responses Card I–X, R, Age, Sex, Marital Status, Sibling Position, Sibling Description, Mother Description, Father Description, Sexual History, F #1–8, L #2, 8, S #8) I was going to put Severe anxiety because of the number of responses and the reaction times to Cards

---

Note: Material contained within parentheses refers to the actual data card selections made by the clinician in obtaining Rorschach information item-by item. Abbreviations are listed and defined in Appendix A.

Clinician #32—Continued   Anxiety problem   62 cards
Beck orientation   Interpreted third 13 minutes

IV–VI. Card IV produced a severe anxiety which was carried over to Card V. Card VI anxiety carried over to Card VII. There's some masochism present. (F #9) That's a nice dependency kind of thing. (F #10–12) That's a withdrawal response. (F #13) She's dependent on others. (F #14, S-L #13–14) I would score that minus. (F #15–16) That's a lot of anxiety. (F #17–20) Always in the wrong direction. (F #21–26)

Answer: Severe anxiety. *Heightening Events:* threat to dependency needs, necessity of assuming adult responsibilities, fear of child-bearing. *Defenses:* withdrawal, masochism, dependency, wanting to change the world but not herself essentially.

Clinician #23   Anxiety problem   24 cards
Beck orientation   Interpreted second 9 minutes

(YF, Y, FT, M, CF, Number of Responses Card III, V #11–13, Number of Responses Card VII, V #20–21, Number of Responses Card IV, V #16, F−, F+, Dd, D, Number of Responses Card X, V #29, F #29 30, 3, 18)

Answer: Severe anxiety. *Heightening Events:* sexual stimuli, threatening social situations (males, authority), stimuli arousing dysphoria (authority, demand). *Defenses:* internalization of affect (withdrawal), attempted reality testing (by not engaging in stressful situations), moderate over-intellectualization.

Clinician #27   Anxiety problem   17 cards
Klopfer orientation   Interpreted first 26 minutes

(V-F #1–5) Still giving more responses. (V-F #6–8) Does this guy ever stop giving responses? He ought to be done pretty soon. (V #9) Yeah. I'll stop there. Let's see what we've got now. Inferentially, there's the perception of the little devil with horns. It suggests a tendency to infantilize, a childish kind of identification. To make things more severe there's the fear of being pierced, bodily, the loss of bodily integration. My assumption is that it's a girl. She may be dealing with some sexual fears of being pregnant. Acting-out would be possible, although it does not appear to be that important.

| Clinician # 27—Continued | Anxiety problem | 17 cards |
| Klopfer orientation | Interpreted first | 26 minutes |

Answer: Severe anxiety. *Heightening Events:* closeness (warm positive relationships), dependency relationships, sex (fear of the destructive aspect). *Defenses:* projection, rationalization, obsessive-compulsive.

| Clinician #7 | Anxiety problem | 69 cards |
| Beck orientation | Interpreted second | 39 minutes |

(Sex, Age, R, F+, Education) I have to know what type of person I'm dealing with. (H, Hd, Approach) M-hm, she's fairly anxious, therefore she probably has a fairly high A%. Let's see how secure she is. (A%, P, M, C, CF, FC) The M:Sum C ratio indicates that she internalizes most of these things. (Affective Ratio) Even less than he (Diagnosis Problem) did. What do I want in order to answer this question? (An, F%) How much dysphoria does she have? (Y, YF, FY) None. Nine non-F responses, F% of 75, 25 out of 34 is probably 74%. I don't have to look at the other nuances. I can figure out the percentages. I'm trying to rule out easy clues to heightening events. (Rejections) She's already internalizing, possibly using fantasy as a defense, a lot of inner living. But she's not able to express her feelings easily. If we're talking about free floating anxiety that's one thing; if we're in the generic thing, that's another. The only way to approach this is to go to the cards themselves. Right now, she's adapting but she has some anxiety. More than the normal anxiety. She keeps things to herself. I don't think that any additional information in the summary will help. It's either exhausted or answered by implication. She's probably regular. (Sequence, S-F-V #1) She's a pretty conventional gal. (S-F-V #2) A little devil. (Location #2, S-F-V #3) My question here is her relationship between her role as a mother and her anxiety. Why a child inside of a devil? Is she really going to go? (S-F-V #4) I get from this response some confirmation of the conflict of little girl versus mother as an important variable for this individual, as a heightening event. A defense which she uses is intellectualization. The response sequence bat-devil-child, then boom—"any number of things I can produce"—is a cover for something. (S-F-V #5) While she's pushing, she doesn't maintain the Dd approach. She's a very immature person. (S-F-V #6) I just got a confirmation of undoing as a defense. The "brown bear face" on the devil is an intellectual undoing. (L #5–6) Too bad she doesn't have more C. (S-F-V-L #7) Card I? Jeez. The stork carrying the body of a child. (S-F-V-L #8) Does she keep this up? That should be the end of it. No? Is she married? (Marital Status) Are her concerns about maternity based on something real in her life, or historical, or intrapsychic? I had been making an implicit assumption about her being married. Why is she so concerned about her role? (Sexual History) I'm glad I put that in parentheses. A heightening event is sexual threat. The piercing, the fear of invasion. I don't know if I want to cite regression as a defense—she's so immature. (S-F-V #9) Oh this childishness is really there. (S-F-V #10) Her anxiety goes up, in my

| Clinician #7—Continued | Anxiety problem | 69 cards |
| Beck orientation | Interpreted second | 39 minutes |

perception of it. (S-F-V #11–12, L #12, S-F-V #13) OK, I'm ready to say that she has much anxiety, and I would say that fantasy is a defense. Also social relations, socialization, being close, of which sexual is a certain special category. She looked sicker as she progressed.

Answer: Much anxiety. *Heightening Events:* motherhood *vs.* childhood roles, sexual threat, close social relations. *Defenses:* intellectualization, undoing, fantasy.

| Clinician #21 | Anxiety problem | 144 cards |
| Beck orientation | Interpreted first | 40 minutes |

A lot of hypotheses are generated when one is giving the test or scoring it. (R, F+%, F%, A%, P) The order of selections here doesn't make a difference. (Avg Reaction Time, RT Achromatic, RT Chromatic, Sex, Age, Education, W, D, Dd, Marital Status, S, Approach, Sequence, Affective Ratio, Rejections, Additionals, F-V-S #1–3, F-L-V-S #4–8, F-V-S #9–10, F #11, Reaction Time Card II, V-S #11, F-V-S-L #12) Even when the percepts are good percepts, plus percepts, the accompanying verbalizations are primary process verbalizations. On Card I the sequence of child, mother goose, and stork suggests concern with pregnancy. On response #12 the "something blinding . . . my eyes dark and cloudy" suggests psychotic concern with decay or attack on one's body. There is real loss of distance between herself and the card she's looking at. So my current hypothesis is that despite the relatively good overall totals, it's just sort of a front. Underneath there's a great deal of psychotic-like process going on. (F-L-V-S #13) "People standing on their heads" makes me feel that she's very concerned perhaps about pregnancy. It reinforces my feeling. (Sexual History) The "little interest in men" would lead me to wonder whether she wasn't an ambulatory schizophrenic. (F-V-S-L #14, F-L #15, Reaction Time Card III, V-S #15, F-V-S #16) This is the kind of thing I was taking about earlier. The percept itself is a good one, but the associated laughter and long, long, long pause suggests that her primary process keeps breaking through. (F-V-S #17–19) These responses again suggest the sexual nature of her conflicts. (F-V-S #20–21) Here she makes a nice recovery from a rather poor original percept. (F #22, Reaction Time Card VIII, V-S #22, F-V-S #23) Here she does it again. She starts out with a minus response and comes back with a P. That's a good sign. (F-V-S #24–26) The notation that this response was given without pause and that the reaction time wasn't recorded suggests that she came on pretty fast, that the color triggered off anxiety. (Reaction Time Card IX, F-V-S #27–29, Reaction Time Card X) Was the person who gave these Ror-

Clinician #21—Continued   Anxiety problem   144 cards
Beck orientation   Interpreted first   40 minutes

schachs experienced at giving the Rorschach? If yes, then probably the verbalizations are a function of the responses and not due to administration errors.
(F-V-S #30–34, L #31, 33, Occupation, Sibling Position, Mother Description,
Father Description, Interests) This would be pretty much how I would go
through the thing. Summaries first. Then the individual responses in some detail.

Answer: Much anxiety. *Heightening Events:* interpersonal contact, especially
            with males, affect-producing situations, public situations in groups.
            Defenses: repression, withdrawal, intellectualization.

Clinician #25   Anxiety problem   142 cards
Klopfer orientation   Interpreted third   27 minutes

Now you're getting into the difficult problems. (Sex, Age, Education, Nationality,
Marital Status, F-V-L #1–7, R, F-V-L #8–11) Edging? I've never seen that
before. (F-V-L #12–34, W, D, d, Dd, S, W%, D%, d%, Dd+S%, Succession,
M, FM, m, k, K, FK, F, Fc, c, C', FC, CF, H, Hd, A, Ad, Avg Reaction Time,
RT Achromatic, RT Chromatic, F%, A%, P, Sum C, 8–9–10%) It's apparent
that there were times when this girl was anxious, especially on Card IV. She was
overstimulated by that card. She's not Severe because she is able to recover,
after this tremendous struggle, and give you some fairly presentable responses.
The ego isn't swamped by anxiety, although it's very vulnerable. The difference
between Much or Severe anxiety would be her recoverability. The speeding up of
responses suggested that either she was trying to get the testing situation over
with before her impulses completely broke down or that she might have been
actually losing contact.

Answer: Much anxiety. *Heightening Events:* primitive hostile associations
            (feelings of inadequacy elicited by Rorschach material), stimulation
            by male connotation of Card IV (departure in stimulus material from
            her own preformed notions), stimulation by color (fear of loss of
            control over impulses). *Defenses:* withdrawal and delay (from testing
            situation), somatization (abortive type), dissociated reactions (Card
            IV).

| Clinician #29 | Anxiety problem | 12 cards |
| Beck orientation | Interpreted second | 11 minutes |

(Y, YF, FY, F #1–2, Rejections, Sexual History, Sex) I know it was a female because of the information in the preceding card. (Age, R, F #3–4) I'm most impressed with the "little devil" response on Card I, the fact that a 26-year-old female has little interest in men, the idea of a child's body, and indications of some poorly controlled aggressive feelings. It is not Severe, due to the fact that she is able to produce 34 responses, without any Y determinants.

Answer: Much anxiety. *Heightening Events:* sexually "tinged" interpersonal relationships, threat to her source of dependency gratification, loss of feelings of capability and competence. *Defenses:* intellectualization, counterphobic maneuvers, denial.

| Clinician #36 | Anxiety problem | 100 cards |
| Beck orientation | Interpreted second | 59 minutes |

I'll be looking for two impressions. First, the "gel" of things fitting together and, second, the transference. (Sex, Age) These are always valuable to have. (F #1, Reaction Time Card I–X, V #1, F #2, L #1–2, V #2, F-L-V-S #3, F-L #4–6) On the question of anxiety, I see her beginning to move toward the edges, picking out faces, handling anxiety by dealing with the surface aspects of things. Not really being too productive at this point. (F-L-V #7, F-L #8) She feels that something is eating away at her. (F-L-V #9, F-L #10–12) I begin to see that while she deals with the whole card to begin with, the whole response, she goes back to a cut-off W and doesn't really capture the whole thing on Card II. And on Card III she avoids this by giving another trite or conventional response. Avoiding human contact I would say. Stereotyped reaction to a small detail. But the defense doesn't really hold up, the "little animal with something blinding it." She indeed really is pulling the wool over her own eyes. (S #12 Beck, Klopfer) I'm not too keen on Beck's scoring all the time. (F-L #13) She seems fearful of manipulating or motorically investigating her environment. There's some inhibition and lack of spontaneity. Finally when she does see humans she sees them out of their usual context, she distorts them, sees them standing on their heads. I see a lot of reference to Mother Goose, storks, puppies, little animals. I don't know if she's just become a mother herself. There are a lot of things I'd expect from a little child. She needs to defend against her own excessive dependency needs. All of these ideas are open-ended a little. (F-L #14) She can't mentally shift here. (F-L-S #15) Again the very infantile quality. The extreme passivity with heads "drooping." (F-L #16) She has some difficulty with the first impact of stimulation, Card II, and then

Clinician #36—Continued   Anxiety problem   100 cards
Beck orientation   Interpreted second   59 minutes

again on Card IV which deals with males. (F-L #17–19, V #18) This is I would guess an inhibited woman, sexually. Yet her attention is drawn to the very thing that she would like to avoid. She's the kind of woman that would walk into the room where there were men and would look at their flies or something. (F-L #20, V #19) Nobody asked her why they were running in the wrong direction? (F-L #21) So far I would assume that this was a person with Much anxiety, more than the average. The long reaction times, attention to the edges of the cards, and her avoidance of human contact and sexually stimulating things. (S #16) The apparent absence of a response would suggest to me that she's not handling her anxiety in an ideational manner. And I find myself at this point eager to see just how it is being handled. Is it being acted out? Discharged? Expressed in some role that she's taking? There's a far out possibility of some sexual perversion. There's no feeling that she somatizes, no concern with skeletons, bodies, organs, etc. I look in the direction of some activity for her to handle her anxiety. (F-L-V-S #22) The whole thing? It's hard to know if the reaction time on Card VII is a carry-over from Card VI. Card VIII is the first really full affective experience. She isn't able to handle reality successfully. She deals with emotional stimulation in a very unproductive, global fashion. (F-L-V #23) Apparently she recovers, snaps back. (F-L-S #24) Here again the emphasis on the heads, childish things. She has never really given up the symbolic aspects of childhood. They stick with her. (F-L #25–29, S #29 Beck, Klopfer) I would score that DW. These have form, but this emphasis on the beginnings of life is parasitic, emphasizing her infantilism, her clinging type of dependency, which she very much has to defend against. This is found in people who are beginning to gain certain insights in therapy. Piotrowski did a study on a group of people who later were hospitalized for schizophrenia. One thing that stood out were fetuses, embryos, things like that. (F-L-V #30) This is a person who tends to regress in emotional situations. (F-L-S #31) Is there some m in there? Yeah. (F-L #32–33) She sort of feels like she doesn't have control of the situation. (F #34–35) In a new situation she feels a need to milk it for everything, but this diminishes as she goes on, as there's nothing later to compare with the first eight responses to Card I. Basically she's a person who has never really evolved proper defenses. She's rooted at an infantile level in many respects, not so much infantile as childish. She never really successfully faced and went through her adolescence. Her sexuality is dealt with in that fashion. She's a lady who is unable to commit herself, and she probably plays a lot of childish games, a teaser. I would expect this person to have difficulty with her own body imagery. I don't see her as having a good concept of self. The heightening events would be new situations. She'd be a bit of a blabbermouth, dealing with all kinds of superficialities. Another one would be situations that are overwhelming emotionally. She's amorphous and primitive in her approach. Contrast the A with the H movement. It's a picture of somebody who doesn't have much to go on. There should be at least some freedom of movement. She's more constricted, literally standing on her head as she grew up. I'm wondering how she related to her mother and father. Was she an only child? She probably didn't go to college, but if she did she didn't do much with it.

Answer: Much anxiety. *Heightening Events:* new situations, any human contact, heterosexual stimulation. *Defenses:* conformity and stereotypy, attention to minutiae, withdrawal.

Clinician # 11	Anxiety problem	120 cards
Beck orientation	Interpreted third	45 minutes

This basically is an assessment of the personality, the same as with diagnosis. It's essentially the same task, namely to find out what this guy is like. (Sex, Age, Education, Occupation, Nationality, Religion, Marital Status, Sibling Position, Sibling Description, Mother Description, Father Description, Sexual History, Military History, Interests) A writing maid. I'll go through a lot of this for a general picture. (W) She's a little light on W. (D, Dd, S, Approach, Sequence, Z Frequency, Z Sum) The Affective Ratio I don't pay attention to. It doesn't have much meaning. (M, C, CF, FC, Y, YF, FY, T, TF, FT, V, VF, FV, F+, F−, F$_0$, Blend # 1) She's more reflective and thought-oriented than action-oriented. (H, Hd, A, Ad, An, Anal, Ar, Art, Ay, Bt, Cl, Fd, Fi, Ge, Hh, My, Na, Oj) Again, for a gal with three years of college it looks like a dismal poverty of content categories. (R, F%, Extended F%, F+%, Extended F+%, A%, P) Another mismatch. I would have expected more F+ with this amount of F and Extended F. She's certainly far from psychotic. She's certainly not a plunger-type gambler. (Additionals, Avg Reaction Time, Rejections) I expect she experiences quite a bit but that others looking at her from the outside wouldn't see it. (S #1–5) She's not having trouble with Card I. (S #6) Oops, not so good any more. Let's go across the board on that. (F-V #6) Let me free associate on that. It's sort of unthreatening, kind of a reaction formation, giving me a general feeling of the child. It's the first F−. Bears are old fathers according to Phillips and Smith, aren't they? Bears are like an ape. Now why is he little? (S #7) She gets a recovery. (S #8) She's really putting out on Card I. (S #9, F-V #8) There's a lot of blocking throughout the inquiry on this one. A bad response is given, then a recovery, then another bad one. It may be another counter-phobic response to threat. Mice generally don't rip bats to shreds. I start getting a picture of lots of hostile fantasies, of not being able to be assertive in any social contacts. She's falling back into dreams of getting even with people. (L #8, S #10–20, F-V-L #19) There are no special problems on Card II. Card III starts out well. Card IV seems OK. There's not much trouble on Card V. On Card VI there's only one response, and it's not a popular. We can get phallic symbolism from that. I'd be willing to assume shock on Card VI. She's fairly productive on everything else. Well Card V isn't that great either. But she's running downhill in quality and productivity. This is somewhat supportive of my hypothesis about working through the Oedipal conflict. (F-V-L #20) I would ask her what the running in different directions meant. For example, were they running to get her or what? And they are "little" rabbits. (S #21–22) Oh she recovers. She manages to come through with a popular. Rabbits are like mice, timid. I wonder if this is a carry-over from Card VI or is it just on Card VII. It's hard to say, but there's recovery with the popular and lots of organizing stuff. I suspect a carry-over from Card II. (S #23) That's a recovery. Card VIII starts bad but there's

Clinician #11—Continued   Anxiety problem   120 cards
Beck orientation   Interpreted third   45 minutes

recovery. (F-V #22) Now I see problems with my carry-over from Card VI hypothesis. Card VIII could be a carry-over. (Reaction Time Card VI–VIII) Not much help. (S #24) We're still on Card VIII. She shows a reasonably good recovery. (S #25–27) Card IX starts OK. (S #28–30) The amebas are getting bad, and it's parasitic. The last ameba was on Card VIII. (F-V #30) Her intellectualizing of problems is better, fitting with her high M. But I doubt that she's the scholarly pedantic type. Psychosis, schizophrenia, is a possibility, especially with those parasitic amebas, but it wouldn't fit with the F+%. (S #31–35) Her Card X recovery seems pretty good. But now I don't know what she's defending against. I'm fighting now between the alternatives Much and Severe anxiety. Also, I've gone off the idea of how much she experiences, forming a composite total between what she's got and what she experiences. It certainly isn't bad enough to interfere with her contact with reality nor her highly active fantasy life. Heightening events would be "life," affect from herself and others which gets into all interpersonal relations, and whether men are more threatening than women. I would say men are more threatening although I'm not sure what that's based on, really. I don't know if I have the data to talk about defenses. I could say sex dependency and hostility, but that's true of everybody and doesn't say much.

Answer: Much anxiety. *Heightening Events:* interpersonal relations particularly when affect is involved, men more so than women, her impulses and her own feelings. *Defenses:* intellectualization, fantasy, emotional constriction, and setting low sights for achievement.

Clinician #14   Anxiety problem   57 cards
Beck orientation   Interpreted third   12 minutes

This one will be a little more difficult. (Sex, Age, Education, Marital Status) Her being single means she's anxious. (Religion, Nationality, Occupation) A maid? (Interests, Y, YF, FY) Now, does that mean she has no anxiety or is she severely repressed? (M) Oh boy. (R, C, CF, FC) She's probably over-ideational and will use intellectual defenses like rationalization and intellectualization, and probably some repression too. We might also expect to find some reaction formation and some denial. (T, TF, FT, V, VF, FV, Approach) She's concrete. (Affective Ratio) She's elated and somewhat euphoric, with no C or very little C, so she's denying. There's little evidence of felt anxiety, but in the raw material there's a lot. There's some real pathology here that's being hidden by the defenses. (F+%, A%, P, S, Number of Responses Card IV, F #16) She's afraid of men, which would be a heightening event. (Number of Responses Card VII, F #20–21,

| Clinician #14—Continued | Anxiety problem | 57 cards |
| Beck orientation | Interpreted third | 12 minutes |

Number of Responses Card VI, F #18–19, Number of Responses Card III, F-L #11–14) She can't tell if people are upside down or what. (F-L #15), Number of Responses Card V, F #17, F+, Extended F+%, Father Description, Mother Description, Sibling Position, Sibling Description, Sexual History, Military History)

Answer: Much anxiety, but less felt distress. *Heightening Events:* contact with men in sexual-genital situations. *Defenses:* intellectualization, rationalization, repression, denial, reaction formation.

| Clinician #26 | Anxiety problem | 41 cards |
| Klopfer orientation | Interpreted third | 31 minutes |

(Age, Sex, Education, Mother Description, Father Description, Sexual History, R, M, Extended F+%, W, D, F #1–6, L #5, V #3, F #7, Occupation, S-L #3, Interests, Sum C) It's becoming fairly obvious that this is a gal who uses fantasy a great deal, whose functioning is largely inner than externally directed. (Fire) This would fit in terms of what I was after, too, a complete inhibition of aggression. (Fd) And here, too, of acknowledging her dependency wishes. (FY, Avg Reaction Time, Number of Responses Card III, F #11, Sibling Position, Sibling Description, m, F #12–14, L #13–14, F #15, 34) I'm wondering whether the main question relates to anxiety as the person is or as the person perceives himself to be. The extreme imbalance between M and C, the depression of all affective indications such as FY, Sum C, and m, the F+ being somewhat high, and no Fire or Fd. It's the conscious anxiety that is fairly minimal, but by the amount of defensive operation I would judge her to be quite anxious.

Answer: Much anxiety. *Heightening Events:* failure, anticipated rejection, interpersonal involvement, awareness of emotion, the unknown and ambiguous. *Defenses:* Intellectualization, reversal of dependency, giving a great deal at first, extensive fantasy.

| Clinician #35 | Anxiety problem | 78 cards |
| Beck orientation | Interpreted third | 18 minutes |

(Sex, Age, Education, Occupation, Nationality, Religion, Marital Status, Interests, Military History, Sexual History, Father Description, Mother Description, Sibling Description) On the basis of this material, the fact that she's been

| Clinician #35—Continued | Anxiety problem | 78 cards |
| Beck orientation | Interpreted third | 18 minutes |

working as a maid and has had three years of college makes you wonder whether she's led a period of up and down in emotions. I wonder if she doesn't take a fairly passive position. I could go in two directions at this point, summaries or qualitative responses. (F #1–8) It's a very long number of responses to Card I. (F #9, V #8) The slowness of her performance in giving these 8 responses indicate a somewhat compulsive and hostile approach to the examiner. (F #10–35) The marked fluctuation in the responses to the cards is important: 8-2-5-1-1-2-2-4-3-6. With the exceptions of responses #29 and #30, I really don't get a—well, maybe #22 with the ameba—I don't get much evidence of the education that's claimed for this gal. And if she has an interest in writing, she doesn't seem to be trying to impress the examiner with her knowledge. (V #1, 33–35) On the basis of that little sample, she's not particularly talkative. Her language is sparse, and task-oriented. Slow they said. I'm asking myself how depressed she is at this point. (F%, F+%, A%, P, Avg Reaction Time) That's not too long. (Additionals, W, D, Dd, S) I didn't think there would be too many. (Z Sum, M, C, CF, FC, Extended F%, Extended F+%) The phrase "brittle" is running through my mind at this point. Let's find out. (F+, F−, Blend #1) She's high in fantasy living, and very incapable of any affective expressiveness. She's highly conventional and stereotyped in her thinking, highly intellectualized. So, the notion of brittleness only comes in relation to fantasy living. (FM, m) These are relatively in keeping with a healthy ratio of M:FM:m. I would say that her defenses included intellectualization, fantasy living, high conformity and conventionality, and withdrawal and social isolation. I wouldn't be surprised if she was a live-in maid, which would be a way for her to try, yet escape. The writing is another distancing factor. (H, Hd) She has that high M. (V #20) There's no explaining of why that's "running in the wrong direction?" There's supposed to be 8M. Looking back over the sequence it does not strike me as an M-ish record, with movement and liveliness pervading the material. I would wonder then if even in her fantasy living her hopes, expressions, and fears would be very much. Thinking about heterosexuality would be threatening for her, also aggression both inner and outer. Proper manners and decorum would be a source of concern for her, if she were out in public or in a social context. Children would bother her. She would be uncomfortable as a nanny, nurse, or surrogate aunt. The physical world would scare her too. She has the old maid syndrome, even though she's not an old maid physically. There's Much anxiety, but it's very diffuse, as contrasted with Severe anxiety in a specific area. Heightening Events would include almost anything that's highly different because it would be threatening to this woman. Any change in her life situation would be threatening. The personal data suggest that she may be making a comeback from an earlier upset.

Answer: Much anxiety, diffuse. *Heightening Events:* heterosexuality, aggression to or from her, children. *Defenses:* intellectualization, withdrawal or social isolation, fantasy living.

| Clinician #2 | Anxiety problem | 76 cards |
| Beck orientation | Interpreted second | 25 minutes |

Well this is the sort of thing I think I'd have to have everything. All right, let's see. A little bit of orientation here. (Sex, Age, Education) Let's see if she's married. (Marital Status) All right, now we know she's anxious. She doesn't want to get married, "What's the matter with me, I don't want to get married." (R, W%, An) Anatomy is supposed to be an indication of anxiety, a certain type, although that's only one type. Let's see if I can establish what her intelligence is. (Z Frequency, Z sum, Affective Ratio, A%) Her anxiety is greater than what would be expected. Now to see what she's afraid of. I usually do a sequence analysis rather than go to the summaries. (F-V #1–8, L #6, Reaction Time Card I) The "body of a child." I assume it's this area here. (F-V #9–12) What was her response time to Card II? (Reaction Time Card II, F-V #13–14) Are responses #13 and 14 the same thing? Each way she looks at it she sees people standing on their head. (L #13–14, F-V #15–16) Big gorilla. (Reaction Time Card IV, VI, F-V #17–18, Sexual History) What's this sexual business? I'm interested. She's scared to death of men, feigning disinterest. (F-V #19–21, Reaction Time Card VII, VIII, F #22, F-V #23–27) Well I think we've got enough to indicate that she probably has more than the normal amount of anxiety. I'm reasonably sure of that. Heightening Events would include anything sexual, anything heterosexual. I'd say it's even broader than that, anything related to problems sexual to the female. Her role as an adult woman. She still feels like a child, especially sexually. As for defenses, I think mostly repression and selective inattention, and probably some belittling. (Occupation, Interests) It would make a difference if she were a maid in a private home or a hotel.

Answer: Much anxiety. *Heightening Events:* anything relating to her role as an adult woman, especially sexual. *Defenses:* selective inattention, repression, "belittling."

| Clinician #8 | Anxiety problem | 80 cards |
| Beck orientation | Interpreted first | 33 minutes |

You're not asking me to pick the minimum number of cards but to approach this the way I usually would approach the Rorschach to answer the referral question. (Sex, Age, Education, Occupation, Marital Status, Sibling Position, Sibling Description, Sexual History, Interests, Mother Description, Father Description, W, D, Dd, S, Approach, Sequence, M, C, Y, YF, FY, F+%, FV, VF, My, An, H, Hd) I'm looking for the indices of anxiety. I heavily use the nature of the interaction between myself and the patient. In the absence of that I'm using the theoretical indices, along with getting a personal picture of the patient. This is like doing a Rorschach "blind." (F-V #1, Number of Responses Card I, F #2, Reaction Time Card I) Anxiety would be influenced a lot by the

Clinician #8—Continued   Anxiety problem   80 cards
Beck orientation   Interpreted first   33 minutes

sequence of the tests, whether or not the Rorschach was the first test administered. (F #3–8, L #7) I want to look at the responses to Card X since there are no color responses, C. I want to see how the patient handled Card X. I have a feeling that she didn't have any color. (Number of Responses Card X, F #29–34, FC, CF) Ah, there is one. I'm trying to get some indication of anxiety and emotional affectivity here. Now I'll shift back to content that might possibly relate to gross ideas that I picked up on Cards I and X. (Anal, Fire, A, Ad) That's 30 of the responses now, with roughly half the cards being A. That means conventionality, stereotypy, and not too much intellect. She has 15 years of education and is a maid. Something else is creating a lot of defensiveness and causing a high A to occur. I need to know more about her than about the anxiety question first. (P, F%) I'm beginning to have a formulation along two lines. One is that this patient has normal or little anxiety on a surface level or, two, conversely, she has a large mass of anxiety that's being held down. I'm leaning toward a more defensive treatment of anxiety, because of the responses on Cards I and X, which don't go along with a 50% A record. I could answer the questions now, but I'm more conservative so I'd like to pull some more cards here. (F−, S-V #2) Since there's some question here of aggression and hostility as well as sex, by the responses on Card I, I'm going to look at Cards IV and VI. (Number of Responses Card IV) Ha. No interest in men, huh? (F #16, Number of Responses Card VI, F #18–19, V-S #18) I'm trying to get a little bit more on her interpersonal relations, so I'll look at Card III. (Number of Responses Card III, F #11–14) Are these, #13–14, the same response repeated? (L #13–14, F-L #15, V #13–14, Avg Reaction Time, Reaction Time Card III, X) OK. There are primarily two defenses here. Also suppression, in view of the long reaction times. For heightening events, there are some fears and concerns about sex, a lot of guilt, maybe about sex. I can't tell you why. And I'm trying to work something in here that doesn't quite fit in, but there's a mixture of regression in some identity problem. Things like seeds, primitive animals, child, puppy dogs, with kind of a little girlish quality. She's an immature person. I might say, in a wild sense, that she might be pregnant, but there's her disinterest in men. But I think there's some identity crisis. I would like information concerning her twenty-first through twenty-fifth years. For example, what's gone on with her writing. There's some creativity here, more elaborate than the A-Ad record. I don't think she's psychotic, but there's a lot of preoccupation with reproduction, phobias, etc. If we assume she's a patient, perhaps something went on of a sexual trauma nature, maybe an employer or the son of an employer. But she's got a real problem with men.

Answer: Much anxiety. *Heightening Events:* fears and concerns about sex, guilt (pregnant?), identity crisis. *Defenses:* intellectualization, isolation, suppression.

Clinician #31   Anxiety problem   37 cards
Beck orientation   Interpreted second   24 minutes

(Sex, Age, Education, Occupation) What, a maid? (Marital Status, R, F%) I
would expect a low F% and it's not that low. My first thought about her, and
it was wrong, was not that she'd be a maid with three years of college. I'm not
assuming that she's a maid at a summer resort, but that this is a stable occupation.
It's hard for me to maintain that she's basically adjusted because of my hospital
work. I thought of hysterical, with the F% quite low, but with C and other
kinds of mixed determinants. Until the F% I wondered "Is she schizophrenic?"
I'm still very much in the air about her. I've got to get a better fix on who she is
before I can tell about her anxiety. (F+%, Extended F+%) She doesn't go to
pot. (A%) Very high. She's not very mature. That should be high. (P) She ought
to have low M. (M) Now I'm in the same spot as before. I have to look at the
actual M. (Number of Responses Card I, F #9–10) There's very little range of
interest. Eight M represent almost one-fourth of her responses, and another one-
half are A. It doesn't leave her much room for anything else. She's interesting.
(Number of Responses Card III, F #11–12) She leaves out the vagina. (F-L #13)
She either has mentally reversed the card or doesn't mean it. I think she's
mentally reversed the card because the hand is extended. (F-L #14) I think she
first mentally reversed it, then turned it. (F-L #15) I would want to specify
anxiety as conscious or unconscious. (Number of Responses Card VII, F
#20–21) She's a very anxious gal. Now, Much or Severe anxiety? "Severe"
should be a decompensating type, markedly decompensating. What do I look
at to make that decision? F+% is OK and extended F+% is even better. For
Severe anxiety the Extended F+% should be lower, if she were on the skids.
I think it's conscious anxiety, much of it is. It's blatant in the content. If I were
to describe her in a report I would say that she acts like a little girl. About the
M, I don't view it in the traditional way as fantasy. I'm not sure she has fantasy
as a resource. If she's got something in the V's it would mean an ability to use
fantasy in a distant-type of retreat manner. Her M's can come on Card IV maybe,
or X, anywhere. (Number of Responses Card IV) Does she see a monster there?
(F #16) Regression is a very broad category, childlike or helpless. (V, VF, FV)
She doesn't have the distancing. (Blend #1) That doesn't leave her with a lot of
resources. "People standing on their heads" while indicating anxiety also involves
people showing off. She may regress and show off in childish ways. So one of the
things that I'm searching for in the M is a retreat to activity of some kind. She's
got to do something. I think I've hit the cards most likely to pull out that sort of
thing; "dancing" is a gay old time. (Affective Ratio, Number of Responses
Card VIII–X) She's not drawn to the color first on Card II, but she is on Card
III. I doubt that she's very active in it. She goes to where the excitement is, but
doesn't participate in it herself.

Answer: Much anxiety. *Heightening Events:* heterosexual contact, being seen as
            personally feminine and attractive, achieving distinction. *Defenses:*
            regression, seeks stimulation, seeks help in the form of dependent
            relationships.

Clinician # 13   Anxiety problem   98 cards
Beck orientation   Interpreted second   20 minutes

(R, F+ %, F%, H, Hd, FC, CF, C, M, W, D, Dd, S, V, T, VF, FV, TF, FT, FY, YF, Y) Doesn't use anything but form. (A, P, Ad, An, Number of Responses Card VIII, F-L # 1, Reaction Time Card I, F-L # 2–9, Reaction Time Card II, V # 8, F-L # 10–11, Reaction Time Card III, F-L # 12–13, 26, Reaction Time Card IX, F-L # 27–28, F # 29, Reaction Time Card X, V # 29, F-L # 22, Reaction Time Card VIII, F-L # 14–16, Reaction Time Card IV, F-L # 17, Reaction Time Card V, F-L # 18, Reaction Time Card VI, F-L # 19–20, Reaction Time Card VII, V # 19–18, F-L-V # 34) Just to make sure of a few things. (Sex, Age, Education, Marital Status, Sexual History)

Answer: Much anxiety. *Heightening Events:* emotional experiences, sexuality, close intimate relations. *Defenses:* fantasy, denial, avoidance of relationships.

Clinician # 6   Anxiety problem   112 cards
Beck orientation   Interpreted third   120 minutes

This question would require going through the whole thing. If the severity of anxiety is the question, then I would start with the reaction times. (Reaction Time Card I–VIII, Rejections, Reaction Time Card IX–X) The behavior must have been disturbed on these last three cards. (Number of Responses Card VII–VIII, F # 22–31) Responses # 29–30 must be identical. (S # 29–30) OK, I see. As far as I'm concerned, two bits of important information relevant to the question are absent, the reaction times to Cards VIII and X. (Sex) I was curious as to whether this was a man or a woman. The responses are ambiguous. Except for the "heads of a doll" I would have guessed it to be a man. But there also are things parasitic and fantasies of pregnancy. The horns of a deer, billy goats, and the scientific aspect of Card X are more masculine than feminine. (Sexual History) The quality of responses to Cards VIII–X led me to become interested in whether the individual was a man or a woman. The responses were confusing, suggesting both masculinity and femininity. When I found that it was a woman I wanted to know the sexual adjustment to see whether she likely was homosexually adjusted or latently homosexually adjusted. There may be failure to achieve heterosexual adjustment. She's a fairly anxious individual. She took 95″ to respond to Card IX. (Age, Education, Occupation) She went to college but is a maid? What's her bag? (Nationality, Marital Status, Sibling Description, Sibling Position, Mother Description, Father Description, Military History, Interests) She's kind of the opposite of what we just had. (F # 1–21, 32–35, S # 1–28, 31–34) Now I'm simply going to read down the free associations for each card and see how the scoring matches up. (L # 29–30) Well I don't wonder that she never graduated from college. I would wonder that she ever

Clinician #6—Continued   Anxiety problem   112 cards
Beck orientation   Interpreted third   120 minutes

got into college. Her intellectual functioning is quite ordinary, quite average. The only intellectual potential that comes through is parasitic, the ameba There's low W and no Z. She's a very immature individual who is really starved for affection and who engages in extremely regressive fantasy, tremendous fantasy. I almost get the impression of her wanting to crawl back into the womb. There's a concern with little things and a preoccupation with heterosexual anxiety, beginning with the little devil with "horns standing up, straight up." Her fantasy to me would have associations with penis included. The devil is not good. On Card IV there's one response, a gorilla. She has curiosity about males but with a great deal of anxiety. On Card I the bat is the conventional popular response. It's easy to give and she takes advantage of the fact that it's easy to give. There also are depressive trends and phobic reactions. The body of a child suggests immaturity. The Mother Goose and the fox both are phallicized and masculinized. The mouse "biting" would strongly support the idea of her affective hunger and frustration of dependent needs. She becomes aggressive in her demands, expressing hostility. Oral aggressivity is very clear on the last response of Card I. The little puppies on Card II is a regressive response, but it's a popular and F+. The color gives her some trouble, but she maintains a good F+%. She recovers a little bit on Card III. Five responses show her to be more productive. (L #11) Notice the anxiety associated with the soft, textured contact. It's wool, but it is blinding the animal. How miserable a person she should be, craving contact but afraid of it. The hands are reaching out, but with no contact. The dolls are small and the heads are drooping, as if they're depressed. She sure begins to sound like a mirror image of the man we just finished. There's lower productivity on Card IV but maintenance of the F+ quality. It's a minimal M, as the man is "sitting" on the stump. (V #3) How was the M on response #3? I wouldn't count it as an M. The experimenter has 3 M but the subject sees only 2 M. On Card V there's only one response but it's F+ and popular. There's some slight increase in productivity on Card VI, but the F+ still is OK. I'm beginning to see what defenses this woman has. Constriction, regressive fantasy that she's indulging in, engaging in vicarious experience, and able to control her anxiety by so doing. Her reality contact is very good, in fact it's almost too good. You can have evidence of inner living without M, you know. If you have associations then you have fantasy. This is a misinterpretation of Rorschach that is very common. M is an enrichment of fantasy life, not merely the presence of it. On Card VII "the rabbits going off in different directions" has some self-reference, as in response #3 on Card I. She sees herself as a small child, confused, while suggesting an underlying preoccupation with sex, especially with adults. Sex is a biological press and one of the pressures of being isolated interpersonally is the frustration of that biological need. The making faces response again is a hostile interpretation reaction. She has difficulties relating constructively interpersonally. The ameba on Card VIII is rather amorphous. The anatomical response indicates anxiety. (L #20) I assume that's correct on Card IX, but hell, let me check Beck's Volume I. Your scoring is sort of severe. If it's truly F—, then it's significant because there's no evidence elsewhere. She's

Clinician # 6—Continued   Anxiety problem   112 cards
Beck orientation   Interpreted third   120 minutes

pathological but not quite that pathological. (L # 22) OK, this makes the record easier to interpret. Card VIII begins another sequence, an F— appearing in a first response to Card VIII indicates color shock. There's such a thing as Rorschach logic. When things go contrary to Rorschach logic, then you have to explain it. Productivity is increased on Card VIII, but the responses remain parsimonious. There's a little increased effort at intellectualizing. There are two populars on Card VIII. On Card X there is the greatest evidence of intellectualization. I mean her verbalizations and concepts—ameba, parasitic, bacterial cells. Suddenly she sounds like a biologist and she's actually a maid. It's erudite. Fortunately she can do this and maintain herself. Wow, she really has become a baby, with little fairies. There are just a couple of things I would like to check in the formal scoring. (F+ %, P) I don't think she had any S. (S) That's right. (RT Chromatic, RT Achromatic) She has color shock, as far as I'm concerned it's an affect shock. She lacks the kind of affect that promotes a relating to others. She can handle self-feeling much better. (Approach, Affective Ratio, M, C, CF, FC) She is just like this other guy. I think I can answer the questions. She has considerable anxiety, but is well-defended against it. It's not severe enough to be disruptive of her defensive armamentarium. She has neurotic defenses, not psychotic defenses. She can get along on a day-to-day basis, can work as a maid, and have a dependent relationship as a maid. It's more personal in a home situation. Now we have an explanation as to why she finds this occupation so acceptable, because it has necessary secondary gains. She fits Berne's idea of being able to relate as a child to adults. She has problems with both sexes but more with males than females.

Answer: Much anxiety. *Heightening Events:* impulses toward or expectations to relate at levels of adult intimacy, threats to dependency needs, heterosexual sex. *Defenses:* constriction of response (withdrawal into fantasy and vicarious experience), reactive hostility, intellectualization.

Clinician # 34   Anxiety problem   85 cards
Klopfer orientation   Interpreted first   53 minutes

(Sex, Age, F%, F+ %, Extended F+ %) I'm assuming that F measures intellectual control. I'm trying to get a picture of what this person's intellectual controls are, and whether there's a breakdown under the influence of color, of which there's no indication. (M, FM, FK+ %, Sum C) That's unexpected. I'm trying to get a picture of the structure of the personality. Also, I'm trying to determine the fewest alternatives. (FK, Fc) I'm working now on the determinants that hypothetically have the most to do with anxiety, the shading responses. (K, k, c, C') That closes out that book. (RT Achromatic, RT Chro-

Clinician #34—Continued	Anxiety problem	85 cards
Klopfer orientation	Interpreted first	53 minutes

matic) There's a time differential of 17″. (F−, 8–9–10%) I would expect this to be rather low. I would like to know the responses scored minus by Beck. (Number of Responses Card I, S-F #1, 9) I'm trying to put some flesh on the content. There are not many anxiety indicators on the surface. What puzzled me was the way this young lady handled color, but not shading. So she responds to the colored areas without using color, and she does not use shading in her percepts. (S-F-V-L #8) I have a hypothesis. I found one of the minuses, on Card I. The breakdown in control may be related to her fears of being pierced in some way, which can have erotic and sexual overtones to it. Perhaps there's some bizarre overconcern with being devoured, but that leaves me with many responses in between which would have to lead up to it. (Number of Responses Card II, S Beck #9, S-F #10, Number of Responses Card III, S-F #11–12, S Beck #12, Number of Responses Card IV, F-V #16, Number of Responses Card VI, F #18–19, V #19, Number of Responses Card VII, F #20–21, V #21, Number of Responses Card VIII, F #22–25, S Beck #22, 24, Number of Responses Card V, IX, F #26–28, V #27, Number of Responses Card X, F #29–35, 2–7, 13–15, 17, V #29–30, 3, S Beck #3, 14) What hangs me up on this is that I can get a notion of the defenses, but is that indicative of the degree of anxiety? In ways, this is an unusual record. There's a concern and preoccupation with small things, children, almost as if this person was very very concerned about mothering. There's some sense of her adequacy as a mother or her maternal role, but also some anxiety connected with her erotic impulses. She doesn't know what to make of the phallic area in sex, she makes it a pole. But let me hazard some guesses. I'm not sure more information would shed any light on it. My judgment is that there is a considerable amount of anxiety, that isn't effected by the usual Rorschach indicators. The question is whether the anxiety is Much or Severe.

Answer: Much anxiety. *Heightening Events:* pregnancy and/or maternal role, heterosexual relationships (husband, boyfriend, father), situations in which there is affective stimulation. *Defenses:* intellectualization, denial, fantasy which borders on the bizarre.

Clinician #5	Anxiety problem	154 cards
Klopfer orientation	Interpreted first	45 minutes

(F-S-V #1) We'll certainly need more than that. (F-S-V #2) I don't have any hunches yet. (F-S-V #3) This is fairly prosaic, except for the devil. It's a little early to be seeing devils, a little unusual. (L #3, F-L-S-V #4–5) This person has some sort of a penchant for unusual things or different things. (F-S-L #6) Where's the face? Another edge detail. That's crummy. (F-S-V-L #7) Must be

the two laterals. There's idiosyncratic thinking going on here. (F-S-V-L #8)
More morbidity is creeping in. The location is more arbitrary, cut. (F-S-V #9)
The atypicality of this suggests some seeming sickness. The verbalizations are
more important here than the formal scoring characteristics. (F-S-V-L #10)
There's somewhat of a recovery here on card II. (F-S-V #11) After a rather
poor beginning this person is back to better things. (F-S-V-L #12) It would have
been useful to find out more about that. It's atypical. (F-S-L-V #13) It's just
plain damned peculiar again. It's scored as popular I guess because of the
people in it, but it's sure unpopular. (F-S-V #14–15, L #14) That must be the
lateral reds. It's a little unusual to describe them as dolls. It's dysphoric. It's
a little confabulatory to put heads of people on dolls. (F-S-V #16) Now we're
on Card IV. It's funny that this person had such a poor first card, seemingly
anyway. It's looking more reasonably healthy. (F-S-V #17–18, L #18) Ah
we're on Card VI. (F-S-L #19, F-S-V #20) Rabbit? What is that? (Age, Sex,
Marital Status, Sibling Position, F-S-V #21) People making faces at each other.
That's a charming female response. (F-S-V #22) Crummy again. (F-S-V #23)
Bears are popular. (F-S-V-L #24) Sometimes the color does diminish. This
response is so-so, with a certain arbitrariness. (F-S-V-L #25–26) Just the tops?
I would have thought the whole thing. (F-S-V-L #27–29) It's a little unusual
again, idiosyncratic, but with control. She didn't mention spermatazoa or any-
thing like that. (F-S-V #30–34, L #31–33, F #35) We've run out. (Avg Reaction
Time, RT Achromatic, RT Chromatic, F%, Extended F%, A%, P, Sum C,
8–9–10%, Additionals, Rejections) I don't particularly have any use for the
Rejections. (H, Hd, A, Ad, At) There are very few At. (AAt, Sex, Succession,
D, d, W, Dd, S) There are 22 out of 35 D's and darn few W's. The S is question-
able. (Education, Occupation) That doesn't make sense at all, a maid? (Mother
Description, Father Description, Sexual History, Sibling Description) I can't
find out anything there. She's probably a little too infantile to be able to stand
relationships. There you are. I don't think I need the rest. It would falsify or
distort the process to have this fragmentation all the time. Usually you have the
Rorschach all in front of you and you can go back and forth. It's too hard to
keep this in your head. This person's a strange creature. There's a lot of anxiety,
but she handles it by dissociation and repression. There's a certain amount of
compulsivity here too. She's probably settled into existence as a maid. That
reduces stimulation greatly for her and she can handle it. She has kind of a
schizoid way of looking at things. Abritrary and idiosyncratic. The ordinary
anxiety indicators don't appear at all.

Answer: Much anxiety. *Heightening Events:* sexual stimulation, close human
contact. *Defenses:* partial dissociation, repression, denial, compulsivity.

Clinician #4   Anxiety problem   46 cards
Klopfer orientation   Interpreted third   20 minutes

First I would want to see how the man starts here, and I would want to see what he's doing. Ordinarily if I had a Rorschach in front of me I'd run through all of the information. (Number of Responses Card I, F-V #1–5) I'm going to review these Card I responses again just to get the number again. (F #6–8) There's no quick way to score this. (Number of Responses Card III, F #9–12, V #12, Number of Responses Card VI, F-V #18–19) Actually my approach to the Rorschach has been completely impressionistic. If you have the age and education you fairly well have it with intelligence estimation. (Number of Responses Card VIII, IV, F #22–23, 16, V #16, Number of Responses Card VII, F # 20–21, V #20, 23, 22) At this point I can make the decision that this is a fairly anxious person, but I'll be cautious here. Were I working with a person I would supplement the data. The Rorschach wouldn't be the important test. (Number of Responses Card X) I have a feeling again that this is a male. I'm going to check that out. (Sex) No. (F #29–30) She repeated this. (Age, Marital Status) I predicted both of these. I thought she would be between 24 and 28 years of age. (Religion, Sexual History) This is what I would have predicted. (F #31) OK, I've had it on this one. Much anxiety would be my estimate. I have an impression here that a single unmarried woman probably has a real fear of sexual stress, possibly with some defensive tendency to turn toward women, but also a defense against that. Immediate stimuli giving rise to anxiety would be sexual intercourse and pregnancy.

Answer: Much anxiety. *Heightening Events:* human socialization, sex, pregnancy. *Defenses:* denial, rationalization, repression, isolation from social contacts.

Clinician #17   Anxiety problem   45 cards
Klopfer orientation   Interpreted third   7 minutes

(Sex, Age, Education, Occupation, Nationality, F #1–3, L #2–4, F #4–14, L #13–14, F #15–35) Heightening events would be outside stimuli. The primary defense would be regression.

Answer: Much anxiety. *Heightening Events:* heterosexual contacts, actual or fantasied, and/or sexual impulses. *Defenses:* regression, denial, distortion.

Clinician # 15   Anxiety problem   46 cards
Beck orientation   Interpreted first   33 minutes

I should start out getting some identifying data. (Sex, Age, Marital Status, Education, R) Now I'm looking for the Experience Balance. (M, Sum C) That's a surprise. No color responses, the total absence of color. (V, Y, T) There are no responses that are undiluted or unmodified by any aspect of F with it. (F%, F+%) I don't think she rejected any. (Rejections, Affective Ratio, Approach, A%, P) I have some feeling I can answer this part here regarding the severity of anxiety, and some of the defenses, but not the heightening events. I think she's probably between Normal and Much anxiety. Defenses go in the direction of intellectualization. There's overattention to the obvious, which is not a defense in Freud's terms. There's a little trend toward stereotypy of thinking. There's certainly a choking off, repression or suppression, of the expression of affect. "Heightening Events" is a little out of my element, unless it comes through sequence analysis. I might get some hints from content. (H, An, Cl) OK. (F-V #1, F-L #2, F-L-V #3) How did you get at the scoring? That's such a deviant response for a girl that carries herself so well usually. This "blind analysis" is used only for a training device. (Number of Responses Card II) I want to see if with the first red there is something like color shock. (F-V-S #9) That certainly doesn't indicate it. (Reaction Time Card I–II, Number of Responses Card IV, VI, VIII, S #16) Then I'm not so curious about that Card VI anymore, with only two responses. Let's see what she did in specific responses to the first chromatic card. (F #22) That's not so hot. Does she recover? (F #23–24) Yes, she does. (L #24) She falls down again. (F-L #25) She has a problem in the area of sexuality. (Sexual History) That doesn't surprise me. (Occupation) That's a surprise. (Interests)

Answer: Much anxiety. *Heightening Events:* emotional stimulation, probably in relation to sex. *Defenses:* intellectualization, overattention to the obvious with a trend to stereotypy in her thinking, choking off of expression of affect.

Clinician # 30   Anxiety problem   96 cards
Beck orientation   Interpreted second   24 minutes

(Sex, Age, Education, Sexual History, Marital Status, R, A%, F+%, Avg Reaction Time, RT Achromatic, RT Chromatic, Rejections, M, C, CF, FC, Y, YF, FY, F-V-S #1–3, Number of Responses Card I) Let's see what happened. (F-V-S #4–6, W, D, Affective Ratio, Sequence, Approach, F-V-S #7–8, Number of Responses Card II, F-V-S #9–10, Number of Responses Card IV, F-V-S #16, Number of Responses Card VI, F-V-S #18–19, Number of Responses Card IX, F-V-S #26–28, Number of Responses Card VII, F-V-S #20–21, Number of Responses Card X) The Affective Ratio is .62, yet there are no

Clinician #30—Continued   Anxiety problem   96 cards
Beck orientation   Interpreted second   24 minutes

color responses. (H, Hd, An, Fi, Anal, Cl, T, V, FV, FT, P) The number of M responses and a deliberate avoidance of color as a determinant created a first impression in my mind of this person being afraid of emotionally arousing situations. She's aroused but defends against it. Then, in her verbalizations, some cards would be disturbing to her—the male figure and sexual stimulation. She responded peculiarly with laughter, long response times, and gave only a few P's. But on those cards she failed to give the popular response, e.g., on the sex card, Card VI. She was getting away from the stimuli, as though she was forgetting what she was doing. She has to be reminded. That would be a way of coping with the feelings aroused by the stimuli and suggests a kind of escape or inhibition. She made a denial type of approach. She wasn't using color as a determinant yet she was responding to the color cards more than to the black and white ones. It's indicative of a repressive trend. There were fairly frequent qualifications of responses also, the "looks like . . . could be . . . this or that." It suggests that compulsivity could be a defense against disturbing feelings. I expected Y responses, but this didn't come out. But there was no color either.

Answer: Much anxiety. *Heightening Events:* relationships to the male figure, stimuli having sexual significance, aggression expressions (hers or others'). *Defenses:* denial, repression, compulsivity.

Clinician #24   Anxiety problem   60 cards
Beck orientation   Interpreted first   29 minutes

(Sex, Age) I need to know the sex and age of the patient, in order to know dynamically the developmental level of the individual. (R) And R because an extreme anxiety would have few responses. (F+%, Extended F+%) If this is a highly anxious person who was constricting you'd get a high F+%, but this is a fairly more relaxed individual. Things don't have to be accurate, yet they are within relatively normal limits. (Avg Reaction Time) This gives me a clue that there is some blocking, so one of my first hunches is either repression or depression. (RT Achromatic, RT Chromatic) It's color that's the longer reaction time. So it's not a depressive reaction time, but more within the neurotic range. (F%) It's 74, indicating an individual who is not that constricted, as the R of 34 suggests. (W, D, Dd) I'm interested in whether this is an obsessive person. (Sum C Klopfer) I would underline repression. (FK+% Klopfer) There's only 9% shading. (m) I sometimes use Klopfer's scores. (Y, YF, FY) Well, I'm getting a picture of some anxiety, but I don't know how much. (F #1–3) I choose Card I to start with because it's an initial exposure to a new and ambiguous task, and what does the individual do with it. I'm getting some suggestion of a great deal of superego anxiety. The little devil. She feels like a little

Clinician #24—Continued   Anxiety problem   60 cards
Beck orientation   Interpreted first   29 minutes

child who feels very much bound by parental restriction. The m means motoric anxiety. (F–L #4–5) This looks like an obsessive-compulsive record to me. I may find other things later, but. . . . All these faces. She's an intellectually striving girl who's producing just to produce, just to impress somebody. (F #6–8) I don't think the location is too essential to know. She keeps going on. Eight of her responses are on the first card. There's a combination of the wish to impress and the first impact is that she is anxious to impress. What is finally elicited is the anxiety over aggressivity, as in response #8 with the biting. (F #9–10) Her response to an ambiguous situation is to be aggressive. She can't control it and it breaks through. She manages to bind the aggression on this Card II. (F #11–14, L #12) I'm laboring between Much and Severe anxiety at this point. She delays the people until the third response. (F-L #15) She recovers on Card III. She was bowled over by the emotionality on Card II, but she recovered on Card III. (F #16–19, L #19) There are some phobic features about this card. I was thinking about a mixed neurosis, but it's more obsessive. (F #20–34, L #21, 24, 27) She had no color. I'm centering on the defenses now. Repression is indicated because of the long reaction times. Intellectualization and isolation because of the number of responses and the empty types of faces. Isolation because of the carving out of areas and the lack of affect. Displacement because of the gorilla, in the phobic sense. Regression because of the bears, dolls, hidden faces. Avoidance because of "something blinding it." Somatization because of the backbone on Card VIII. Although it's a common response, it might be an outlet for her. The reason I don't say Severe Anxiety is that this woman's defenses are binding. The one way she is in trouble is that she does not use color. She's attracted to it, but blocks. The anxiety is not Severe because the defenses seem to be operating. She holds herself aloof and isolated from experience.

Answer: Much anxiety. *Heightening Events:* affective stimulation, ambiguity, anger, sexuality, superego pressure. *Defenses:* repression, intellectualization, isolation, displacement (phobic).

Clinician #9   Anxiety problem   83 cards
Beck orientation   Interpreted first   21 minutes

I have to know what the Rorschach is like. I have to start with the number of responses and go right down here, in order to know what the face sheet would look like. (R, F%, F+%, Rejections, M, C, CF, FC) The order really is of no importance to me. (Y, YF, FY, T, TF, FT, V, VF, FV, F+, F−, F$_0$, Blend #1, W, D, Dd, S, A%, P, H, Hd, A, Ad, An) OK, 34 responses and I now have 31, so I don't have to bother going further. (8–9–10%) I have no real information at this point. I'm going to go now card-by-card. (Number of Responses Card I,

Clinician #9—Continued   Anxiety problem   83 cards
Beck orientation   Interpreted first   21 minutes

F #1–8, V #3, Sex, Age, Marital Status, Sexual History) I'm only picking this up because it sounds good. (Interests, Number of Responses Card II, F #9–10, Number of Responses Card III, F #11–15, Number of Responses Card IV, F # 16, Number of Responses Card V, F #17, Number of Responses Card VI, F #18–19, Number of Responses Card VII, F #20–21, Number of Responses Card VIII, F #22–25, Number of Responses Card IX, F #26–34, Extended F+%) There's at least Much anxiety. Adult heterosexual encounters—a whole complex of things—would be heightening events, the idea of pregnancy, not just screwing but the whole business. Also, any kind of awareness of feelings that are intrapsychic. Her defenses are of a little girl, a dependent orientation, and isolation from feelings.

Answer: Much anxiety. *Heightening Events:* adult heterosexual encounters, pregnancy, awareness of feelings. *Defenses:* little girl dependent orientation, isolation from feelings, refraining from closeness, i.e., all relationships are spotty, conventional, and sweet but no real investment.

Clinician #16   Anxiety problem   75 cards
Beck orientation   Interpreted second   13 minutes

(W, D, Dd, M, C, CF, FC, Y, YF, FY, V, VF, FV, T, TF, FT, F+, F−, F$_0$, Blend #1, An, Hd, Fi, Fd) None of the traditional things that indicate anxiety are present. (RT Achromatic, RT Chromatic, Rejections, A%, P, F+%, R, 8–9–10%, H, A, Ad, F #1–8, V #8, F #9–16, L #13–14) Is this the same response? (F #17–20, V #20, F #21–31, V #29–30, F #32–34)

Answer: Much anxiety. *Heightening Events:* pain as in illness, physical assault, criticism, erotic stimulation, feelings of inadequacy. *Defenses:* denial of affect, ego constriction.

Clinician #18   Anxiety problem   60 cards
Klopfer orientation   Interpreted first   48 minutes

(F-V-S #1, 13) That's a lucky one. (F-S-V #31) I don't have any anxiety indicators yet, except I don't like this one here on Card III. (m, Fc, F-V #20, A) There are a lot of A's. (H, Hd) I want the white space card. (S) He's got two upside down responses and upside down people and rabbits moving the wrong way, which I don't like. I want to see his populars. There shouldn't be too many.

Clinician # 18—Continued   Anxiety problem   60 cards
Klopfer orientation   Interpreted first   48 minutes

(P) The M's should be high. (M, FK, FC, CF) I don't think this guy has much anxiety. (K, C', F) There are no Originals available here. (W, D, R, d) There's no dd available either. (Dd) I want to see how mature he is. (FM, Rejections) I usually go by anxiety on the basis of K and FK. There are no K, no C', no Fc. (c) No c. Those would be my anxiety indicators apart from the content. Fm would indicate a certain amount of inner tension and a need for personality transformation, and it's a quiet one. There's nothing violent or explosive. This guy has a certain amount of passivity. He likes people to carry him along. He wants his dependency needs met from people. On the basis of that I'd put down Little Anxiety. He's a bright guy. Humans are upside down and rabbits are running away. Yet I get no S. You'd think he'd be more oppositional. He likes to look on both sides of the coin. (Fire) I should have got that from the lack of C. I'll look at this for anxiety. (At) The Art shouldn't be much because he doesn't have much color. (Art, k) There's nothing on phobic responses. He has less anxiety than the average individual. It's hard for him to have warm adient feelings. He's interested in things rather than people. There's not too much overcontrol, but too little, the d's. He's not compulsive. He sees broad principles but beyond that he handles things in a comfortable way. He's not a creative scientist but would be a good worker at a high level. He intellectualizes, in terms of the things he plays with. I'm not bothering with the percentages. (F #21) Again, there's avoidance of people, social events, cocktail parties, social engagements. He's not capable of warm relationships. He likes to read and study, he likes solitude. (Sex) That certainly ruins it for me since I've been calling him "he." (Age, Education) She should be single. (Marital Status) Her occupation would be a student. I gave no thought to sex. Now with the avoidance of art and color I would change the thing to Much Anxiety. But she's terrific in defending against it. (Sibling Position, Father Description, Mother Description, Sexual History) I went into that already. I think I said there was trouble in the sexual area. But at the moment she's quite buffered. (Religion, Occupation) The anxiety is not expressed in the Rorschach scores. She is handling her anxiety. She's very much at home with things that are unrelated to people, mathematics and the scientific. She's constantly questioning reality as it's ordinarily seen. She's using the null hypothesis all the time. I ordinarily look at the actual responses, but I've got so many good things here already. (F #29) Now, I said the guy would be interested in the physical sciences. (F #37, 30, 23, Number of Responses Card III–IV, VIII) There are more responses given on the human card, but not too many more. I would revise my concept. This guy would have normal responses, maybe more. (Number of Responses Card V) There is only one response here too. I'm beginning to revise my hypothesis. There are a lot of problems adjusting to male authority. (Number of Responses Card VI–VII, IX–X) This guy has had trouble with male authority. He's trying to get away from human relationships, to things around him, where there is no emotional involvement. Let's see if we get out the authority problem. It's immobilized, so he has a very calm facade. His defenses lie in his interests. He immerses himself in a world of science. He defends through an avoidance of people. There's a certain amount of immaturity.

Answer: Much anxiety. *Heightening Events:* encounters with male authority, encounters involving emotional relations, social engagements. *Defenses:* intellectualization, immersion in work, solitude for reading.

| Clinician #33 | Anxiety problem | 24 cards |
| Klopfer orientation | Interpreted first | 23 minutes |

(Age, Sex) I need to get a feel for this person. I will take one of her responses and behavioral observations, to see what this person is like. (F-V #1, F%, m, F #2, Number of Responses Card I, F #9–10, Number of Responses Card II, F #11–13, L #12–13) Was this seen right side up I wonder? I'm beginning to wonder how well this girl is functioning. Is she a passive or inadequate person who is frightened? My next thought is how well she had functioned with regard to education and marriage. (Education, Marital Status) She didn't make it through college, which doesn't surprise me. It backs up the hypothesis that this girl isn't functioning too well. I get a picture of a child who's inadequate or emotionally unstable and who's really threatened by what's around her. She's not developed enough to have sexual problems. (Sexual History) Yeah, that backs up what I just said. It could mean a lot of things. Homosexuality I dismiss because I don't think she's developed enough. I can make a pretty good guess at this point. How sure do you want me to be? No one has "No Anxiety," and where do you draw the line for Normal? The anxiety is not so overwhelming that she ceases to function entirely, but that she is handicapped. I think I could make some good guesses at this point. Have I really ruled out homosexuality, though? (A%) That's pretty high. It strengthens my feeling about infantilism. I wonder just how much this anxiety interfered with her functioning. Did she reject any of the Cards? (Rejections) No, she didn't. So that strengthens my feeling of Much Anxiety. (R) That's not bad. (F+%) No, I just don't think that homosexuality is any problem. She's still too small of a child. (Occupation) That doesn't change my mind. I'm still bugged by the homosexuality idea. There's pressure. She may be putting herself in a situation that she could not control or handle well. If she can get through three years of college there must be something there. But she's over-qualified for a maid, and she's under-working. There's not much expected of her, intellectually and emotionally, that would make her feel uncomfortable. She leans on people.

Answer: Much anxiety. *Heightening Events:* stress with regard to adult responsibilities, close emotional relationships, situations which she feels not qualified to deal with or control. *Defenses:* withdrawal, reducing stress by putting herself in positions or situations which she does feel she has some control over or in which not too much will be asked of her, leaning on other people.

Clinician #22   Anxiety problem   45 cards
Beck orientation   Interpreted second   14 minutes

(R, H, Hd, A, Ad) I'm trying to see how few cards I would need to answer the question. (An, Anal, Fi, F+%, F%, Rejections, S #1, F #1–8, S-V #8, F #9–14, L #13–14, F #15–28, V #27) I can stop now. The big problem is transactions with other people. People arouse anxiety. Part of it is their unpredictability. And apparently they're a danger as he perceives it. And his own aggressive impulses and feeling of inadequacy. Repression certainly is one defense. I'd like to take another look at some of this. I've got several that I'm not too sure of at the moment. Isolation is another defense. I think there's present in this person something on the order of denial, but more like a minimization. It's not so much to deny but to reduce the significance of the experience, the impact of the experience.

Answer: Much anxiety. *Heightening Events:* transactions with others (unpredictability as a danger), own aggression and feelings of inadequacy, uncertainty. *Defenses:* repression, isolation, minimization.

Clinician #1   Anxiety problem   62 cards
Beck orientation   Interpreted second   10 minutes

(Sex, Age, Occupation, Y, YF, FY, Hd, Ad, R, Extended F+%, Extended F%, V #1–3, F #1–34) She's very concerned about children, pregnancy, sex, that sort of thing. And this gorilla! (M, C, CF, FC) I need these for the M:Sum C ratio. (Marital Status, Sexual History, T, TF, FT, V, VF, FV, P) It's a very odd sort of thing, not one of the shading determinants appears in the record. I wonder if Klopfer has something about it. (C′)

Answer: Normal anxiety. *Heightening Events:* fears of men, sex, pregnancy and childbirth. *Defenses:* denial or negation, reversal in fantasy, intellectualization.

Clinician #28   Anxiety problem   47 cards
Beck orientation   Interpreted third   41 minutes

(R, F+%, Y, YF, FY, Approach, F%, FC, Blend #1, CF, C, M, Extended F+%, F #1–7, V #2) There are a lot of young type responses. I wonder how old a person this is? (Age, F #8–32) On anxiety I certainly was hung-up. This seems like a disturbed person, but maybe not an overtly anxious person. It would be

Clinician #28—Continued   Anxiety problem   47 cards
Beck orientation   Interpreted third   41 minutes

more of a withdrawn individual who in a fairly protected situation just doesn't manifest anxiety unless there are demands made upon him. So I tried to find a middle ground, but I don't feel very comfortable about that. The Rorschach determinants had a lot to do with my thinking here. This is a withdrawn person, with the M and minimal color sensitivity. The childish content of the responses was another factor, suggesting a kind of infantile mind. Someone who was less comfortable with the world maybe and more dwelling in fantasy. This type of person would not be so vulnerable to an ongoing anxious state.

Answer: Normal anxiety. *Heightening Events:* another person attempting to establish a relationship with the subject, pressing the subject to meet adult demands and responsibilities, taking away one of the subject's personal possessions. *Defenses:* withdrawal with refusal to communicate, preoccupation with fantasy, delusional constructs.

Clinician #10   Anxiety problem   55 cards
Klopfer orientation   Interpreted third   29 minutes

The questions are getting harder and harder. I'll pull the whole psychogram, to get the full picture. (R, M, F, C', K, k, P, A%, At, Hd, Ad, H, A, FM, CF, FC, C, FK, Fc, c) Do you want anxiety that's observable or bound? (Age, Marital Status, Education, Occupation) Maid, so I know it's female. (Mother Description, Father Description, Sexual History) She has little interest in anything. She hasn't got any anxiety. There's a heck of a lot of M. She internalizes very well. She's very inhibited and repressed, with no spontaneity. There's no outward indication of much of anything. Certainly there's no reaction to color, which would make people a heightening event. OK let's take a color card, to see how she handles that. (Number of Responses Card X, F #29) And she's working as a maid? (F #30–33) Well she responds all right. I wonder what her comments are. (V #29) Some view this as the father card, a dependency card. (Number of Responses Card IV, F #16, Number of Responses Card VI, F #18–19) She didn't even pick up the bear skin at all. I know what Card VII is. Let's see what she does with the mother card. (F #20–22, Number of Responses Card III, F #11, F-L #12–13) Is this card turned? (Sibling Position, Sex content) She doesn't have any sex responses. (F-L #10, F #9–8, S #31) That's the only m response.

Answer: Little anxiety. *Heightening Events:* contact with others, sexuality, authority-dependency relations, her own aggressive feelings. *Defenses:* repression, intellectualization, constriction, avoidance.

| Clinician # 3 | Anxiety problem | 95 cards |
| Beck orientation | Interpreted first | 40 minutes |

The thing is that I'm so accustomed to scoring the whole thing that I would need all of the information. I'll go down the whole thing. Well let's see how the thing first hit him. (F #1) Hm, that's exciting, but not really. Let's see what else he did on Card I. (F #2–6) Boy he spent a lot of time on Card I. (F #7–8) Card I still. What the hell is going on here? (F #9) Ah, so he starts out with populars and then goes wild. What happens after this? (F #10–14) And again people standing on their heads. (S #13–14) This is P? And this he turned upside down? (S #1) What kind of a bat was that? It's a W, just as I thought. Was he self-conscious about the bat? (V #2–3, 7, m) Where's this m from? (YF, Y, FY, T, TF, FT, V, VF, FV, Blend #1–3) No V? Well . . . and no blends. There's a suspicious man for you. I kind of begin to get the idea that there may not be very much subjective anxiety. (M, C, CF, FC, S #11) Where is that FC? Nope, I guessed wrong. (W, D, Dd, S) Now what should I want to know about his anxiety? This is an inhibited kind of schizoid individual. (FM) Ha, at least he's got some FM. (Age, Sex) It's about time I wanted to know that. What a dumb thing to overlook. (Marital Status, Sexual History) Well that goes with the lack of texture. What makes this girl anxious? (F-S #15) Let's find out what else she saw. Her productivity sure drops. It looks like she's suppressed her interest in affection. (S #16–18) I've got no shading whatsoever. (F #16, 19–21) However, we've got a big gorilla, sitting on a stump. The M is all in humans, and not very active. Is there anything more on Card VI? Let's see what heightens her anxiety, if anything does. I get the impression that probably females in authority might heighten it. She defends by inhibition and fantasy. (A%) Aha, it's high. There's anxiety all right. (P) That's it. (F+ %) This is kind of low for somebody with 56% A. (Extended F%, Anal) Oh you're randomizing. You stuck me with that. (F-S #22) I've got to find the m. She's got a weak ego you know, but it's defended pretty well. (F #23–25) She's sure obsessed with kiddies isn't she? (F #26–27, S #27) Where are the populars? (F #28–30, S #29) She repeats herself, unless these are not the whole thing. (F-S #31) All this science, and that's her FC. (F #32–35) That's it. I didn't find the m, did I? I suppose it's the seeds carried away by the wind. (S #31 Klopfer) Well I think she's afraid of men. I would put that before females in authority. Of course her defense is avoidance of men. But what's the significance of these people always standing on their head? (FC Klopfer, Affective Ratio) So she's kind of stimulated by social situations but she doesn't let her feelings out. (Occupation) Well I'll be damned, and I said she was made anxious by females in authority. Do I stick with that? (Nationality) Nothing of significance. (Z Sum) This is rather average. She's not off too badly in her intelligence. She's certainly not ambitious with only 4W and 8M. (Sibling Position, Sibling Description, Mother Description, Father Description, Interests, Religion, Military History, Education) Oh she's had some college. Well I found out all the personal data I could, looking at everything. I'm still bothered by the people standing on their heads percept. Does she think she's better than the people she works for? (V #34) Nothing much here. Well she's afraid of open spaces, like being downtown in a crowd. It says she's a maid, but it doesn't say to whom. That question is pretty important. (RT Achromatic, RT Chromatic) There's slowness

Clinician #3—Continued   Anxiety problem   95 cards
Beck orientation   Interpreted first   40 minutes

on color. (Additionals) Naturally there are none. She got by once so why the hell
should she add some others. And her religion's not known. Well I think her anxiety is Little as she goes about her business. I think it's heightened by closeness
to men, by crowds to some extent, and by social gatherings. I didn't leave anything for this authority idea, the making faces at each other. She didn't know her
mother. So we have for her defenses fantasy, inhibition of emotion, avoidance of
intimate proximity of men, and I think denial.

Answer: Little anxiety. *Heightening Events:* closeness to men, crowds, social
gatherings. *Defenses:* fantasy compensation, inhibition of emotion,
avoidance of intimate proximity to men, denial.

Clinician #12   Anxiety problem   116 cards
Beck orientation   Interpreted second   26 minutes

(Sex, Age, Education, Occupation) It's fascinating to see her as age 26, with three
years of college and a maid. Something is haywire. (Nationality, Religion, Marital History, Sibling Position, Sibling Description, Mother Description, Father
Description, Sexual History, Military History, Interests) She's interested in writing, which is ridiculous. Anybody with three years of college and working as a
maid must be deteriorating rapidly. I want to look at the Experience Balance
first. (M, R, C, CF, FC, Blend #1) OK, the M:C is 8:1. Since we're talking about
anxiety, you'd expect to have some Y's. (Y, YF, FY, T, TF, FT, V, VF, FV) No
T's? No V's? (F+, F−, F₀, Approach, W, D, Dd, S, Sequence, Affective Ratio,
Z Sum) At this point, judging from the M and Z, there's good intellect, and
F+%. It's surprising in terms of her working as a maid. (F+%, Extended F%,
F%, Extended F+%, A%, P, H, Hd, A, Ad, Na, Oj, My, Hh, Ge, Fi, Fd, Cl,
Bt, Ay, Art, Ar, Anal, An, Number of Responses Card I–X, RT Achromatic,
RT Chromatic) I don't think a lot of anxiety is shown in terms of the Rorschach.
The anxiety is relatively bound. (S #9–10 Klopfer, F #9–10) There are problems
in terms of relationships with people. She jumps down from eight to two responses and there are no M's on Card II. A problem in relation to people, again
with three years of college and her ending up as a maid. She's a pretty sick gal.
(V #9–10) There's not only a diminution of the number of responses but a blocking in reaction time. (S-F-V #11–12, S-F #13–15) I think this gal is psychotic,
with the edging and disturbance on Cards II and III. So this is where the M's
come. Maybe she isn't psychotic. I would have scored this as M but as a different
type of M. It's a childish M. (V #13–16) On Card I she takes off and gives a
number of responses. On Card II she gets thrown by color as well as people. On
III there's recovery but a regressed recovery, a different type of M from the

Clinician #12—Continued   Anxiety problem   116 cards
Beck orientation   Interpreted second   26 minutes

healthy. On Card IV she comes back down with one response. With Card IV you'd expect problems with the father. (S-F #16) Aha, a very "threatening" figure. So, this is a little disturbing. You'd wonder about the father, where he comes into the picture. (S-F-V #17, Reaction Time Card V) She does recover here. No, she doesn't have much anxiety. You can expect problems with sex. (S-F-V #18–19) You don't find her aware of her anxiety, of her problems in relationship to people. She makes people a nonthreat by making them dolls. This is an aggressive type of response, making them into dolls. (S-F-V #20–21) This is probably something you'd find in somebody ten years younger than she is. There's a regression. Women are unsafe too. People are unsafe. There are some compulsive-constricted defenses.

Answer: Little anxiety. *Heightening Events:* relationships to people, particularly men. *Defenses:* constriction, regression, compulsivity.

Clinician #20   Anxiety problem   43 cards
Klopfer orientation   Interpreted first   28 minutes

(Sex) Females have higher anxiety. (Age) Is she married? If not, then her anxiety's high. (Marital Status) She's not, so she's anxious. If she's approaching age 26 then she might be anxious about getting married. I'm trying to locate her demographically. Then I'll go to a few things on the Rorschach that will answer my specific questions. (Education) She dropped out before she completed. (Occupation) A maid? That's a high class maid, also an ambulatory schizophrenic. (Interests) Let's go to her interests. Maybe that'll pin her down. Introspective, with pretensions. A well-educated maid who likes to write. That's a heck of a case. (Nationality) Might be important. (Religion, Sibling Position, Mother Description, Father Description, Sexual History) Let's find out how anxious she is, with the shading. (R) She can't be too anxious, with obsessive defenses. Of course she is intelligent, but 34 responses is too many. (FK + %) 65? Oh, it includes F. (F%) About the only other thing I want to know is the M's. I doubt if she has any C. (M, FM, m) She sure does sound like a color responder, but let's see. (FC, CF, C) She's not very anxious, manifestly. She's tight. We know, statistically, that anxiety drives the number of Rorschach responses down. What's the shading ratio? There are defenses of constriction. I'll bet those aren't very good M's. Seven M's, she just can't be an obsessive-compulsive. One of the heightening events has got to be sex. I'll bet that her step-mother's a son of a gun. This girl went back to child care. This format doesn't lend itself to zeroing in on the richness, e.g., the M's. From that daydreaming she's likely to be a masturbater. I'll bet she's got authority problems with mother. (F-V #1, F-V-L #2–4) That's unusual. The verbalizations and behavioral observations are turning out to be useless. That's

| Clinician #20—Continued | Anxiety problem | 43 cards |
| Klopfer orientation | Interpreted first | 28 minutes |

kind of bad form in response #4. I should have done this before, going back to F+%. (F+%, F-V-L #5, F-L #6–8) Are you sure you scored this right? F+? There are three minuses on Card I. (F #9) Now we're on Card II. Card I certainly conveyed an extreme amount of information in clarifying this person. She's able to see things conventionally. She's childish. Mother Goose is a phallic stepmother, then the attacking of the body.

Answer: Little anxiety. *Heightening Events:* sexual stimuli from others, other peoples' angry responses to her rebelliousness, dominating mother figures. *Defenses:* maintaining distance from others (from constriction to formality, nonemotionality), daydreaming, regression and identification with the children with whom she works.

THE CASE OF ADOLESCENT GIRL

Rorschach Interpretation by R. Bochner and F. Halpern*

In this record the numerical results show no outstanding discrepancies when compared with expectancy for a normal adolescent of high average to superior intelligence. The number of responses, thirty-seven, corresponds to accepted standards, shows freedom of association, lack of inhibition, and a general cooperativeness of spirit combined with interest in the test procedure.

The relationship of W to D is weighted on the side of the W but this is to be expected in a person of her intelligence and drive. The rare details fall within normal limits, and since they never come as first responses to a plate and are not characteristic of her approach, acquire significance from their content and not from their numerical frequency (11%).

The total number of form responses (51%) falls just at the limits of the postulated normal frequency. In other words, she does not stress the intellectual and controlled outlook to the constriction of affective living. The Experience Range is ambiequal, the ratio of M:C being 4M:3½C. The potentialities expressed in the FM + m:C' + c ratio show a slight bent toward introversion. The subject says she feels it wiser to be one of a crowd, to make contacts, rather than to lead a withdrawn though possibly more intense and creative life. This suggests that her 3½C are in part at least consciously determined.

As evidenced by the chiaroscuro responses, this girl has definite anxiety, but this is not all of the vague, free-floating kind. Rather she has given her disturbance specificity. Two of her K's are combined with M, which suggests that she is using her disturbance as a springboard to creativity. The attitude, which is a typical adolescent one, is that true art will come from her suffering. Her FM and m are numerically slightly more frequent than the M, showing undeveloped and misconceived abilities. This argues for her relative immaturity. That her abilities are misconceived is substantiated by the fact that her drive is greater than her ability, witness the W to M ratio. She is capable of good emotional adjustment (FC), but her moodiness (K) and her impulsive outbursts (CF) preclude consistently good adjustment to others. She is probably not too easy to live with, particularly since her moodiness may take a depressive turn (FC').

The contents show the wide variety of interests common to an alert and not too mature adolescent.

Her relationship with people has apparently not been a happy one, and although she is able to make good contact this disappears when the adults in question are those with whom she has an emotional tie. This probably explains her excessive delay (24″) on Card III followed by the interpretation of skeletons. It is evident that this is not because she cannot complete the gestalt since she does so immediately following, but because of emotional blocking. The second response, an interpretation of women in a very domestic role, leads to the suspicion

*R. Bochner and F. Halpern, 1942, pp. 125–127.

that the maladjustment is primarily in relation to a family member, probably her mother.

On Card VI, by her introductory comment, she shows some sex shock but this should not be over-weighted since it is natural for an adolescent to have some embarrassment and lack of sophistication on sexual matters.

Although in a more mature person the degree of color shock shown here might be considered significant of poor adjustment, in this girl it only reflects adolescent unsureness.

Answer form presented to clinicians at beginning of Intelligence interpretation.

Question: Estimate the present *level of intellectual functioning* of this individual, on the basis of the Rorschach data available.

As soon as you feel quite sure of the estimated intellectual level, check one of the three intellectual levels below and write your own more specific clinical impression.

Below Average   _____
Average (90–109)   _____
Above Average   _____

Specific Clinical Impression _____

INTELLIGENCE

Listing of cards available for selection (*Items*) by clinicians and information contained on reverse side of cards (*Information*) for the Intelligence question. (Refer to Chapter 5 for detailed explanation of method used for presenting information to clinicians.)

Personal Data

Items	*Information*
Sex	Female
Age	17 years
Education	12 years
Occupation	Unemployed. Plans to look for job.
Nationality	Irish
Religion	Roman Catholic
Marital Status	Single
Sibling Position	½
Siblings	Sister is submissive type. Adores mother. Plans to be a nun.
Mother	S not get along with mother. S has lived with grandmother.
Father	Says little.
Sexual	Too many friends, male and female. No deep ones. No affairs. Doesn't give marriage a thought. Supposes marriage someday.
Military	
Interests	Theatrical ambitions.

Locations—Klopfer

W	W = 13
D	D = 21
d	d = 0
Dd	Dd = 3
S	S = +2
W%	W% = 35 (expect 20–30%)
D%	D% = 57 (expect 45–55%)
d%	d% = 0 (expect 5–15%)
Dd + S %	Dd + S % = 8 (expect <10%) + 2S
Succession	Succession = orderly

Locations—Beck

W	W = 10
D	D = 23
Dd	Dd = 4
S	S = +2
Approach	Approach = W! (D) Dd
Sequence	Sequence = irregular
Aff. ratio	Aff. ratio = .61
Z freq.	Z freq. = 18
Z Sum	Z Sum = 49.0

Determinants—Klopfer

Items	Information
M	M = 3 + 1
FM	FM = 1
m	m = 3 + 1
k	k = 0
K	K = 4
FK	FK = 0
F	F = 19
Fc	Fc = 0
c	c = 1
C'	C' = 2
FC	FC = 2
CF	CF = 2
C	C = + 1

Content—Klopfer

Items	Information
H	H = 5
Hd	Hd = 1
A	A = 11
Ad	Ad = 4
At	At = 0
AAt	AAt = 0
Art	Art = 0
Chapel	Chapel = 1
Cl	Cl = 2
Dust	Dust = 1
Fd	Fd = 2
Fire	Fire = 1
Light	Light = +1
Na	Na = 0
Obj	Obj = 6 + 1
Pl	Pl = 2
Prison	Prison = 1

Determinants—Beck

M	M = 3
C	C = 0
CF	CF = 2
FC	FC = 2
Y	Y = 0
YF	YF = 0
FY	FY = 2 (1−)
T	T = 0
TF	TF = 0
FT	FT = 0
V	V = 0
VF	VF = 3 (1−)
FV	FV = 0
F+	F+ = 18
F−	F− = 5
F_0	F_0 = 0
Double	Double = V·M+
Double	Double = TF·C+
Double	Double = 0

Content—Beck

H	H = 4
Hd	Hd = 1
A	A = 11
Ad	Ad = 4
An	An = 1
Ar	Ar = 3
Art	Art = 2
Bt	Bt = 2 + 1
Cl	Cl = 2
Fd	Fd = 2
Fi	Fi = 1
Hh	Hh = 1
My	My = +1
Na	Na = 2 +1
Oj	Oj = 1
Prison	Prison = +1
Rc	Rc = +1
Rl	Rl = +1

Totals and Percentages—Klopfer Summaries

Items	*Information*
R	R = 37
Avg RT	Avg RT = 15″
RT Achrom	RT Achrom = 13″
RT Chrom	RT Chrom = 18″
F%	F% = 51
FK + F + Fc %	FK + F + Fc % = 51
A%	A% = 41
P	P = 4 (10 possible)
Sum C	Sum C = 3
VIII–IX–X %	VIII–IX–X % = 38
Additional Responses	Additional Responses = 0
Rejections	Rejections = 0

Totals and Percentages—Beck Summaries

R	R = 37
F%	F% = 62
Ext.F%	Ext.F% = 81
F+%	F+% = 78
Ext.F+%	Ext.F+% = 80
A%	A% = 41
P	P = 7 (21 possible)
Avg RT	Avg RT = 15″
RT Achrom	RT Achrom = 13″
RT Chrom	RT Chrom = 18″
Additional Responses	Additional Responses = 0
Rejections	Rejections = 0

Number of Responses to Each Card

Card I.	Card I.	4	(#1–#4)
Card II.	Card II.	4	(#5–#8)
Card III.	Card III.	2	(#9–#10)
Card IV.	Card IV.	3	(#11–#13)
Card V.	Card V.	3	(#14–#16)
Card VI.	Card VI.	4	(#17–#20)
Card VII.	Card VII.	3	(#21–#23)
Card VIII.	Card VIII.	4	(#24–#27)
Card IX.	Card IX.	4	(#28–#31)
Card X.	Card X.	6	(#32–#37)

Reaction Times to Each Card

Items	*Information*	
Card I.	Card I.	2″
Card II.	Card II.	6″
Card III.	Card III.	24″
Card IV.	Card IV.	16″
Card V.	Card V.	27″
Card VI.	Card VI.	13″
Card VII.	Card VII.	5″
Card VIII.	Card VIII.	18″
Card IX.	Card IX.	25″
Card X.	Card X.	18″

Individual Response Scorings—Klopfer

# 1	# 1 Card I.	W	F	A
# 2	# 2 Card I.	W	KF	Cl
# 3	# 3 Card I.	W	F A	P
# 4	# 4 Card I.	W,s	KF,m	Pl,Light
# 5	# 5 Card II.	W	CF	Fire
# 6	# 6 Card II.	W	FC	Obj
# 7	# 7 Card II.	W	M	H
# 8	# 8 Card II.	W	FM	A
# 9	# 9 Card III.	W	F (H)	P
#10	#10 Card III.	W	M H	P
#11	#11 Card IV.	D	F	Obj
#12	#12 Card IV.	W	FC′	A
#13	#13 Card IV.	W	KF	Cl
#14	#14 Card V.	D	F	(H)
#15	#15 Card V.	W	Fm	Dust O
#16	#16 Card V.	D	F	Fd
#17	#17 Card VI.	D	F	Obj
#18	#18 Card VI.	D	F	A
#19	#19 Card VI.	dr	Fm	Chapel O
#20	#20 Card VI.	dr	FC′	Prison O
#21	#21 Card VII.	D	M	(Hd)
#22	#22 Card VII.	D	K,M	H,Obj
#23	#23 Card VII.	D	F	Ad
#24	#24 Card VIII.	D	F	A P
#25	#25 Card VIII.	D	cF,C	Obj
#26	#26 Card VIII.	D	FC	Pl
#27	#27 Card VIII.	D	CF	Fd
#28	#28 Card IX.	D	Fm	Obj
#29	#29 Card IX.	D,s	F	Obj
#30	#30 Card IX.	D	F	Ad
#31	#31 Card IX.	D	F	A
#32	#32 Card X.	D	F	Ad
#33	#33 Card X.	dr	F	Ad O

Individual Response Scorings—Klopfer—Continued

Items		*Information*		
#34	#34 Card X.	D	F	A
#35	#35 Card X.	D	F	A
#36	#36 Card X.	D	F	A
#37	#37 Card X.	D	F	A

Individual Response Scorings—Beck

# 1	# 1 Card I.	W	F+	A	1.0
# 2	# 2 Card I.	W	VF+	Cl	1.0
# 3	# 3 Card I.	W	F+	A P	1.0
# 4	# 4 Card I.	Ws	VF−	Bt,Na	3.5
# 5	# 5 Card II.	W	CF+	Fi	4.5
# 6	# 6 Card II.	W	FC+	Art	4.5
# 7	# 7 Card II.	W	M+	H P	4.5
# 8	# 8 Card II.	D	F−	A	
# 9	# 9 Card III.	D	F−	An	
#10	#10 Card III.	D	M+	H P	3.0
#11	#11 Card IV.	D	F+	Art	
#12	#12 Card IV.	W	FY+	A	2.0
#13	#13 Card IV.	W	VF+	Cl	2.0
#14	#14 Card V.	D	F+	H,Rc	
#15	#15 Card V.	W	F+	Na	1.0
#16	#16 Card V.	D	F+	Fd P	
#17	#17 Card VI.	D	F+	Na	
#18	#18 Card VI.	D	F+	A	
#19	#19 Card VI.	Dd	F−	Ar,Rl	2.5
#20	#20 Card VI.	Dd	FY−	Ar,Prison	
#21	#21 Card VII.	D	M+	Hd,My P	3.0
#22	#22 Card VII.	D	V·M+	H,Bt	1.0
#23	#23 Card VII.	D	F+	Ad	
#24	#24 Card VIII.	D	F+	A	
#25	#25 Card VIII.	D	TF·C+	Hh	
#26	#26 Card VIII.	D	FC+	Bt P	
#27	#27 Card VIII.	D	CF+	Fd	3.0
#28	#28 Card IX.	D	F+	Ar	
#29	#29 Card IX.	Dds	F+	Oj	5.0
#30	#30 Card IX.	D	F+	Ad	
#31	#31 Card IX.	D	F−	A	2.5
#32	#32 Card X.	D	F+	Ad	4.0
#33	#33 Card X.	Dd	F+	Ad	
#34	#34 Card X.	D	F+	A	
#35	#35 Card X.	D	F+	A P	
#36	#36 Card X.	D	F+	A	
#37	#37 Card X.	D	F−	A	

Free Associations

Items		*Information*
# 1	# 1 Card I.	Eagle. (Wide spread of wings.)
# 2	# 2 Card I.	Clouds. (Odd shape. Uneven spread.)
# 3	# 3 Card I.	Bat.
# 4	# 4 Card I.	Section of tree. Sunlight through it. (Foliage. Sun coming through holes.)
# 5	# 5 Card II.	Smoke and fire. (Coloring. Like burning building.)
# 6	# 6 Card II.	Surrealist painting.
# 7	# 7 Card II.	Men. Without their heads. (Helmets. Coats blowing.)
# 8	# 8 Card II.	Polar bears. Standing on their hands.
# 9	# 9 Card III.	Skeleton.
#10	#10 Card III.	Women. On windy day. With basket of clothes.
#11	#11 Card IV.	Petty drawing. (Slim girl.)
#12	#12 Card IV.	Dragon. (Shape. Color. Dark.)
#13	#13 Card IV.	Storm cloud.
#14	#14 Card V.	One of the Seven Dwarfs. (Shape.)
#15	#15 Card V.	Dust cloud. From back of car. (Dust cloud goes up and settles down in this shape.)
#16	#16 Card V.	Leg of lamb. (After its cooked.)
#17	#17 Card VI.	Icebergs. (Down the center. Goes to point at top.)
#18	#18 Card VI.	Odd bird. (Shape.)
#19	#19 Card VI.	Entrance to chapel. Flicker of light.
#20	#20 Card VI.	Prison wall. (Drab.)
#21	#21 Card VII.	Devils. Making faces at each other. (Horn.)
#22	#22 Card VII.	In distance. Somebody walking. Between two hedges.
#23	#23 Card VII.	Rabbits' heads.
#24	#24 Card VIII.	Cats.
#25	#25 Card VIII.	Beautifully blue satin pillows. (Nice and shiny.)
#26	#26 Card VIII.	Pine tree. (Shape. Color.)
#27	#27 Card VIII.	Delicious orange and strawberry sundaes. (Color mainly.)
#28	#28 Card IX.	Fountain. (Sprays out.)
#29	#29 Card IX.	Door. With things to see through. To see who's outside.
#30	#30 Card IX.	Animal's faces.
#31	#31 Card IX.	Row of turkeys. (Shape.)
#32	#32 Card X.	Animal's face. Big long something coming out.
#33	#33 Card X.	Horses' head.
#34	#34 Card X.	Octopuses. (Shape.)
#35	#35 Card X.	Dogs. (Shape.)
#36	#36 Card X.	Angry looking creatures. (Shape.)
#37	#37 Card X.	Crocodiles. (Shape.)

Location Areas

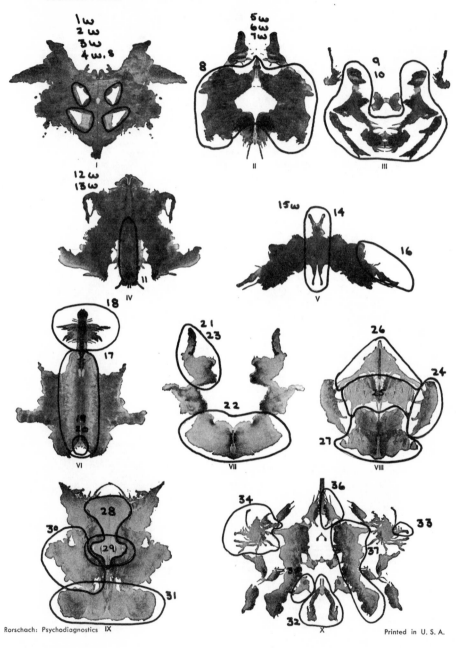

Verbalizations and Behavioral Observations

Items	Information

Items		*Information*
# 1	# 1 Card I.	
# 2	# 2 Card I.	
# 3	# 3 Card I.	
# 4	# 4 Card I.	Looks like_____. Should I see something else?
# 5	# 5 Card II.	
# 6	# 6 Card II.	Could be_____. Could I say it? They all could be that.
# 7	# 7 Card II.	I saw it in a daze.
# 8	# 8 Card II.	
# 9	# 9 Card III.	
#10	#10 Card III.	
#11	#11 Card IV.	Reminds me of_____. I could say it about all of them.
#12	#12 Card IV.	
#13	#13 Card IV.	
#14	#14 Card V.	I could take part of it.
#15	#15 Card V.	
#16	#16 Card V.	
#17	#17 Card VI.	This is awful. My imagination will have to go wild_____, I suppose.
#18	#18 Card VI.	Looks like_____.
#19	#19 Card VI.	
#20	#20 Card VI.	
#21	#21 Card VII.	(*Laughs.*) Looks like_____.
#22	#22 Card VII.	Looks like_____. You could never see this. This is something I alone can see.
#23	#23 Card VII.	
#24	#24 Card VIII.	Suppose we call it_____.
#25	#25 Card VIII.	
#26	#26 Card VIII.	
#27	#27 Card VIII.	
#28	#28 Card IX.	
#29	#29 Card IX.	
#30	#30 Card IX.	
#31	#31 Card IX.	
#32	#32 Card X.	Hmm, saving this for the end.
#33	#33 Card X.	
#34	#34 Card X.	It's field day for animals.
#35	#35 Card X.	
#36	#36 Card X.	
#37	#37 Card X.	_____, shall we say for a conclusion.

Clinician #34   Intelligence problem   39 cards
Klopfer orientation   Interpreted second   11 minutes

(Sex, Age) I'll first pick out the usual indicators of intellectual level. (R, A%, F+%, Extended F+%, M, W, D, d, Dd, Succession, Avg Reaction Time, P, m, Z Frequency, Z Sum) I wanted to get some idea of the cognitive processes, and then some specific responses to the cards. (Number of Responses Card III, F-V #9–10) Card IX is a difficult card. (Number of Responses Card IX, F #28–31, 1, V #28–29, F%, Extended F%) Now I want to see if there are some W responses to Card X. (Number of Responses Card X, S #32–37)

Answer: Average intelligence. IQ = 95.

Clinician #1   Intelligence problem   74 cards
Beck orientation   Interpreted third   14 minutes

(Sex, Age, Education, Occupation, Interests, W, R) There's no information about original responses. (M, Approach, Z Sum, S, Dd, Extended F+%, Extended F%, F #1–37) I just want to get a sampling of the way she talks. (V #9–17, 21–23, 25–27, 2–3, C, CF, FC, Art, Sexual History, Sequence)

Answer: Average intelligence. IQ = 90–109. Her thinking is relatively childlike, superficial. She is probably on the impressionable side and given to a certain amount of unrealistic thinking. Outgoing and impulsive.

Clinician #22   Intelligence problem   48 cards
Beck orientation   Interpreted third   9 minutes

(R, F%, Extended F%, F+%, Rejections, W, Z Sum, D, Approach, Sequence, M, C) I wish I knew where the different cards were represented. (H, A, Art, My, Na, F #1–29, L #11, V #6) This guy is kinda pretentious. He could give the impression of being pretentious. "Surrealist" suggested that the intelligence could be a little more than it turns out to be. Response #4 caught my eye, the way it was organized. The IQ probably is somewhere above 100, but leave it that way.

Answer: Average intelligence. High average. IQ = 105 ±3.

Note: Material contained within parentheses refers to the actual data card selections made by the clinician in obtaining Rorschach information item-by-item. Abbreviations are listed and defined in Appendix A.

Clinician # 6	Intelligence problem	112 cards
Beck orientation	Interpreted first	51 minutes

The first thing I want to find out is something about the person taking the test, so I'll probably go right down here. There's no sense in doing the interpretation in vacuo. (Sex, Age, Education, Occupation, Nationality, Religion, Marital Status, Sibling Description, Sibling Position) In other words, she's the oldest. (Mother Description, Father Description, Sexual History, Military History, Interests, F # 1–6, Reaction Time Card I–II, F # 7–10, Reaction Time Card III, F # 11–14, Reaction Time Card IV–V) As far as I'm concerned the most important part of the Rorschach is the sequence of the free associations. Card-by-card analysis is the way I learned it. (F # 15–20, Reaction Time Card VI, F # 21–24, Reaction Time Card VII–VIII) The reaction time is one of the most important pieces of Rorschach information, but not the amount of time taken per card. In addition to the reaction time, the number of responses per card also is important. (F # 25–30, Reaction Time Card IX–X, F # 31–37) I assume that's all. Now what I'm doing is reading the responses again. I want to read the responses in terms of their card groupings. Ordinarily I would be looking at two things at once, scoring and locations. I would look at the location first and then the scoring. (S # 1–2) What contributed to the vista? I don't see any information for the vista response either in the free association or the inquiry. (S # 3, V # 2, S # 4) Also, I don't see any particular evidence for the vista on Card IV either. I see S but not the vista. (S # 5–8) Also on Card II, response # 7, I see no evidence for M. There's m but no M. Well let's take a look. (V # 7) Hm, "I saw it in a daze." For response # 8, Card II, there might be support for M here. Bears don't have hands but humans do. It's anthropomorphic. Beck doesn't use an FM but he does often score an M for human movement in animals. Many people in the Chicago area follow this approach. The reason I'm concerned about it is that it's a minus, if the hands are down in this section. Let me refer to Beck's Volume I. (S # 9–10) For an intelligence estimate I would say in general that I've ruled out the fact that she's Below Average, because of the quality of responses. On Card II there's the surrealist painting which automatically rules out Below Average. On Card IV there's the Petty drawing of a slim girl. Evidently this Rorschach was given some time ago. That response would rule out a below average person. She's at least 100 in IQ. Primarily I'm going on the basis of vocabulary. An average person wouldn't use the term "foliage" either. So now the decision is whether essentially she is Average or 110 or better. The use of the Rorschach for intelligence estimation is quite different than for answering other questions. The quality of vocabulary is important, the complexity of concepts, then the formalization of the free association, how it matches. (S # 11–13) If there are a lot of emblems or multiple determinants then these are above average. Then would come the ratios, the W:M rating for example. (S # 14–16) What I suspect is that the person who scored this wasn't familiar with Beck. (S # 17–27) If I were to take a short cut, then I'd go to the formulations. It's just a course of habit. When one scores a Rorschach one usually has the whole record. OK, here's something else, "An entrance to a chapel." This is not a below normal kind of conceptualization. Also she says "beautifully blue satin pillows . . . delicious orange and strawberry sundae" on Card VIII. Primarily it's the verbalizations and vocabulary, then the organization of responses and the use of determinants. Regarding the scoring, I'm sad to say that the "beautifully blue satin pillow" is not a correct Beck scoring. The color is the thing that's emphasized, more than the texture. The "shiny" is not a texture determinant but a light determinant. It's a "Y" response according to Beck. The scoring errors in the Beck here would not interfere in answering the question about intellectual functioning of the patient. (S #28–31) And another thing is that because of the way the data is arranged here it's taking longer to arrive at an interpretation. (S #32–37) Now I want to quickly run down the locations in general, in terms of W, D, Dd. I notice that there are quite a lot of W on Card I and Card II. Card II is difficult to integrate W-wise. The men without heads while a pathological response is good for intellectual level. It's better than the smoke and fire or surrealist painting responses. Card III is extremely hard to integrate and she does not integrate it, which isn't against her. On Card VI there is no W probably because it's a little threatening, some form of anxiety. Card VII for the same reason, nor IX nor X. It is interesting that her last W was on Card V. She doesn't have a single W after that. I'm trying to determine whether the slough off of W is due to anxiety or the level of intellectual functioning. I rather think it is the anxiety. Something which is often an indication of pathology is that the further along the less W. Three-quarters of her W came on Cards II–V. The more she's exposed to the test, the more anxious she becomes. But in terms of the basic question this pattern is not due to her lack of basic capacity. Now what I'd like to do is uh. . . . (Additionals, M, Blend #1–3) The blends would depend on the scoring accuracy. (W, Approach, Z Sum, F+, F−, F₀, F+ %) I don't usually score Z. I don't consider it that important actually. Well OK. I think I can answer the question now. I must specify that I'm talking about capacity and functioning separately.

Answer: Average intelligence. IQ = 105. Potential IQ = 120.

(R, F+ %, M, F #1–4, V #1, Education, Occupation, F #5–6, F-V #7–9, 25, 28, F #30, 34, 23, 22) There's nothing to suggest a Below Average kind of person. The R is pretty good, the F+ is not too poor. The high school graduation confirmed someone who was at least average. The language of the responses on the other hand suggested nothing that was especially intellectual. From the language I would place the intelligence around Average. I would use vocabulary as the basis, without anything very impressive there.

Answer: Average intelligence. IQ = 106.

Clinician # 18   Intelligence problem   31 cards
Klopfer orientation   Interpreted third   18 minutes

I wish I had Halpern's textbook for this one. (Sex, Age, M, F, H, R, P, A, FM, W) Do you have the W:D information? (W%, D, D%, d, Dd, FC, 8–9–10%, Education) You don't have any combinatory W's. Where human movement is involved I like more W information, like on Card I with the dancing around the maypole. I rely heavily on that. The M's are not enough for 37 responses. There are too many D's and not enough W's. (Sexual History) This is a typical high school kid, average or nearly average in IQ. There are too many populars too. (F, #17, 10) That's not too bad. It's even sexually normal. (F #26, 34) Those aren't too bad either. (Number of Responses Card X, F #32, 37, Number of Responses Card III, F #9, Number of Responses Card VII, F #21, 23) I don't see anything extraordinary.

Answer: Average intelligence. IQ = 105–109.

Clinician # 33   Intelligence problem   30 cards
Klopfer orientation   Interpreted third   6 minutes

(Sex, Age, Education) A high school graduate at age 17. That puts her at least Average in intelligence. (F+ %, R, F%, Number of Responses Card I, F #1, 5, V #1–4, Number of Responses Card II, F #9–10, Number of Responses Card III, F #11) This is a man named Petty. (F #12–13, Number of Responses Card IV, F #14–15, W%) The toughest card is IX. Let's see what she did. (Number of Responses Card IX, F #28–32)

Answer: Average intelligence. IQ = 107.

Clinician # 16   Intelligence problem   59 cards
Beck orientation   Interpreted third   8 minutes

(R, F+ %, M, V, VF, FV, Z Frequency, Z Sum, W, D, Dd, C, CF, FC, Sex, Age, Education, Occupation, Nationality, Interests, F #1–37, Religion, Marital Status)

Answer: Average intelligence. IQ = 109.

Clinician #10   Intelligence problem   24 cards
Klopfer orientation   Interpreted second   10 minutes

(Education, Occupation) It doesn't make a difference if the person is unemployed. (Age, Sex, W, R, Succession, D) Let's see, how else can we estimate intelligence? Intellectual level. (Extended F+ %, P, M, FM, F%, A%) Where are the Originals? (Avg Reaction Time) Well I better get some quality of the response. (Number of Responses Card III, F-L #9, F #10) That's pretty good. Let's take another one, where she can show some ingenuity. Card IX's a hard one. (Number of Responses Card IX, F #28–31) Is this the row of turkeys down here?

Answer: Above Average intelligence. IQ = 110.

Clinician #25   Intelligence problem   151 cards
Klopfer orientation   Interpreted second   26 minutes

(Sex, Age, Education, Nationality, R, F-V #1, F #2, L #1, V-L #2, F-V-L #3–11) "Petty" refers to the man who took those pictures? (F-V-L #12–27) That's the obvious location. (F-V-L #28–37, M, FM, m, k, K, FK, F, Fc, c, C', FC, CF, C, Avg Reaction Time, RT Achromatic, RT Chromatic, F%, FK+%, H, Hd, A, Ad, A%, P, Sum C, 8–9–10%, W, D, d, Dd, S, W%, D%, Dd+S%, Succession) She's functioning within the bright normal range of intelligence. The form quality of the record, subjectively, would be relatively high. There are few departures from good form and there are a large number of W's made with apparent ease. She has a fair number of M's, for her. The content is not stereotyped, rather there's a variety. There's been no scoring for originals, but I would have scored one or two as original. Response #4 would be at least an additional original and response #19 would be original. There are two main reasons why she's not functioning near her potential. First, she has difficulty elaborating her responses. She could give more but can't. Second, there's a relatively large amount of free floating anxiety. She's a girl who has relatively severe psychoneurotic problems. Hysterical components are suggested. There are relatively severe problems in her percepts of male sexuality. Obsessive components are suggested as well. She's in need of treatment, but would have difficulty relating. I would say that her potential is superior, around 130.

Answer: Above Average intelligence. IQ = 110–119. Functioning is at the Bright Normal range of intelligence, with significantly higher intellectual potential which is hampered by neurotic problems and easily elicited anxiety.

| Clinician # 3 | Intelligence problem | 74 cards |
| Beck orientation | Interpreted second | 25 minutes |

(Age, Education) I don't think I'm going to use all of these personal data cards. (W, D, Dd, S) Here you want the level of functioning and not the potential intelligence. (M) This suggests overstriving. (Z Frequency) Not uncommon for that age. (Blends #1–3) How the hell are you scoring this? Also that "Prison" content. What are these, tricks? (P, F+ %) That's all right. (A %) Well so far so good. I would say that he might be Above Average. What else do I need to know? (S #31–32) He's not giving any color here. (S #33–37) He really recoups. I think this kid has been disturbed. (F #32) I doubt this 4.0. (S #30) Another F+ Ad. (S #31, 29, F #29) There's an object, but poor. You know what you don't have here? The Experience Balance. (S-F #28–27) Well he's oral. (RT Achromatic, RT Chromatic) There's nothing there. (m) I'm thinking about anxiety here. (FM, Prison) What the hell kind of a response is this? (Sexual History, Interests, S-F #26) Bt, tree, green tree, with very weak color. (C, CF, FC) I still haven't seen all the color yet, have I? (S #1–5) Aha. (S #6–7, F #6) And there's the P. (S #8–10, F-V #10, S Klopfer #10) The wind, and I was tricked on that scoring. (S-F #25) That's not scored right, sorry. (F %) He leans toward some acting out, but probably is not that aggressive. I've got a lot of things here. (Reaction Time Card II–III) That's fast, and he's got a homosexual conflict. (F #17–10, L #14) A member of the seven dwarfs is cousin to a fairy. He's a resistance guy, in some ways. I don't have to find out if he's a homosexual or not, really. He's above average, but not much. From the looks of it his creativity has originality, his use of his intelligence has gone down within the past few years. I'm saying that primarily because of the sequence. By the time he gets to Card X he's not doing much. (A, Ad) Three of the four Ad are on the last card. He's probably not a homosexual although his sexual identity sure isn't the clearest. Out of all that Z, a big chunk of it is on Card II. I'm not real good at estimating intelligence from the Rorschach but I would say that this guy has had a potential of 120 ± 5 and that his functioning is at the 110–115 level right now. I probably could have reached this conclusion earlier. (Reaction Time Card X) He had something of a comedown, his functioning has constricted probably related to his concern over his identity. I'd guess that that's a little longer, too. (Reaction Time Card IX) Thank you. There's delayed neurotic shock, anxiety, regressive tendencies, which are other reasons to suspect that it has gone down a little bit.

Answer: Above Average. IQ = 110–115, functioning lately. Potential IQ = 120 ± 5.

| Clinician # 29 | Intelligence problem | 5 cards |
| Beck orientation | Interpreted first | 5 minutes |

(Education, Interests, R, W, M)

Answer: Above Average intelligence. IQ = 110–115.

Clinician #13   Intelligence problem   14 cards
Beck orientation   Interpreted third   3 minutes

(R, Z Frequency, Z Sum, Sex, Age, Education, W, M, A, H, Art, FV, F%, Avg Reaction Time)

Answer: Above Average intelligence. IQ = 115 ± 5.

Clinician #2   Intelligence problem   12 cards
Beck orientation   Interpreted first   10 minutes

The first thing I'd want is the age and education. (Education, Age, Sex, Occupation) These are all I think I have to have. You don't have the total? (R) Already she's just Above Average. (M) Three M, that's pretty good. (Z Sum, F+%, A%) Oh it looks like a pretty bright gal. Let's take this. (W) The W is 10. Thus far my best guess is that she's slightly Above Average. What degree of confidence do you want? You're never quite sure. I'll put it in terms of percentages, 70% odds would be good I suppose. (Affective Ratio, Z Frequency) I'll say she's Above Average. I would say 115, plus or minus 5.

Answer: Above Average intelligence. IQ = 115 ± 5.

Clinician #17   Intelligence problem   16 cards
Klopfer orientation   Interpreted first   10 minutes

(Sex, Age, Education, Occupation, Nationality, W, R, M, Sum C, D, Dd, F #1–5) This is the actual verbalization, "foliage, sun coming through the trees?" There's a high number of responses, even though it's somewhat constricted—3 M—in terms of affect. And the use of just the term "foliage." It indicates a person probably Above Average. If I went further I'd find her probably higher than my estimate.

Answer: Above Average intelligence. IQ = 115 or above.

Clinician #12	Intelligence problem	87 cards
Beck orientation	Interpreted first	13 minutes

I don't want to use the Education item. It's not Rorschach data. (R, F+ %, Extended F+ %, Extended F%, F%, Approach, Z Sum, Sequence, W, D, Dd, S, M, F+, F−, F₀, Klopfer contents Na, Obj, Pl, Prison, Light, Art, Chapel, Cl, Dust, Fd, AAt, H, Hd, Rejections, Additionals, P, Number of Responses Card I–X, S-F-V #28–37, F #5–7, S-V #7) I would disagree with the scoring there. There's not enough movement for M. (S-F-V #8, 10–11, S #9) OK. I can make a judgment about that.

Answer: Above Average intelligence. IQ = 115.

Clinician #8	Intelligence problem	36 cards
Beck orientation	Interpreted third	10 minutes

(Education, Age, Sex, Occupation) I'm going to look for some formal scores, to see what the ego is doing. (W, R, F+ %, A, Ad, M, Dd) I would tend to be surprised, although it's early yet, if this girl is very much Below Average. What I want to get now is a little bit of the quality, some idea as to how she expresses herself, her verbalizations. (Number of Responses Card I, F #1–4, L #4) The "eagle" is pretty good. "Sunlight coming through the tree" is pretty good too. That's a pretty good response. I like that. Although there's a little anxiety in this gal. Let's see how she expresses that. Yeah, she's a little insecure. (FY, YF, Y, Additionals) Her F+ % is 78. I don't need to know her F+ and F−. (Number of responses Card X) That's a fair number. (F #32–37) Not as good as I thought, but "octopuses" is pretty good. (L #34, 36, Z Sum) I want to see what she does with a stereotyped card. (Number of Responses Card V, F #14–16, L #14)

Answer: Above Average intelligence. IQ = 115.

Clinician #26	Intelligence problem	28 cards
Klopfer orientation	Interpreted second	17 minutes

(Age, Sex, R, M, FM, H, Hd, A, Ad, Sum C, W, D, Extended F+ %, 8–9–10%, F #1–4) The problem to clear up here is whether this is a gal of Above Average functioning which is impaired or of Average intelligence who is over-extending herself. (F #5, P, F #6, F%, F+ %, S #4, Education, Number of Responses Card III, F #9–10) I don't use the Rorschach too much for intellectual level.

Clinician #26—Continued   Intelligence problem   28 cards
Klopfer orientation   Interpreted second   17 minutes

I'm taking into account the W which is fairly high. The M and C are not high, but she is not unduly constricted. The P is reasonably good. F+ is good. The content of the cards shows a little more than the usual imagination. R is high, but there are some pretty vague responses that might inflate the R. There's some inhibition here also. And, she's a high school graduate. So you would anticipate at least Average ability.

Answer: Above Average intelligence. IQ = 115.

Clinician #27   Intelligence problem   14 cards
Klopfer orientation   Interpreted third   7 minutes

I never use the Rorschach for intelligence estimation. Let's take a look at the M's. (M, R) There are so many responses. These probably are all college kids, not psychiatric cases at all. (W) Either she's overstriving or she's pretty damn bright. The 13 W is almost absurd. To tell you the truth, I doubt if I can estimate any closer, but I'm going to look at the responses. (F #1–5) That one looks all right. It's pretty nice. (V #1–3) He's up tight, doesn't say a word. (Number of Responses Card III, F #9–10) It's best not to get too much information. This one is not consistent with the other response, it's confusing because she doesn't verbalize. I wonder what her education is, but you want only the Rorschach data to be used. You don't believe that people can rate IQ, do you? It couldn't be much higher than 115. Important here are the M, W, R, and then response #4 which is kind of nice. But then you see response #9 and think she's not above average at all. So I just ignored that. And then you look at response #10 and she integrates that OK.

Answer: Above Average intelligence. IQ = 115.

Clinician #23   Intelligence problem   5 cards
Beck orientation   Interpreted first   2 minutes

(Z Sum, W, M, VF, CF)

Answer: Above Average intelligence. IQ = 115–122.

Clinician # 11   Intelligence problem   105 cards
Beck orientation   Interpreted first   17 minutes

The intelligence question is the worst one to try to do for a Rorschach. One of the problems has to do with the type of intelligence you're looking for. (Z Frequency, Z Sum) My memory's hazy but I would say that 49 is pretty good. I'd want a fairly big overview for IQ. (W, D, Dd, S, Approach, Sequence, Affective Ratio) This really has no meaning for me. Now I'm trying to get at the breadth of areas of interest. (H, Hd, A, Ad, An, Ar, Art, Bt, Cl, Fd, Fi, Hh, My, Na, Oj, Prison, Rc, Rl, V-F #1, Education, Occupation, Military History, Interests, F #2–4) Simple addition tells me that there are 37 responses. (F #5–37) I'm sure I'm forming other hypotheses at the same time. (V #2–37) She's bright normal or something. Well, some time ago I decided that her intelligence was Above Average. Now as far as zeroing in, you want as tight a range as I would feel comfortable making, right?

Answer: Above Average intelligence. IQ = 115–120.

Clinician # 32   Intelligence problem   78 cards
Beck orientation   Interpreted first   18 minutes

(Sex, Age, Education, Occupation, Nationality) I wanted to see if she was English-speaking. She must be Catholic. (Mother Description, Father Description) I was looking for information on their education. (R, Z Sum) I would want to know the qualitative forms of the responses. (Number of Responses Card I, F-V #1) That's W. (F-S #2–3) I would consider that W and P. (F-S #4, Number of Responses Card II, F-S #5–6, F-L-S #7, F-S #8–9, L #9, F #10–11, S #11, Number of Responses Card III–IV, L #11, F #12–14, S #12, Number of Responses Card V, S-L #14, F #15–17, Number of Responses Card VI–VIII, F #24–27, S #24, Number of Responses Card IX–X, F #28–29, S-L #29, F-L #30, F-S-L #32, F-S #33, F #34–37, F+, F−, M, FM, m, Approach) The number of responses was one aspect which may not be too important. I wanted to see whether there were any cards on which there was constriction, any cards where there was a release of association. I tried to look at the popular association, to see how concrete this person was. I could gauge the form responses, and look at the movement. I used the Beck Z score to get an idea of how he would score it, to see whether there was Z in it. I tried to get some estimation of anxiety, of feelings of inadequacy that might be great enough to disturb the profile, and to see what the individual would give. My estimation was that the individual was fairly concrete in many respects, but she had enough additional material that would indicate to me that she was Above Average in intelligence. But she's not highly above average. There were a few responses that were somewhat higher than what I would have given her—the "surrealistic painting"

Clinician #32—Continued   Intelligence problem   78 cards
Beck orientation   Interpreted first   18 minutes

—but the total Rorschach was what I would expect. I would like to say some general things about the Rorschach, from the background of having had experience with many thousand Rorschachs. I do not use the summary scores, although maybe students do. Sequential analysis is most important for diagnosis problems. Anxiety questions are relatively easy ones to answer. I look especially for what occurs on Cards IV and VI because when anxiety is high these cards usually are rejected and avoidance is a typical response to them. Frankly, I don't use diagnosis in my Rorschach work, unless the medical chart report is needed or there is someone who doesn't understand the psychodynamics. I avoid diagnosis because it's meaningless to put persons into categories. The Rorschach does not pick up the sociopathic type of individual. While I use the whole Rorschach protocol, I give emphasis to certain areas—the actual responses, the locations, the reaction times, and inquiry. The scorings are determinable from the responses themselves. I don't think you can make a good estimate of intelligence. I frequently do a Testing of the Limits. I do not rely on the Rorschach alone for interpretation, preferring to use such tests as the Thematic Apperception Test and Sentence Completion Test as well.

Answer: Above Average intelligence. IQ = 115–120.

Clinician #30   Intelligence problem   88 cards
Beck orientation   Interpreted first   24 minutes

(F-V-S #1) It's not an additive W, not much integration involved. (F-V-S #2–3, Reaction Time Card I, F-V-S #4) That's a little better. (F-V #5, Sex, Age, Education, F-V-S #6–7, S #5) I want to go through a few more responses first. (F-V-S #8–12, R, F+%, M, W, Z Frequency, Z Sum, A%, P, My, Art, H, A, Na, Ar, Additionals, F%, Number of Responses Card IX, F-V-S #28–31, Number of Responses Card X, F-V-S #32–33, F-S #34–37, D, Approach, Reaction Time Card IX–X).

Answer: Above Average intelligence. IQ = 116.

Clinician #7   Intelligence problem   76 cards
Beck orientation   Interpreted third   31 minutes

Let me be consistent. (Age, Sex, Education, R) The responses do go as high as 37. (Approach) That's interesting, W! For the first time I want to look at Z. (Z Sum) It's pretty high. How good is the F+%? (F+%) Oh 78 is pretty good. A% would be lower for a person with a higher level of intelligence. (A%) Forty-one is OK. (M, C, CF, FC) I like to know the Experience Balance. (W, P, Number of Responses Card V and X) Card V pulls the strongest against multiple responses. She can free herself. I already feel that she's Average or above. She's not Below Average. F+ is high with W expanded. She's able to mobilize energy to have a meaningful Experience Balance of 3:3, with an Experience Actual of 6 and a Z of 49. The F+% is staying up high enough. She can mobilize her intellectual energies toward constructive pursuits. A% is within range. She's seventeen and has graduated high school. In the past she has been able to utilize her intelligence. In order to answer this question I have to see how she organizes her thinking. In sequence she'd be regular. (Sequence) Oh, it's irregular. Let me look at Cards I, V, and X. (S-F-V #1–2) I'm not happy about that. (S-F-V #3) Still not happy about that. (S-F-V #4) This makes me want to see how she did on her Extended F+%. (Extended F+%) F− occurs when emotionality is involved. Is this characteristic or spotty? 86% is OK. Her F− is isolated. (S-F-V #5) She asks directions. Her passivity comes out. I've now exhausted Card I. Hm. Two of her heavily laden Z scores or W's are not that delineated, responses #4 and #5, constituting one-sixth of her total Z score. There's a nonprecise delineation, an "easy W" sort of thing. There might be a C and Y blend in response #5. You'd need more inquiry. Is she able to organize her percepts? (S-F-V #6) Here's the same thing again. This surrealistic painting is a global thing. There's a lack of differentiation. (S-F-V #7) This is more acceptable because she's a 17-year-old. If she were an adult the response would indicate sickness, "without a head." Thirty-seven responses are significantly above the mean. According to Ames, 20 responses could be expected from a 16-year-old. She has productive energy. (S-F-V-L #8–9) I wanted to know if the area was D1 or D2. Let me go back to my original question. (S-F-V #14–16) This is a very poor inquiry. She has a lot more Y than you give her credit for. On Card II with the smoke and fire, a good inquiry would help me to understand the degree of blending. The Y probably involves good integration, but I have no basis for the latter. (S-F-V #32–37, L #32, 34) Her intelligence would be Average or Above Average. Her basic intelligence probably is higher. There's a certain diffuseness and she uses up a lot of her energy in defending herself. When she finds herself more then she'll be able to apply it, but it doesn't interfere with the Above Average range. Most important are her verbalizations and conceptualizations, the "sunlight coming through the trees," the exhaust from the car going down the road, the crocodile. She organizes her language.

Answer: Above Average intelligence. IQ = 116.

Clinician #31   Intelligence problem   28 cards
Beck orientation   Interpreted third   33 minutes

(Age, Sex, Education, Interests, W% Klopfer) The W% is a little high. I don't know the norms for the Z. (R, F+%, Extended F+%, M) I want to know if she has a lot of unusual content. Ordinarily, I would look at the Wechsler IQ first, the Verbal and Performance scores, then maybe the Rorschach to see if it's consistent. If there's no consistency then I would see it as a diagnostic problem. I would go to the content. (F #1) She's ambitious. (F #2) She's not impressing me. (F #3) That's not impressive either. (F #4) Oh now, that's better. (L-V #4) She might make a good actress with this esoteric response #4. There's a suspicion of some histrionic stuff, looking at the card and sensing the prison. The tree with sunlight through it. If it were a special part of the card I would say she's striving for dramatic effects. M is important to me, the quality of the inner life. (Number of Responses Card II, F #5–7) Doesn't she wish. (F #8–10) That's kinda nice. (F #11) My guess is that she stopped there, and she did. That is gorgeous. Denial at it's very best. (Number of Responses Card VII, F #21) What? (F #22) I want to see if that's got V in it. (S #22, F #23) She's obviously not Below Average. The problem is she's not a terribly, terribly bright person, but Above Average at that age. It's arbitrary at this point.

Answer: Above Average intelligence. IQ = 117.

Clinician #5   Intelligence problem   134 cards
Klopfer orientation   Interpreted third   20 minutes

(Sex, Age, Education) She can't be an idiot. (Occupation) That's to be expected. (Nationality, Religion, Marital Status, Sibling Position, Sibling Description, Mother Description, Father Description, Sexual History, Military History, Interests) That sure is a potpourri. (F-S-V #1–4) There's a little hostility in that one. Now we're on Card II. (F-S-V #5) She can act out too. (F-S-V #6) She can reflect. (F-S-V #7) Oh my, she can kill her old man for being so ineffectual. (F-S-V #8) So, cooling off, literally and figuratively. (F-S-V-L #9) That's all? Anyway, the first response isn't a human one. (F-S-V #10–11) The Petty girls are buxom. Maybe that's what she sees. What happened to her M? (F-S-V #12–15, L #14) I still think she relates more to her mother than to her ineffectual father who "says little." He should have been protecting her with her mother, controlling blow-ups. (F-S-V #16) She shows a fairly wide range of response. (F-S-V #17) You could easily give that a CF−. She has to tone it down, putting it on ice again. (F-S-V #18) She still stays with that area. (F-S-V #19) Maybe religion will help. I hope she doesn't become a nun. (F-S-V #20) Maybe there's nothing but a drab prison wall. She's investing herself in sex and human relationships, especially with her parents, but she's ambivalent about the whole

Clinician # 5—Continued   Intelligence problem   134 cards
Klopfer orientation   Interpreted second   20 minutes

business. (F-S-V #21) Maybe the devils are mother. (F-S-V #22–23) She gets more conventional after having expressed her anxiety. (F-S-V #24) And we go on to cats. (F-S-V #25–26) She is a responsive kid, the color and texture. (F-S-V #27) This is a nice CF for a 17-year-old, by no means constricted or inhibited. (F-S-V #28) She's not distorted in her thinking. (F-S-V #29) The door probably described her present frame of mind. (F-S-V #30–31, L #31) Is that the top stuff? (F-S-V-L #32) There's a certain amount of originality, "saving this for the end." (F-S-V-L #33–37) Well, neither fish nor fowl. I don't think it's too important to do those other things. I've got the general flow of this.

Answer: Above Average intelligence. IQ = 116–119. A relatively bright, normal adolescent with some conflict, nothing per se pathological.

Clinician # 36   Intelligence problem   117 cards
Beck orientation   Interpreted first   64 minutes

(F-V #1–2, F #3, F-L #4, F #5, L #1–3, F-L #6–9, S #2 Klopfer) An intelligent person. There's a large number of responses and the quality holds up. The W's vary, from good to poorly organized, with a high degree of compulsivity. Everything so far seems to be a W. The vista response "behind" things can be used as an index of intelligence. As for the content analysis, which I do a good deal of, the "eagle" is a good response. It has to do more with status than with an animal. She apparently does get anxious after this, she recovers and gives a stereotyped response. Then she gives a sensitive one, the tree with sunlight. Is it minus? Well I'll still stick with this. (S #4–5) In Piotrowski's scoring system I'd score the smoke in here as well, CF:c. This is somebody with some degree of difficulty, turmoil. I have seen such responses in enuretics. The fire responses. (Sex, Age, S #6) She deals with reality testing more, but then. . . . I associate to this, Alice in Wonderland, the Queen saying "Off with their heads." I would have to determine whether this were hostility or inability to deal with humans. The color cards give a sense of feeling, of movement. Where's the information about her turning the cards? (V #8) Piotrowski's analysis of movement has some value. Animal movement represents the earliest learned rule in life. The M is more recently acquired. This gal was maybe forced to stand on her hands when she was a kid. (Mother Description, Sibling Position, Father Description, V-S #9, F #10) She recovers. I begin to get a picture of somebody who has a degree of health, but struggling with problems of dehumanization. It would be helpful to know whether the movement were standing, helping, etc. (F-L-S #11) This is an unusual response. It would be pretty original, but more than that. Why does she suddenly avoid dealing with the whole? There may be some exhibitionistic needs in this area. (Sexual History) My curiosity would be aroused to see what she did with Cards VI and VII. Is she avoiding some of the darker

Clinician #36—Continued   Intelligence problem   117 cards
Beck orientation   Interpreted first   64 minutes

tone? (Reaction Time Card I-X, F-L #12–14, S #13 Beck, Klopfer, V #14)
This is a person who likes to indulge here. Smart, not a terribly original response,
seen as a ballet dance. It's somewhat childish, but not infantile. A question I have
is why the W's until Card IV, at which point she moved away from that approach?
(F-S Beck, Klopfer #15) I wonder why she hasn't seen a bat or butterfly by now.
The m is an important determinant. Whatever is giving her this pervasive anxiety
she has is felt as coming from outside of her. She's a person who feels that things
are fated in life, destined, a leaf being blown off a tree, the wind. (F-S-L #16)
I'll assume it's a minus. Oh, it must be over here. The diagnostic clues so far are
enuresis and oral activity, following generalized anxiety. (Education, F #17) I
would say the Above Average category. Her intelligence would be 118 or something. (L #17) Here's a cold, detached response to sexuality. I might have
thought she had a negative sexual experience. Like in some women I've seen who
have had abortions. She's focusing on this section of the card, deep compensation. (F-L #18, S #17, F-L-S Beck, Klopfer #19) Her first response of light
coming through is something I wonder about. There's a very erratic progression
of responses, quite wholesome at times, with some F−. (F-L-S #20) This shows
attention to detail, m, and poor form quality. (F-L-S #21) On the one hand she
decapitates, and on the other she gives you just a head. (F-L #22) Here again a
vista response, which indicates a degree of intelligence. The classical Freudian
would look at this area as female sexuality, but I would hold off on that. It's
more of a dealing with minutia. (F-L #23–24, V #24) She can reverse those
devils. I would have pushed the inquiry here, looking for movement, especially
in animals. (S #24, F-L-S #25, F-L #26–27) Here it's not so much ice cream or
sundaes, but she adds the "delicious" to it. She sees the P, then color, in a conventional way, but then she begins to come through with some affect. She's more
food oriented. (F-L #28) This is a puzzling protocol, starting with W's, then
the d's, with reality and then away from it. Cross-sectionally there's a sharp contrast. She's getting a lot of m in this. Things are beyond her control. "Fountain"
responses are not uncommon in the enuretic. (F-L-S #29) Is it an Original?
Again things "coming through" something to suggest mild paranoia and sus-
piciousness, which she likes to deal with in a circumscribed and tiny way. She's
able to hold it down to something manageable. (F-L #30) Fine. She recoups
very nicely again. (F-L #31–33, 35–37, S #31–32 Beck, Klopfer, V #32, L #34)
I would begin to eliminate certain things. There's no evidence of organicity, nor
psychosis. What does that leave me? Certainly she isn't an acting-out type of
person, but there's impulsivity in "smoke and fire." I would need some other
test. She misses some popular responses, e.g., on Card V. There's evidence of
internal struggle here. She's quite an intelligent young lady, high average. There
are a number of originals. She tends to be more on the C type than the M. Almost hard to say. With such a wide range of responsivity she may be unpredictable at times. She's certainly concerned with oral gratification, especially when
her anxiety is aroused. She probably would tend to freeze up with men. I would
diagnose her as an anxiety hysteria, maybe with some somatization of symptoms.

Answer: Above Average intelligence. IQ = 118.

Clinician #19   Intelligence problem   11 cards
Beck orientation   Interpreted first   7 minutes

There are some artificialities with this board setup. It doesn't have the location numbers and you can't scan the whole Rorschach. (Z Sum, R, A%, F+%, Extended F+%, Extended F%, Number of Responses Card VIII, F-S-V #24, P)

Answer: Above Average intelligence. IQ = 118.

Clinician #35   Intelligence problem   45 cards
Beck orientation   Interpreted second   15 minutes

(R, F%, F+%, Extended F+%, A%, Avg Reaction Time, Rejections, M, W, D, S, Affective Ratio, Blend #1–3) At this point I'm certain that this person is not Below Average. I'm inclined to put Above Average as the most likely choice. (FM, m, F+, F−, F$_0$, H, Hd, Prison, A, Ad, An, Fi) I have to assume a fair amount of spread here, beyond H and A. There are only 5 H with 15 A's. The spread should be fairly good through the rest of those content categories. Fi is of interest because it represents something destructive. What I'm trying to judge at this point is whether there's much inefficiency, or constriction, or affective disruptions, which may have thrown the subject. (C, CF, FC, Y, YF, FY, T, TF, FT) These being low are not surprising to me. (V, VF, FV) But the high jump in VF is surprising. The high VF and V means that this guy would be extremely critical of himself, a little hesitant betting on his own intellectual potential. I would predict his IQ for the WAIS. (Sex, Age, Education, Occupation) I would assume single. (Marital Status, Sexual History) I'm a little surprised that it's a female.

Answer: Above Average intelligence. IQ = 118 ± 2, on the WAIS.

Clinician #15   Intelligence problem   8 cards
Beck orientation   Interpreted third   4 minutes

(Age, F+%, R, M, P, A%, Z Sum, Approach)

Answer: Above Average intelligence. IQ = 120.

| Clinician #9 | Intelligence problem | 19 cards |
| Beck orientation | Interpreted second | 4 minutes |

(Education, Age, W%, Approach, Sequence, R, M, F%, F+%, A%, Number of Responses Card I, F #1–8) I probably would want to see more of her W's.

Answer: Above Average intelligence. IQ = 120's, a superior intelligence.

| Clinician #14 | Intelligence problem | 14 cards |
| Beck orientation | Interpreted second | 4 minutes |

(Sex, Age) I'm glad I pulled that item. (Education) If she's completed high school already she's bright. (Occupation, Marital Status, R) She's bright, above average. Do you want me to stop now? (Approach, M) Where are the M's? I always figure a W:M ratio. (P) I have an impression already but I don't know how valid it is. My educated guess would be 120–130 IQ. (Blend #1–3) She has two blends. (F+%, Extended F+%) That's a little low. It might be a dilated record because of some loosening of thought processes, but I'll stick to it.

Answer: Above Average intelligence. IQ = 120–130.

| Clinician #21 | Intelligence problem | 41 cards |
| Beck orientation | Interpreted second | 7 minutes |

This is the kind of task I don't think the Rorschach is good for. (Sex, Age, Education, Occupation, Sibling Position, Sibling Description, Mother Description, Father Description, Sexual History, Nationality, Interests, R, F%, F+%, P, A%, W, D, Dd, Approach, Sequence, Z Sum, F-S-V #1, F-V-S #2–3, F-L-V-S #4, F-V-S #5–6) The words "foliage" and "surrealist" are interesting. The "foliage" is a lovely response even though it's a minus.

Answer: Above Average intelligence. IQ = 120–130.

| Clinician #4 | Intelligence problem | 17 cards |
| Klopfer orientation | Interpreted second | 10 minutes |

(Education, Age) I wanted to see how far the person would be in school. (Number of Responses Card X, F #32–37) This person looked a little constricted in a sense. I'm impressed with the octopus and crocodile. (V #35–37, Number of Responses Card I, F #1–4) These responses also include the inquiry.

Answer: Above Average intelligence. IQ = 130.

Clinician #20   Intelligence problem   11 cards
Klopfer orientation   Interpreted second   6 minutes

Looking at the actual responses to Card I could show the actual intellectual capacity. (Sex, Age, Education, F+%, Extended F+%, R, M, FM, m, W, Z Frequency) You don't have the Originals. That Z Frequency looks pretty high. Her intelligence is going up, I'd say 128–130, but not more.

Answer: Above Average intelligence. IQ $= 130 \pm 5$.

Clinician #24   Intelligence problem   47 cards
Beck orientation   Interpreted second   8 minutes

(Sex, Age) This is my bailiwick now. I'm more an adolescent and child psychologist. I feel more comfortable with that. (R) It's productive, but I do not know how good it is. (W) It depends on how good the W's are. (Z Sum) I haven't used that in a long time, but it's pretty high. (M) Only 3 M. (FT) I'm looking for evidence of integration capacity. This is somebody who pushes to be productive, with a high level of integration, but who is repressed in other ways. (Sum C Klopfer) The push is in intellectual areas rather than the affect or fantasy. That's good for intelligence. (F+%, Extended F+%) I want to look at some of the organization of the individual responses. (F #1–5) Well, on verbalization—the clouds, smoke, and fire—she's a much more volatile person who shows anxiety. She uses words like "foliage" and "surrealist painting." (F #6–8) Everything is differentiated. (F #9–10) I have the impression of somebody with a 120–130 IQ. I have to remind myself that this is a 17–year-old kid. This is very good for a 17–year-old kid. (F #11–20) She's definitely Above Average. (F #21) Everything is so differentiated. (F #22–23) There's a lot of FV here, to me. (F #24) The satin pillows are "beautifully" blue. (F #25–28) She's at least 130–140. (F #29–37).

Answer: Above Average intelligence. IQ $= 130$–140.

Appendix A

List of Abbreviations

A B,K*	Animal content
A% B,K	Animal content percent
AAt K	Animal anatomy content
Ad B,K	Animal detail content
Additionals B,K	Additional responses
Affective Ratio	Affective ratio, R(VIII, IX, X) ÷ R(I–VII)
Age	Age of subject
An B	Anatomy content
Anal B	Anal content
AObj K	Animal Object content
Approach B	Approach (locations)
Ar B	Architecture content
Art B,K	Art content
At K	Anatomy content
AvgRT B,K	Average reaction time
Ay B	Anthropology content
Blend 1, 2, 3 B	Double determinant or blend
Bt B	Botany content
C B,K	Undiluted chromatic color determinant
c K	Shading as texture determinant
C' K	Achromatic surface color, determinant
CF B,K	Chromatic color modulated by form
Cl B,K	Cloud content
D B,K	Large usual detail location
D% K	Large usual detail percent
d K	Small usual detail location
d% K	Small usual detail percent
Dd B,K	Unusual or rare detail location

*B indicates Beck and K indicates Klopfer score.

Dd+S% K	Unusual detail and white space percent
Education	Education of subject
8–9–10% K	Percent responses to last three Rorschach cards
Extended F% B	Percent of responses beginning with form
Extended F+% B	Percent of accurate form responses
F #	See "Free Associations"
F B,K	Pure form determinant
F% B,K	Pure form percent
Father Description	Father information
FC B,K	Definite form dominant over chromatic color, determinant
Fc K	Differentiated shading determinant, as surface appearance
Fd B,K	Food content
Fi B	Fire content
Fire K	Fire content
FK K	Shading determinant, as three-dimensional expanse of vista or perspective
FK+% K	Three-dimensional shading percent
FM K	Animal movement determinant
F– B	Inaccurate form determinant
F+ B	Accurate form determinant
F+% B	Accurate form percent
F₀ B	Form determinant, accuracy not known
Free Associations	Qualitative responses #1–#37 (e.g., "Bat")
FT B	Form dominant over texture, determinant
FV B	Form dominant over vista, determinant
FY B	Form dominant over shading, determinant
Ge B	Geography content
Geo K	Geography content
Individual Scorings B,K	Quantitative scoring of each free association #1–#37 (e.g., W F+ A P)
H B,K	Human content
Hd B,K	Human detail content
Hh B	Household content
Interests	Interests of subject
K K	Shading as diffusion, determinant
k K	Shading as three-dimensional expanse on two-dimensional plane, determinant
L #	See "Location Areas"
Location Areas	Location of individual responses #1–#37, as appearing on the standard location chart
M B,K	Human movement determinant
m K	Inanimate movement determinant
Marital Status	Marital status of subject
Mother Description	Mother information
Military History	Military history of subject
My B	Mythology content

Na B,K	Nature content
Nationality	Nationality of subject
Number of Responses	Number of responses to each Rorschach Card I–X (e.g., Card I = 4 responses, #1–#4)
Obj K	Man-made objects content
Occupation	Occupation of subject
Oj B	Man-made objects content
P B,K	Popular percepts
Pl K	Plant content
R B,K	Total number of scored responses
Reaction Time	Initial reaction time to each Rorschach Card I–X (e.g., Card I = 14″)
Rejections B,K	Rejection of card
Religion	Religion of subject
RT Achromatic B,K	Average reaction time to achromatic cards
RT Chromatic B,K	Average reaction time to chromatic cards
S #	See "Individual Scorings"
´S B,K	White space location
Sc K	Science content
Sequence B	Sequence of locations
Sex	Sex of subject
Sex K	Sex content
Sexual History	Sexual information about subject
Sibling Description	Information about siblings of subject
Sibling Position	Sibling position of subject
Succession K	Succession of locations
Sum C K	Sum of color determinants
T B	Undiluted texture determinant
TF B	Texture modulated by form, determinant
V #	See "Verbalizations and Behavior"
V B	Undiluted vista determinant
VF B	Vista modulated by form
Verbalizations and Behavior	Subject verbalizations and examiner observations accompanying each free association #1–#37 (e.g., "Oh what a pretty color" . . . S giggles)
W B,K	Whole location
W% K	Whole location percent
Y B	Undiluted shading determinant
YF B	Shading modulated by form, determinant
Z Frequency B	Frequency of organization scorings
Z Sum B	Sum of weighted organization scorings.

Appendix B

Summary of Clinician
Interpretations by Page Number

Rorschach Problems

Clinicians	Diagnosis	Anxiety	Intelligence
1	123	171	188
2	106	156	194
3	120	173	193
4	128	164	205
5	125	162	200
6	110	159	189
7	101	147	199
8	115	156	195
9	128	167	204
10	105	172	192
11	113	152	197
12	122	174	195
13	130	159	194
14	108	153	204
15	129	165	203
16	116	168	191
17	128	164	194
18	116	168	191
19	127	145	203
20	122	175	205
21	103	148	204
22	129	171	188
23	107	146	196
24	124	166	205

Rorschach Problems—Continued

Clinicians	Diagnosis	Anxiety	Intelligence
25	100	149	192
26	119	154	195
27	123	146	196
28	124	171	190
29	100	150	193
30	130	165	198
31	117	158	200
32	126	145	197
33	121	170	191
34	118	161	188
35	108	154	203
36	104	150	201

Bibliography

Abt, L. A., and L. Bellak, (Eds.) *Projective psychology*. New York: Grove Press, 1950.

Ainsworth, M. D. Problems of validation. In B. Klopfer, M. Ainsworth, G. Klopfer and R. Holt, *Developments in the Rorschach technique*. Vol. I. *Technique and theory*. New York: Harcourt, Brace & World, 1954.

Allport, G. W. *Becoming*. New Haven: Yale University Press, 1955.

Ames, L. B. Rorschach responses of Negro and white 5- to 10-year olds. *J Genet Psychol*, 1966, *109*, 297–309.

Ames, L. B., J. Learned, R. W. Metraux, and R. N. Walker. *Child Rorschach responses: Developmental trends from two to ten years*. New York: Hoeber-Harper, 1952.

Ames, L. B., J. Learned, R. W. Metraux, and R. N. Walker. *Rorschach responses in old age*. New York: Hoeber-Harper, 1954.

Ames, L. B., R. W. Metraux, and R. N. Walker. *Adolescent Rorschach responses: Developmental trends from ten to sixteen years*. New York: Hoeber-Harper, 1959.

Armitage, S. G., P. D. Greenberg, D. Pearl, D. G. Berger, and P. G. Daston. Predicting intelligence from the Rorschach. *J Consult Psychol*, 1955, *19*, 321–329.

Armitage, S. G., and D. Pearl. Unsuccessful differential diagnosis from the Rorschach. *J Consult Psychol*, 1957, *21*, 479–484.

Baughman, E. E. A comparative analysis of Rorschach forms with altered stimulus characteristics. *J Project Techn*, 1954, *18*, 151–164.

Baughman, E. E. The role of stimulus in Rorschach responses. In B. I. Murstein, (Ed.) *Handbook of Projective Techniques*. New York: Basic Books, 1965, 221–255.

Beck, S. J. Problems of further research in the Rorschach test. *Amer J Orthopsychiat*, 1935, *5*, 100–115.

Beck, S. J. Error, symbol and method in the Rorschach test. *J Abnorm Psychol*, 1942, *37*, 83–103.

Beck, S. J. *Rorschach's test*. Vol. II. *A variety of personality pictures*. New York: Grune & Stratton, 1945.

Beck, S. J. *Rorschach's test*. Vol. III. *Advances in interpretation*. New York: Grune & Stratton, 1952a.

Beck, S. J. The experimental validation of the Rorschach test. IV. Discussion and critical evaluation. *Amer J Orthopsychiat*, 1952b, *22*, 771–775.

Beck, S. J. Review of the Rorschach. In O. K. Buros (Ed.) *The fifth mental measurements yearbook*. Highland Park, N.J.: Gryphon Press, 1959, 273–276.

Beck, S. J. *The Rorschach experiment. Ventures in blind diagnosis*. New York: Grune & Stratton, 1960.

Beck, S. J., A. G. Beck, E. E. Levitt, and H. B. Molish. *Rorschach's test*. Vol. I. *Basic processes*. (3rd ed.) New York: Grune & Stratton, 1961.

Bell, J. E. Case studies. The case of Gregor: Interpretation of test data. *Rorschach Research Exchange*, 1949, *13*, 155–168.

Bialick, I., and R. M. Hamlin. The clinician as judge: Details of procedure in judging projective material. *J Consult Psychol*, 1954, *18*, 239–242.

Binder, A. The Rorschach test: A perceptual bias. *Perceptual and Motor Skills*, 1964, *18*, 225–226.

Bochner, R., and F. Halpern. *The clinical application of the Rorschach test*. New York: Grune & Stratton, 1942.

Bower, D., and L. E. Abt. *Progress in clinical psychology*. New York: Grune & Stratton, 1952.

Bower, P. A., R. Testin, and A. Roberts. Rorschach diagnosis by a systematic combining of content, thought process, and determinant scales. *Genet Psychol Monogr*, 1960, *62*, 105–183.

Bradway, K., and V. Heisler. The relation between diagnoses and certain types of extreme deviations and content on the Rorschach. *J Project Techn*, 1953, *17*, 70–74.

Brockway, A. L., G. C. Gleser, and G. A. Ulett. Rorschach concepts of normality. *J Consult Psychol*, 1954, *18*, 259–265.

Brown, F. An exploratory study of dynamic factors in the content of the Rorschach protocol. *J Project Techn*, 1953a, *17*, 251–279.

Brown, F. Reply to a critique of "An exploratory study of dynamic factors in the content of the Rorschach protocol." *J Project Techn*, 1953b, *17*, 462–464.

Buros, O. K. (Ed.) *The fifth mental measurements yearbook*. Highland Park, N.J.: Gryphon Press, 1959.

Caldwell, B. M., G. A. Ulett, I. N. Mensh, and S. Granick. Levels of data in Rorschach interpretation. *J Clin Psychol*, 1952, *8*, 374–379.

Challman, R. C. Clinical methods: Psychodiagnostics. *Ann Rev Psychol*, 1951, *2*, 239–258.

Chambers, G. S., and R. M. Hamlin. The validity of judgments based on "blind" Rorschach records. *J Consult Psychol*, 1957, *21*, 105–109.

Corsini, R. J., W. E. Severson, T. E. Tunney, and H. F. Uehling. The separation capacity of the Rorschach. *J Consult Psychol*, 1955, *19*, 194–196.

Crenshaw, D. A., S. Bohn, M. R. Hoffman, J. M. Matheus, and S. G. Offenbach. The use of projective methods in research: 1947–1965. *J Project Techn*, 1968, *32*, 3–9.

Cronbach, L. J. Statistical methods applied to Rorschach scores: A review. *Psychol Bull*, 1949, *46*, 393–429.

Cronbach, L. J. Statistical methods for multi-score tests. *J Clin Psychol*, 1950, *6*, 21–25.

Cronbach, L. J. Assessment of individual differences. *Ann Rev Psychol*, 1956, *7*, 173–196.

Cummings, S. T. The clinician as judge: Judgments of adjustment from Rorschach single-card performance. *J Consult Psychol*, 1954, *18*, 243–247.

Davis, H. S. Judgments of intellectual level from various features of the Rorschach including vocabulary. *J Project Techn*, 1961, *25*, 155–157.

Elizur, A. Content analysis of the Rorschach with regard to anxiety and hostility. *Rorschach Research Exchange*, 1949, *13*, 247–284.

Epstein, S., E. Lundborg, and B. Kaplan. Allocation of energy and Rorschach responsivity. *J Clin Psychol*, 1962, *18*, 236–238.

Eysenck, H. J. *Sense and nonsense in psychology*. Baltimore: Penguin, 1957.

Fiske, D. W., and E. E. Baughman. Relationships between Rorschach scoring categories and the total number of responses. In B. I. Murstein, (Ed.) *Handbook of projective techniques*. New York: Basic Books, 1965, 257–271.

Frank, J. D. *Persuasion and healing: A comparative study of psychotherapy*. Baltimore: The Johns Hopkins Press, 1961.

George, C. E. Stimulus value of the Rorschach cards: A composite study. *J Project Techn*, 1955, *19*, 17–20.

Goldfried, M. R. The connotative meaning of some animal symbols for college students. *J Project Techn*, 1963, *27*, 60–67.

Gordon, J. Rorschach responses as verbal behavior. *J Project Techn*, 1959, *23*, 426–428.

Grant, M. Q., V. Ives, and J. H. Ranzoni. Reliability and validity of judges' ratings of adjustment on the Rorschach. *Psychol Monogr*, 1952, *66*, 1–20.

Griffith, R. M. Rorschach water percepts: A study in conflicting results. *Amer Psychol*, 1961, *16*, 307–311.

Gunn, H. E. An analysis of thought processes involved in solving clinical problems. Unpublished doctoral dissertation, Loyola University, Chicago, 1962.

Haley, J. V. Effects of training on diagnostic skills. Publication No. 30, Loyola Psychometric Laboratory, Loyola University, Chicago, 1963.

Halpern. F. *A clinical approach to children's Rorschach*. New York: Grune & Stratton, 1953.

Halpern, H. M. A Rorschach interview technique: Clinical validation of the examiner's hypothesis. *J Project Techn*, 1957, *21*, 10–17.

Hamlin, R. M. The clinician as judge: Implications of a series of studies. *J Consult Psychol*, 1954, *18*, 233–238.

Hamlin, R. M., and W. T. Powers. Judging Rorschach responses: An illustrative protocol. *J Clin Psychol*, 1958, *14*, 240–242.

Harrower, M. R., and M. E. Steiner. *A manual for psychodiagnostic inkblots*. New York: Grune & Stratton, 1946.

Hertz, M. R., and R. B. Rubenstein. A comparison of three blind Rorschach analyses. *Amer J Orthopsychiat*, 1939, *9*, 295–314.

Hertz, M. R. Rorschach: Twenty years after. *Psychol Bull*, 1942, *39*, 529–572.

Hertz, M. R. Current problems in Rorschach theory and technique. *J Project Techn*, 1951, *15*, 307–338.

Hertz, M. R. The Rorschach: Thirty years after. In D. Bower, and L. E. Abt, *Progress in clinical psychology*. New York: Grune & Stratton, 1952, 108–148.

Hertz, M. R. The use and misuse of the Rorschach method: I. Variations in Rorschach procedure. *J Project Techn*, 1959, *23*, 33–48.

Holtzman, W. H. *The inkblot test*. Austin: University of Texas Press, 1958.

Horn, J. L. The utility of projective techniques and the function of the clinical psychologist. *Ment Hyg*, 1969, *53*, 654–656.

Howard, K. I. Ratings of projective test protocols as a function of degree of inference. *J Educ and Psychol Meas*, 1963, *23*, 267–275.

Hunt, H. F. Clinical methods: Psychodiagnostics. *Ann Rev Psychol*, 1950, *1*, 207–220.

Hunt, W. A. The future of diagnostic testing in clinical psychology. *J Clin Psychol*, 1946, *2*, 311–317.

Hunt, W. A., M. L. Schwartz, and R. E. Walker. Reliability of clinical judgments as a function of range of pathology. *J Abnorm Psychol*, 1965, *70*, 32–33.

Hunt, W. A., and R. E. Walker. Validity of diagnostic judgment as a function of amount of test information. *J Clin Psychol*, 1966, *22*, 154–155.

Hunt, W. A., R. E. Walker, and N. F. Jones. The validity of clinical ratings for estimating severity of schizophrenia. *J Clin Psychol*, 1960, *16*, 391–393.

Jackson, C. W., Jr., and J. Wohl. A survey of Rorschach teaching in the university. *J Project Techn*, 1966, *30*, 115–134.

Jensen, A. R. Personality. *Ann Rev Psychol*, 1958, *9*, 295–322.

Klopfer, B. *Developments in the Rorschach technique*. Vol. II. *Fields of application*. New York: Harcourt, Brace & World, 1956.

Klopfer, B., M. Ainsworth, G. Klopfer, and R. Holt. *Developments in the Rorschach technique*. Vol. I. *Technique and theory*. New York: Harcourt, Brace & World, 1954.

Klopfer, W. G., B. V. Allen, and D. Etter. Content diversity on the Rorschach and "Range of Interests." *J Project Techn*, 1960, *24*, 290–291.

Kobler, F. J., and R. G. Doiron. Book reviews [on four Rorschach texts]. *Psychometrika*, 1968, *33*, 126–132.

Kurtz, K. H. *Foundations of psychological research*. Boston: Allyn and Bacon, 1965.

Lazarus, R. S. The influence of color on the protocol of the Rorschach test. *J Abnorm Psychol*, 1949, *44*, 506–515.

Levine, D. Rorschach genetic-level and mental disorder. *J Project Techn*, 1959, *23*, 436–439.

Levy, L. H. In J. Zubin and K. M. Young, *Manual of projective and cognate techniques*. Madison, Wisconsin: College Typing Company, 1948.

Levy, L. H., and T. B. Orr. The social psychology of Rorschach validity research. *J Abnorm Psychol*, 1958, *58*, 79–83.

Lindner, R. M. The content analysis of the Rorschach protocol. In L. A. Abt, and L. Bellak (Eds.) *Projective psychology*. New York: Grove Press, 1950, 75–90.

Loehlin, J. C. *Computer models of personality*. New York: Random House, 1968.

Long, F. J., and K. P. Bertram. Rorschach validity as measured by the identification of individual patients. *J Project Techn*, 1969, *33*, 20–24.

Lorenz, M. Language as index to perceptual modes. *J Project Techn*, 1959, *23*, 440–452.

McCully, R. S. Process analysis: A tool in understanding ambiguity in diagnostic problems in Rorschach. *J Project Techn*, 1965, *29*, 436–444.

Meyer, M. L. Psychotherapy and problem solving process. Unpublished doctoral dissertation, Loyola University, Chicago, 1963.

Mills, D. H. The research use of projective techniques: A seventeen year survey. *J Project Techn*, 1965, *29*, 513–515.

Mitchell, M. B. Preferences for Rorschach cards. *J Project Techn*, 1952, *16*, 203–211.

Mohrbacher, J. W. The diagnostic approach of three disciplines to minimal intracranial pathology in children. Unpublished doctoral dissertation, Loyola University, Chicago, 1961.

Murray, H. A. *Manual for the Thematic Apperception Test*. Cambridge: Harvard University Press, 1943.

Murstein, B. I. *Theory and research in projective techniques (emphasizing the TAT)*. New York: Wiley, 1963.

Murstein, B. I. (Ed.) *Handbook of projective techniques*. New York: Basic Books, 1965.

Newton, R. L. The clinician as judge: Total Rorschachs and clinical case material. *J Consult Psychol*, 1954, *18*, 248–250.

Osgood, C. E. The nature and measurement of meaning. *Psychol Bull*, 1952, *49*, 197–237.

Pauker, J. D. Relationship of Rorschach content categories to intelligence. *J Project Techn*, 1963, *27*, 220–221.

Phillips, L., and J. G. Smith. *Rorschach interpretation: Advanced technique*. New York: Grune & Stratton, 1953.

Powers, W. T., and R. M. Hamlin. Relationship between diagnostic category and deviant verbalizations on the Rorschach. *J Consult Psychol*, 1955, *2*, 120–124.

Powers, W. T., and R. M. Hamlin. The validity, bases, and process of clinical judgment, using a limited amount of projective test data. *J Project Techn*, 1957, *21*, 286–293.

Pribyl, M. K., W. A. Hunt, and R. E. Walker. Some learning variables in clinical judgment. *J Clin Psychol*, 1968, *24*, 32–36.

Ranzoni, J. H., M. Q. Grant, and V. Ives. Rorschach "card-pull" in a normal adolescent population. *J Project Techn*, 1950, *14*, 107–133.

Reidel, R. G. A study of the relationship between complex problem solving ability and a measure of scholastic aptitude. Publication No. 32, Loyola Psychometric Laboratory, Loyola University, Chicago, 1963.

Richards, T. W., and D. C. Murray. Global evaluation of Rorschach performance versus scores: Sex differences in Rorschach performance. *J Clin Psychol*, 1958, *14*, 61–64.

Rimoldi, H. J. A. A technique for the study of problem solving. *Educational and Psychological Measurement*, 1955, *15*, 450–461.

Rimoldi, H. J. A. A new technique for appraising diagnostic ability. Unpublished paper, Loyola University, Chicago, 1956.

Rimoldi, H. J. A. Thinking and language. *Arch Gen Psychiat*, 1967, *17*, 568–576.

Rimoldi, H. J. A. Analysis of the interrelationships between logical structure, language and thinking. *Interdisciplinary Topics in Gerontology*, 1969, *4*, 127–146.

Rimoldi, H. J. A., and J. R. Devane. Training in problem solving. Publication No. 21, Loyola Psychometric Laboratory, Loyola University, Chicago, 1961.

Rimoldi, H. J. A., J. R. Devane, and T. F. Grib. Testing skills in medical diagnosis. Commonwealth Fund Project. Unpublished paper, Loyola University, Chicago, 1958.

Rimoldi, H. J. A., J. V. Haley, and H. M. Fogliatto. The test of diagnostic skills. Publication No. 25, Loyola Psychometric Laboratory, Loyola University, Chicago, 1962.

Rimoldi, H. J. A., and K. W. Vander Woude. Aging, and problem solving. *Arch Gen Psychiat*, 1969, *20*, 215–225.

Rodgers, D. A. Sources of variance in student's Rorschach interpretations. *J Project Techn*, 1957, *21*, 63–68.

Rorschach. H. *Psychodiagnostics*. (Trans. P. Lemkau) Berne: Hans Huber, 1942.

Rychlak, J. F. Forced associations, symbolism, and Rorschach constructs. *J Consult Psychol*, 1959, *23*, 455–460.

Sapolsky, A. An indicator of suicidal ideation on the Rorschach test. *J Project Techn*, 1963, *27*, 332–335.

Sarason, S. B. *The clinical interaction, with special reference to the Rorschach*. New York: Harper & Row, 1954.

Sargent, H. D. Projective methods: Their origins, theory and applications in personality research. *Psychol Bull*, 1945, *42*, 257–293.

Schachtel, E. G. *Experiential foundations of Rorschach's test*. New York: Basic Books, 1966.

Schafer, R. *The clinical application of psychological tests*. New York: International Universities Press, 1948.

Schafer, R. *Psychoanalytic interpretation in Rorschach testing: Theory and application*. New York: Grune & Stratton, 1954.

Schneider, L. I. Rorschach validation: Some methodological aspects. *Psychol Bull*, 1950, *47*, 493–508.

Shapiro, D. The integration of determinants and content in Rorschach interpretation. *J Project Techn*, 1959, *23*, 365–373.

Sherman, M. A comparison of formal and content factors in the diagnostic testing of schizophrenia. *Genet Psychol Monogr*, 1952, *46*, 183–234.

Siegel, S. *Nonparametric statistics for the behavioral sciences*. New York: McgrawHill, 1956.

Siipola, E. The influence of color on reactions to ink blots. *J Personality*, 1950, *18*, 358–382.

Sommer, R. Rorschach M responses and intelligence. *J Clin Psychol*, 1958, *14*, 58–61.

Strauss, M. E. Examiner expectancy: Effects on Rorschach Experience Balance. *J Consult Psychol*, 1968, *32*, 125–129.

Sundberg, N. D. The practice of psychological testing in clinical services in the United States. *American Psychol*, 1961, *16*, 79–83.

Symonds, P. M. A contribution of our knowledge of the validity of the Rorschach. *J Project Techn*, 1955, *19*, 152–162.

Tabor, A. B. Process analysis of Rorschach interpretation. Unpublished doctoral dissertation, Loyola University, Chicago, 1959.

Trier, T. R. Vocabulary as a basis for estimating intelligence from the Rorschach. *J Consult Psychol*, 1958, *22*, 289–291.

Turner, D. R. Predictive efficiency as a function of amount of information and level of professional experience. *J Project Techn*, 1966, *30*, 4–11.

Vander Woude, K. W. Problem solving and language: A comparison of the problem solving processes used by matched groups of hearing and deaf children. Publication No. 54, Loyola Psychometric Laboratory, Loyola University, Chicago, 1969.

Wagoner, R. A. The Rorschach test: A perceptual or a grammatical device? *Perceptual and Motor Skills*, 1963, *17*, 419–422.

Wagoner, R. A. Comment: "The Rorschach Test: A perceptual bias." *Perceptual and Motor Skills*, 1964, *18*, 282.

Walker, R. E., and W. A. Hunt. The difficulty of WAIS comprehension scoring. *J Clin Psychol*, 1965, *21*, 427–429.

Wheeler, W. M. An analysis of Rorschach indices of male homosexuality. *Rorschach Research Exchange*, 1949, *13*, 97–126.

Williams, G. J., and I. D. Nahinsky. Frequency of the Rorschach human-movement response in Negro and white emotionally disturbed children. *J Consult Clin Psychol*, 1968, *32*, 158–163.

Zubin, J. The non-projective aspects of the Rorschach experiment: I. Introduction. *J Soc Psychol*, 1956, *44*, 179–192.

Zubin, J., L. D. Eron, and F. Sultan. A psychometric evaluation of the Rorschach experiment. *Amer J Orthopsychiat*, 1956, *26*, 773–782.

Zubin, J., and C. Windle. Psychological prognosis of outcome in mental disorders. *J Abnorm Psychol*, 1954, *49*, 272–281.

Zulliger, H. *Der Behn-Rorschach test*. I. *Band: text*. Berne: Hans Huber, 1952.

Author Index

Allen, B. V., 14
Ainsworth, M. D., 4, 6
Allport, G. W., 26
Ames, L. B., 9
Armitage, S. G., 6, 14, 15, 17, 21, 22, 23, 32

Baughman, E. E., 4, 44
Beck, S. J., 6, 7, 8, 17, 19, 37, 38, 44, 45, 59, 72, 75, 77, 78, 86, 132
Bell, J. E., 45, 87
Berger, D. G., 14
Bialick, I., 13, 82
Bochner, R., 44, 46, 86, 178
Bower, P. A., 18, 24, 33
Bradway, K., 24
Brockway, A. L., 9
Brown, F., 4, 5
Buros, O. K., 4

Caldwell, B. M., 22, 23
Challman, R. C., 6
Chambers, G. S., 6, 9, 10, 11, 18, 33
Corsini, R. J., 13, 33
Crenshaw, D. A., 3
Cronbach, L. J., 3, 5, 6, 27
Cummings, S. T., 10, 11, 32

Daston, P. G., 14
Davis, H. S., 14
Devane, J. R., 30

Elizur, A., 5
Epstein, S., 9
Etter, D., 14
Eysenck, H. J., 4

Fiske, D. W., 44
Frank, J. D., 5

George, C. E., 4
Gleser, G. C., 9
Goldfried, M. R., 25
Gordon, J., 5
Grant, M. Q., 4, 10
Greenberg, P. D., 14

Griffith, R. M., 9
Gunn, H. E., 30

Haley, J. V., 30
Halpern, F., 25, 44, 46, 86, 178
Halpern, H. M., 26
Hamlin, R. M., 6, 9, 10, 11, 13, 18, 19, 20, 21, 22, 31, 32, 33, 82
Harrower, M. R., 4
Heisler, V., 24
Hertz, M. R., 3, 6, 8, 19, 32, 85
Holtzman, W. H., 4
Horn, J. L., 4
Hunt, H. F., 3
Hunt, W. A., 9

Ives, V., 4, 10

Jackson, C. W., Jr., 3, 4, 18
Jensen, A. R., 4

Kaplan, B., 9
Klopfer, B., 4, 6, 17, 19, 37, 38, 44, 45, 47, 59, 72, 75, 76, 78, 81, 86, 87
Klopfer, W. G., 14

Lazarus, R. S., 4
Levine, D., 19, 21
Levy, L. H., 4
Lindner, R. M., 5
Loehlin, J. C., 22
Lorenz, M., 12
Lundborg, E., 9

McCully, R. S., 17
Meyer, M. L., 30
Mills, D. H., 3
Mitchell, M. B., 4
Mohrbacher, J. W., 30
Murray, D. C., 13, 33
Murray, H. A., 9, 21
Murstein, B. I., 5

Nahinsky, I. D., 9
Newton, R. L., 10, 12

219

Subject Index